The Neurobiology

In this book, psychiatrist Erik Goodwyn reviews decades of research to put together a compelling argument that the emotional imagery of myth and dreams can be traced to our deep brain physiology, and discusses how a sensitive look at this data reveals why mythic or religious symbols are indeed more "godlike" than we might have imagined.

The Neurobiology of the Gods weaves together Jungian depth psychology with research in evolutionary psychology, neuroanatomy, cognitive science, neuroscience, anthropology, mental imagery, dream research, and metaphor theory into a comprehensive model of how our brains contribute to the recurrent images of dreams, myth, religion and even hallucinations. Divided into three parts, this book provides:

- definitions and foundations
- an examination of individual symbols
- conclusive thoughts on how brain physiology shapes the recurring images that we experience.

Goodwyn shows how common dream, myth and religious experiences can be meaningful and purposeful without discarding scientific rigor. *The Neurobiology of the Gods* will therefore be essential reading for Jungian analysts and psychologists as well as those with an interest in philosophy, anthropology and the interface between science and religion.

Erik D. Goodwyn is a practicing military psychiatrist for the Air Force in North Dakota, involved in teaching, research and patient care, including that of deployed soldiers. His essays on archetypes, Jungian theory and neuroscience as well as dreams reported by soldiers in combat have appeared in *The Journal of Analytical Psychology*.

The Neurobiology of the Gods

How Brain Physiology Shapes the
Recurrent Imagery of Myth and Dreams

Erik D. Goodwyn

Routledge
Taylor & Francis Group

LONDON AND NEW YORK

First published 2012
by Routledge
27 Church Road, Hove, East Sussex BN3 2FA

Simultaneously published in the USA and Canada
by Routledge
711 Third Avenue, New York NY 10017

Routledge is an imprint of the Taylor & Francis Group, an Informa business

British Library Cataloguing in Publication Data
A catalogue record for this book is available from the British Library

Library of Congress Cataloging in Publication Data
Goodwyn, Erik D., 1970–
The neurobiology of the gods: how brain physiology shapes the recurrent imagery of myth and dreams / Erik D. Goodwyn.
   p. cm.
   Includes bibliographical references and index.
   ISBN 978-0-415-67299-3 (hbk.) – ISBN 978-0-415-67300-6 (pbk.)
1. Symbolism (Psychology) 2. Mythology–Psychological aspects. 3. Dreams.
4. Psychology–Religious aspects. 5. Neurobiology. I. Title.
   BF458.G66 2012
   154.2–dc23

                                                                   2011027643

ISBN: 978-0-415-67299-3 (hbk)
ISBN: 978-0-415-67300-6 (pbk)
ISBN: 978-0-203-14152-6 (ebk)

Typeset in Times by Garfield Morgan, Swansea, West Glamorgan
Paperback cover design by Andrew Ward

MIX
Paper from
responsible sources
FSC® C004839
www.fsc.org

Printed and bound in Great Britain by
TJ International Ltd, Padstow, Cornwall

For my grandfather

Contents

Acknowledgment

C. G. Jung (1977). *The Collected Works of C. G. Jung.* © Princeton University Press and Routledge. Reprinted by permission of Princeton University Press and Routledge.

Foreword

Life's mysteries – birth, love, compassion, death, to name a few – are no less mysterious when we have developed complex rituals and meaning systems to relate to and articulate them. Historically, this has been the province of religion. In the "wonder" full text that Dr. Erik Goodwyn has assembled, you will encounter a rich and thought-provoking approach to the mysteries. He does not reduce religious experience to materialistic mechanisms, childish regression, or culturally conditioned wish fulfillment, but places the realm of the gods in nature, expressed through our biology, as phenomenologically "real" and potent for us today as for our ancestors. His effort is elegant in that it brings impressive explanatory power while also leaving room for the ineffable – no small feat.

Humankind has long sought to appease and control the unseen powers that surround us on every side – and also to simply experience the awe, fascination, and ecstasy that they carry. Dr. Goodwyn explains how this business of the gods is shaped by brain physiology, which expresses itself through recurrent imagery in our myths, dreams, and religious icons and imagery. He casts a wide net, pulling together independent research in affective and cognitive neuroscience, cultural anthropology, evolutionary psychology, psycholinguistics, and neurobiology – all to explore the link between biology and symbol.

Like the Swiss psychiatrist Carl Jung in the first half of the twentieth century, Dr. Goodwyn draws upon a broad spectrum of research to refute the "blank slate" model of mind that continues to hold sway in American psychology, and, like Jung before him, he makes a cogent argument for a psychic system of a collective, universal, and impersonal nature.

To demonstrate archetypal patterns, Jung stacked up comparisons of symbols and metaphors that appeared cross-culturally, which he felt were reflective of archetypes. Dr. Goodwyn, too, assembles reference upon reference, analogy upon analogy, as he builds a psychological model that is broad and deep.

Such methodology, coupled with the broad range of his inquiry and the fact that Jung's collected works were spread out over twenty volumes (and as many volumes of unpublished seminars, letters and speeches), have contributed to Jung being misunderstood and too easily dismissed. Then, too, some of Jung's followers have eschewed evidence-based research and advanced one-sided interpretations of his work. For example, archetypes are sources of typical actions, reactions and experiences that characterize the human species, primordial roots of patterns that structure behavior, images, affects and thoughts as these emerge in typical situations of life. They are *both instinct and image*. This definition is true to Jung's original intuition of the archetype, and it is one that Dr. Goodwyn shows to be supported by evidence-based research. Along with contemporaries such as John Haule, Dr. Goodwyn is one of a new generation of depth psychologists to show us that Jung's most important theories not only hold up quite well in the light of empirical study, they were amazingly prophetic.

Of course, we live in a time of great specialization, in which narrowly focused researchers have a hard time keeping up with their own fields of study. It has been rightfully said that today researchers know more and more about less and less. But when one trawls through the evidence assembled since Jung's death in 1961, one finds Jungian concepts being rediscovered and restated using new vocabulary with nary a mention of Jung in the footnotes. Jungian theory of complexes, developed in the 1920s, reemerges as neural networks, archetypes are re-postulated as domain-specific algorithms, and the collective unconscious is redeployed in neuroscience as core human psyche.

In this book, Dr. Goodwyn is a generalist in the best sense. A generalist possesses the broad curiosity, mental acuity – and probably the personality type – to see the forest for the trees. He/she assembles diverse data and pulls it together to create useful new gestalts for theory and practice. Of course, in doing so generalists leave themselves open to criticism by specialists for oversimplifying, obscuring controversies, and cherry-picking data. There is always some truth to such charges, but without general theories we are left with bits of cognition, dribbles of behaviorism, and a divisive split between those who conduct research and those who pursue clinical practice. Such has been the state of American psychology for too long.

By bringing together evolutionary psychology and Jungian analytical psychology, and subjecting both to the discipline of research most appropriate for the process under study, we are taking a powerful and inclusive approach to psyche that can rightfully include cognitive, behaviorist, humanist, and psychodynamic theory and technique under a unifying umbrella or meta-theory.

One might ask: how is an understanding of brain/mind possible given differences in methodology between the empirical sciences and psychological phenomenology? "Subjective" experiences of the "outside world" are created by the mind. The quality of color is not something that exists "in itself" and can only be verified through subjective reports of human subjects who presumably have the same experience. Physical and mental worlds are linked in a mysterious way – Descartes postulated it was through the pineal gland. Today, we believe the mind uses raw, incomplete and poorly characterized sensory data in remarkable ways to construct the reality we take for granted, not only color but shape, contour, spatiality. There is no Cartesian divide between subject and world: everything we observe is raw physical sensory data plus unconsciously constructed meaning. As Dr. Goodwyn points out, neither is reducible to the other and both require the other to create a coherent experience. What brings them together are psychological processes, which manifest outwardly as behaviors and inwardly as subjective imagery and feeling. Outward manifestations can be effectively studied empirically, while subjective states are best studied using other methods. One should not exclude the other, and we need both.

As Dr. Goodwyn further shows, the conceptual system we use to understand the "subjective" world of experience is highly metaphorical. The metaphors we use to attribute meaning to the world are not arbitrary nor consciously dictated – they are almost entirely unconscious in origin, biologically derived, and involuntary. The phrase "I have a deeper understanding" makes sense despite the fact that understanding is not something that can literally be made deeper. We are innately metaphorical and symbol-making creatures utilizing a deeply embedded metaphorical system. It is impossible to discuss anything without referring to common shared metaphors such as: "passage of time", "climbing out of depression", "giving" someone an idea. The mind creates experience, not only through our perceptual system but also through our conceptual system, generating a fabric of experience.

In his study, Dr. Goodwyn avoids three fallacies that have tripped up three generations of Jung's critics as well as more than a few Jungians in making sense of the archetypal underpinnings of all human experience: 1) Reifying fallacy would imagine the archetypes as some kind of neurochemical mechanism or brain region. This is an overly concrete interpretation, as archetypes are highly complex processes relating to the way we understand, orient and relate to the world. They are not "things" in your head or DNA. Their origin lies in the brain insofar as processes emerges out of interaction in which physical sensory data are used to construct lived experience; 2) Reductionistic fallacy would find some kind of neurobiological correlate of archetypal images and reduce them to "nothing but" the neurological. For example, love has neurobiological correlates but stating this tells us nothing of how love is experienced; and 3) Naturalistic fallacy would give undue weight to the physical as "more real" than the psychological realm to which it is inextricably linked.

Dr. Goodwyn makes an interesting case for Jung as a proto-evolutionary psychologist. In his autobiography Jung wrote, "If the unconscious is anything at all, it must consist of earlier evolutionary stages of our conscious psyche . . . Just as the body has an anatomical prehistory of millions of years, so also does the psychic system" (Jung, 1961: p. 348).

Jung posited a strong evolutionary basis for behavior, frequently referring to anthropology and "primitive" psychology (i.e. the psychology of tribal cultures), as well as comparative animal behavior. He wrote, "Consciousness began its evolution from an animal-like state which seems to us unconscious, and the same process of differentiation is repeated in every child" (Jung, 1961: p. 348).

Compare this to the work of the evolutionary psychologists Tooby and Cosmides, who suggested in 2005,

> Organisms come factory equipped with knowledge about the world, which allows them to learn some relationships easily and others only with great effort, if at all. Skinner's hypothesis – that there is one simple learning process governed by reward and punishment – was wrong . . . The mind is not like a video camera, passively recording the world but imparting no content of its own.
>
> (Tooby and Cosmides, 2005: 15)

Rather than, like the behaviorists, assuming a few generic learning mechanisms, evolutionary psychologists such as Tooby and Cosmides "expect a mind packed with domain-specific, content-rich programs specialized for solving ancestral problems" (Tooby and Cosmides, 2005: 15).

Consciousness, as Jung surmised long ago, rests upon an edifice of unconscious processes that do not depend upon it, but without which consciousness would be nonfunctional. Dr. Goodwyn cites evidence that as little as 5 percent of our actions are consciously determined, leaving the other 95 percent to unconscious processing. This cohering consciousness is imperfect and fragile, as well as subject to disintegration via various processes, including trauma. "Older" systems are more universal and "closed" with respect to environmental learning and able to dominate conscious processing much more than conscious processing can influence them. The implications of this for therapies based purely on the power of will are obvious.

Jung anticipated a link between mind (psyche) and physical matter. He wrote,

> Psyche cannot be totally different from matter, for how otherwise could it move matter? And matter cannot be alien to psyche, for how else could matter produce psyche? Psyche and matter exist in one and the same world, and each partakes of the other, otherwise any reciprocal action would be impossible. If research *could only advance far enough,*

therefore, we should arrive at an ultimate agreement between physical and psychological concepts.

(Jung, 1959a: para 413)

Today, research has advanced far enough.

Dr. Goodwyn's speculations about the neurobiological substrates of goddess symbols and soul images within men, as well as the "ideal man" carried within every woman, are invaluable for understanding how our intimate relationships become muddled. We typically carry unreasonable expectations of our partners based on our longing for the gods and goddesses within. There are many more implications for therapeutic practice in this book, such as the affective underpinnings of dreams, and the ways we hold and process trauma.

I am very pleased to recommend this book to anyone who is interested in inner work. Most books today contain at best a handful of new ideas. This one has dozens, and will reward careful, slow, and repeated readings. It is only the first of what I expect will be many contributions to depth psychology by Dr. Erik Goodwyn.

Jerry M. Ruhl, Ph.D.
Executive Director, C. G. Jung Educational Center of Houston
September 2011

Part 1

Definitions and foundations

Chapter 1

Symbols, biology and depth psychology

Gods, demons, angels . . . muses, spirits, ghosts . . . fairies, devils, imps, fauns, unicorns, dragons, poltergeists, ghouls, vampires, djinns, werewolves . . . saviors . . .

Have you ever wondered why humans have spent so much time writing and worrying about, praying to, running from, blessing, cursing, exorcizing, and placating these entities? If there is so little physical evidence that any of these things exist, why do we spend so much energy thinking about them? Philosophers as early as Epicurus argued that they are pure nonsense, yet since the dawn of our existence humankind has been convinced of the power of these "spiritual" entities. Isn't this irrational? Illogical? Even potentially harmful? Why would such a propensity evolve, when clearly a more rational animal would never waste precious biological resources on self-sacrifice, burnt offerings, or self-mutilation in the name of a god?

Many have tried to explain this phenomenon. Some speculate that religions evolved because certain cultural constructs passed down through the generations survived better than others in the human imagination (Dennett, 2007; Dawkins, 2008). Others argue that religion promotes social "cohesion" (Wilson, 2003), or that it is an "evolutionary by-product" of our propensity to think in anthropomorphic terms (Atran, 2002b; Barrett, 2004; see also Pyysiäinen, 2009). This view holds that our brains are hardwired to detect agency and intent in the environment, so ideas about spirits and gods are naturally "intuitive," making them memorable and impressive. While these arguments are compelling and have much to recommend them, they are only part of the picture. Explaining the transmission, social function, or ease of construction of religious ideas in cognitive terms still does not address the question of what they *mean*. Theoretically, any set of arbitrary ideas could be passed on easily, promote social cohesion or be intuitive and we would still have no idea what they represented. Thus we must not only ask why these ideas are so persistent and ubiquitous but also what they *are*, and why they are so emotionally stirring.

This is obviously no easy question. I will approach it from a medical perspective, based on the scientific literature and my experience with patients in psychotherapy. Unlike the authors referenced above, I am neither an evolutionary biologist nor an anthropologist, but a psychiatrist; I therefore argue primarily from a neuropsychiatric perspective. This awareness should alert you to any potential biases I may have. I am not interested in asserting dogma; rather I seek an explanation that agrees with the best medical and basic research available. I propose to show how we can understand what gods and spirits are by understanding them as a subset of special ideas known as *symbols* – to which I hasten to add that this is no light statement, reducing the mighty gods to "ideas." No, hopefully, by the end of the book, you will see how *symbols* carry the weight of the gods in the human heart, and are very real and potent forces acting on us.

By symbols I don't mean archaic scribbles or mathematical equations, but rather *metaphorical representations* of thoughts, feelings, actions, environments, and everything else we experience. This may seem like a trivial construct in which to house the gods, but bear with me. As we will see, symbols are a fundamental part of our existence, and they have their origin in our neurobiology – in other words, they are not arbitrary creations of whimsy or poetic conceits, but originate from deep-rooted, innate predispositions as they interact richly with the environment. And some of them are highly charged with emotion – these are the symbols that become gods, not because we "mistake" them for gods, but because *that is how they are best represented.*

The link between biology and symbol according to early depth psychology

For Freud, most symbolism was sexual, and he believed that dream imagery was rooted in our deepest emotional drives. Thus Freud was perhaps the first of the major depth psychologists of the late nineteenth and early twentieth centuries to link dream symbols to our innate human biology, specifically to the most evident of all human instincts, the sex drive. His student and later rival, Carl Jung, had a fundamental disagreement with this emphasis on sex as the primary source of dream symbol meaning. He argued that although, as Freud observed, dream images *are* symbolic, sex is simply one of many instincts they might portray. For Jung, symbols used basic universal meanings; they emerge from the "collective unconscious"; that is, the unconscious ground that all of us share as humans. This collective unconscious was built over millennia by natural selection and is inextricably bound with the environment. It was the source of the meaning behind these symbols, and included much more than the sex drive. He argued that the universal core of meaning behind each important symbol was the "archetype," an instinctual prototype, sexual or otherwise, related to the symbol in human consciousness. Jung felt that recurrent images were not mere arbitrary images that could mean *anything*, but rather they had a relatively fixed, emotionally powerful meaning that was frequently only dimly grasped and hard to verbalize, but nonetheless was widely shared. As we will see, many of the opinions of Jung and many later theorists can be revisited in light of modern empirical research, with some important modifications.

From the very beginning, Freud envisioned a "scientific psychology" in which empirical research in neurology could be used to better understand psychopathology (Freud, 1923). However, lack of neurobiological knowledge made this impossible at that time, and he abandoned this goal. Later psychoanalysis branched off into Adler's "individual psychology," and then Jung's "analytical psychology." Freudian psychoanalysis further subdivided into various schools of thought, including drive theories, object relations schools, and self psychology. During the early part of the twentieth century, these schools developed largely independently of empirical research in psychology. This was because the school of behaviorism (Skinner, 1953), which at that time prevailed, presumed that the mind was not only a "blank slate," imprinted by experience, but also a "black box." Truly rigorous scientific inquiry, it was argued, must discard "unscientific" concepts like Freud's unconscious, repression, or even mental states in general. This ultra-positivistic viewpoint caused a rift in psychology, the effects of which are still present. In the meantime, discussion of symbols and their meanings went by the wayside when it came to empirical research and was relegated to the depth psychology schools.

The 1950s and 1960s saw the decline of behaviorism with the advent of cognitive psychology (McDonald and Okun, 2004). For the first time in decades, the mind was being studied in terms of its internal structure, rather than as a collection of stimuli and responses, and the success of cognitive psychology has revolutionized the field. Meanwhile, the neurobiology research Freud wished for has progressed tremendously. Neuro-imaging techniques enable researchers to investigate the brain *in vivo*, giving us an unprecedented ability to correlate neurobiology with function. This revolution in the study of the mind began in the 1970s with John Tooby and Leda Cosmides (Tooby, 1976a, 1976b; Cosmides and Tooby, 1992; Tooby and Cosmides, 2005; Tooby *et al.*, 2005) when evolutionary theory, long since neglected in the study of the mind, began to be rigorously applied to psychology.

Understanding symbols neurobiologically

Because of the historical progression of psychology since Freud, the interpretation of symbols has remained largely detached from neurobiological research. But this situation need not continue, as we now have an abundance of data from the neurobiological sciences that should shed some new light on the older ideas that dream and fantasy symbols had their origin in the biological "drives" bequeathed to us by evolution. The primary focus of this book, then, is to propose a model for understanding dream, fantasy, and religious symbols in terms of our brain physiology. As I will show, there is a great deal of data from a variety of sources that we can use to address these questions. Despite the fact that Freud originated the idea of linking dream symbols and neurobiology, you will find that I refer to Jung quite a bit more than Freud. I have two reasons. First, Jung did not limit himself to sex, aggression and the Oedipal complex – rather, he considered these aspects of the mind to be among the many "archetypal" processes (Jung, 1990). Second, the hypothesis that symbols can be understood in terms of our neurobiology was expanded a great deal by Jung's theory, whereas Freud concerned himself less with symbols and more with defense analysis and transference – very important concepts that are beyond the scope of this work.

Jung and his students developed the most complete system for the interpretation of symbols that can be compared to those used by empirical science. In fact, several recent Jungian analysts have already attempted to work along these lines (Knox, 2003; Stevens, 2002) – Jungian analyst John Ryan Haule (2010), for example, in his *Jung in the 21st Century*, reviews many of the finer points of Jung's theory in light of modern research in a variety of fields, and finds Jung's theory agrees very well with the data of anthropology, evolutionary biology and primatology. Furthermore, the Jungian analyst David Rosen and his colleagues (Sotirova-Kohli *et al.*, 2011) have produced empirical evidence that supports the existence of a collective unconscious – in this case, evidence for an underlying universal mechanism of symbol construction.

This study is therefore a synthesis – an attempt to organize and combine many fields under one framework that we can use to understand spontaneous, emotionally meaningful symbols. In so doing, one rapidly encounters Jung, because he had so many observations about the subject. As we will see, many of his ideas hold up remarkably well despite their age, and are not inconsistent with many other theoretical positions.

The "collective unconscious": Jung's universal human nature

Before we can investigate what empirical research has to say about the existence of a "collective unconscious" (a term that unfortunately conjures up metaphysical ideas Jung did not intend), or any universal human nature from which symbols emerge, we must first try to understand what exactly Jung was trying to describe. Jung attempted to define the term in his paper "The concept of the collective unconscious," first published in 1936:

In addition to our immediate personal conscious . . . (even if we tack on the personal unconscious as an appendix), there exists a second psychic system of a collective, universal and impersonal nature which is identical in all individuals and is inherited. It consists of pre-existent forms, the archetypes, which can only become conscious secondarily and give form to psychic contents.

(Jung, 1959b: 43)

This idea, radical for its time, was essentially a rejection of the "blank slate" concept that was prevalent in the surrounding social and cultural environment at the time (Pinker, 2002); Jung repeatedly attacked the idea of the blank slate, stating:

It is in my view a great mistake to suppose that the new-born child is a *tabula rasa* [blank slate] . . . Insofar as the child is born with a differentiated brain that is predetermined by heredity and therefore individualized, it meets sensory stimuli coming from outside not with *any* aptitudes but with *specific* ones. . . . These aptitudes can be shown to be inherited instincts and preformed patterns, the latter being the *a priori* and formal conditions of apperception that are based on instinct. Their presence gives the world of the child and the dreamer its anthropomorphic stamp. They are the archetypes.

(Jung, 1959b: 66, emphasis in original)

The good thing is that psychologists do not believe in the "blank slate" anymore (Goodwyn, 2010a), so the question therefore becomes "what is the nature of the innate mind?" and what about these "archetypes"? As later Jungians have pointed out (Hogenson, 2004), Jung struggled to define the archetype, which seemed to be a deeply felt, but elusive, intuition. One attempted definition was to identify archetypes as "inherited instincts and preformed patterns . . . typical mode[s] of apprehension . . . wherever we meet with uniform and regularly recurring modes of apprehension we are dealing with an archetype" (Jung, 1919: para 280). He also often compared archetypes to biological instincts:

instincts are not vague and indefinite by nature, but are specifically formed motive forces which . . . pursue their inherent goals. Consequently they form very close analogies to the archetypes, so close, in fact, that there is good reason for supposing that the archetypes are the unconscious images of the instincts themselves, in other words, that they are *patterns of instinctual behavior*.

(Jung, 1959b: para 91, emphasis in original)

Similarly, he stated that there is "no justification for visualizing the archetype as anything other than the image of instinct in man" (Jung, 1959a: para 278). Jung frequently emphasized the instinctual origin of the archetype – this speaks to the same issue of symbol neurobiology that we are exploring. Because humans are capable of articulation, he argued, we come to know these instinctual forms through themes found in myth and folktale, and in highly elaborated form in religious doctrine, but their *source*, he argued, was *instinctual*. This is the crucial element I am considering in the present work, in particular with respect to the experiences of gods and spirit beings.

Jung proposed that much of human life is directed by a group of universal instinctual processes he termed the "collective unconscious" and its archetypes, though he acknowledged that experience is important in the development of individual "complexes" (Jung, 1959b: 42). Jung argued that emotional ideas and concepts have an "archetypal core," meaning that they are under the direction of a highly specific preexisting archetype/instinct that forms the scaffold for the images and experiences that surround it. For Jung, the mother complex, for example, does not emerge spontaneously via some generic learning mechanism that associates a child's mother with food or "rewards," but rather emerges from an innate, specific mechanism that orients the child toward its mother, and makes emotional associations to those stimuli that are enduring – the mother complex. In his words:

> The mother archetype forms the foundation of the so-called mother complex . . . [however] My own view differs from that of other medico-psychological theories principally in that *I attribute to the personal mother only a limited aetiological significance*. That is to say, all those influences which the literature describes as being exerted on the children do not come from the mother herself, but rather from the archetype projected upon her, which gives her a mythological background and invests her with authority and numinosity.
>
> (Jung, 1959b: 81–85, emphasis added)

Thus for Jung our actual mother is not as important as the internal *idea* of *mothering* that makes our actual mother so important to us and forms "mother" symbols. This "mother archetype" therefore acts as an independent player in our minds. I will have more to say on mothers (and fathers!) later on.

Jung's archetypes

Jung felt that archetypes, or instincts, were a fundamental part of human psychological existence.[1] He maintained this opinion throughout his life:

The psyche of the child in its preconscious state . . . is already preformed in a recognizably individual way, and is moreover equipped with all specifically human instincts, as well as with the a priori foundations of the higher functions.

(Jung, 1961: 348)

Jung's theory assumed a great deal of innate structure and predispositions for the mind, and the recent work of evolutionary psychologists, cognitive scientists and ethologists appear to support this idea, demonstrating that organisms utilize many types of learning that is gene-directed and "domain-specific" rather than domain-general – this is just a fancy way of saying that we learn some things, like social exchanges and predator/prey detection, more easily than Sudoku or vector calculus.

Jaak Panksepp, a pioneer in affective neuroscience, or the study of emotions from the perspective of the brain, has pointed out that "experience is more influential in changing the *quantitative* expression of neural systems rather than their *essential nature*" (Panksepp, 1998: 17, emphasis added).[2] In other words, emotions are essentially innate and relatively specific. Echoing this idea, Joseph LeDoux observes that "Evolution tends to act on the individual modules [of emotional processing] and their functions rather than the brain as a whole. . . . Most likely attempts to find an all-purpose emotion system have failed because such a system does not exist" (LeDoux, 1996: 105–106).

The ethologist Gallistel (1995) has shown that throughout the animal kingdom, learning proceeds according to a multiplicity of specialized mechanisms. Like evolutionary psychologists, affective neuroscientists and ethologists feel that animals have a constellation of specialized learning mechanisms. The increasing support for the existence of these "problem-specific learning mechanisms" (Marler, 1991), which are called "domain-specific algorithms" by human evolutionary psychologists, lead cognitive neuroscientists to conclude:

As we ascend into the human brain, we can see from an evolutionary perspective how humans must possess special devices for learning. Our human brains are larger because they have more devices for solving problems, and the devices are *shared by all members of the species* . . . Complex capacities like language and social behavior are not constructs that arise out of our brain simply because it is bigger than a chimpanzee's brain. *No, these capacities reflect specialized devices that natural selection built into our brains* . . .

(Gazzaniga *et al.*, 2002: 606–608, emphasis added)

Finally, cognitive anthropologists agree that the mind has a large array of innate predispositions that play a large part in explaining why world religions and rituals have such striking similarities (Whitehouse and Laidlaw, 2007). All this research leads to the conclusion that Jung was on to something when he proposed that the mind had a significant amount of innate structure, though this view was unpopular in his day. What follows, then, is a review this innate structure with respect to how the mind appears to formulate symbols. From there, we can revisit the old idea of "archetypes" to see how this plays into the recurrent imagery of dreams, myth and religion.[3] Thus, although I use Jung's considerable intuitions as a guide, one need not be a "Jungian" to see how this plays out.

Chapter 2

Foundations

In this chapter I will use the existing literature to lay the foundations for the "instinctual psychological processes" I talked about earlier; as I will show, these instinctive workings hold the key to understanding recurrent universal symbols. What follows is a review of a number of different fields that I will draw upon in later chapters, where I get into more specific examples of symbols in action. This chapter is therefore by necessity a bit technical, since I am trying to lay down a valid empirical framework for the later subjective experiences of spirits and gods, but it will be worth the effort later on.

Carl Jung: Proto-evolutionary psychologist

Jung posited a strong evolutionary basis for behavior, frequently referring to anthropology and "primitive" psychology (i.e. the psychology of indigenous cultures), as well as comparative animal behavior in his works:

> If the unconscious is anything at all, it must consist of earlier evolutionary stages of our conscious psyche. . . . Just as the body has an anatomical prehistory of millions of years, so also does the psychic system. And just as the human body today represents in each of its parts the result of this evolution, and everywhere still shows traces of its earlier states – so the same may be said of the psyche. Consciousness began its evolution from an animal-like state which seems to us unconscious, and the same process of differentiation is repeated in every child.
>
> (Jung, 1961: 348)

As I will show, these sentiments have been arrived at independently, and in great detail, by evolutionary psychologists, and in fact the many broad similarities of evolutionary psychology and analytical psychology have already been observed (Haule, 2010; Stevens, 1995, 2002; Stevens and Price, 2000; Walters, 1994). One might therefore consider Jung as one of the world's first evolutionary psychologists after Darwin, though evolutionary psychology (EP) has developed independently of analytical psychology and appears largely ignorant of Jung's work (Stevens, 2002). Moreover, it is a new discipline, having developed only within the last 30 or so years – well after Jung's death.

In a review of EP, Tooby and Cosmides (2005) outline the fundamental findings of the field:

> Research in animal behavior, linguistics, and neuropsychology [has shown] that the mind is not a blank slate, passively recording the world. Organisms come "factory equipped" with knowledge about the world, which allows them to learn some relationships easily and others only with great effort, if at all. Skinner's hypothesis – that there is one simple learning process governed by reward and punishment – was wrong.
>
> (15)

They continue:

> The mind is not like a video camera, passively recording the world but imparting no content of its own. Domain-specific programs organize our experiences, create our inferences, inject certain recurrent concepts and motivations into our mental life, give us our passions, and provide cross-culturally universal frames of meaning that allow us to understand the actions and intentions of others. They invite us to think certain kinds of thoughts; they make certain ideas, feelings, and reactions seem reasonable, interesting, and memorable . . . that is, they play a crucial role in shaping human culture.
>
> (Tooby and Cosmides, 2005: 18)

Jung once said that the infant "meets sensory stimuli coming from outside not with *any* aptitudes but with *specific* ones" (Jung, 1959b: 66, emphasis in original); compare this observation with that of Tooby and Cosmides, who state that "there does not appear to be a single program that causes learning in all domains . . . evidence strongly supports the view that learning is caused by a multiplicity of programs . . ." (2005: 32). They are stating practically the same thing: that our genes, along with universal aspects of our environment, organize a lot of what goes on in our minds. The evolutionary psychologist Hagan (2005) elaborates:

> The universal architecture of the body is genetically specified . . . Because psychological adaptations such as vision are no different from other adaptations in this regard, they, too, are genetically specified human universals.
>
> (146)

Tooby and Cosmides elaborate:

> Evolutionary psychologists expect a mind packed with domain-specific, content-rich programs specialized for solving ancestral problems . . . human cognitive architecture contains many information processing mechanisms that are domain-specific, content-dependent, and specialized for solving particular adaptive problems.
>
> (2005: 46; see also Cosmides and Tooby, 1992, and Tooby *et al.*, 2005)

As it turns out, humans are genetically more like each other than most species; this is due to a genetic "bottleneck" that occurred in our relatively recent evolution. Mitochondrial DNA evidence suggests that all humans on earth share essentially the same bloodline some 200,000 years ago, and may even be descended from a single so-called "mitochonrial Eve" (Cann *et al.*, 1987). This and other evidence has led neuroscientists to conclude:

> Most scholars are beginning to concede the existence of a *core human psyche* that is largely a product of biological evolution (specifically a result of natural selection). . . . Evolutionary psychiatrists are beginning to agree that much of human mental activity is driven by the ancient affective emotional and motivational brain systems shared with other animals.
>
> (Panksepp, 2006: 790, emphasis added; see also Gardner and Wilson, 2004; Jones and Blackshaw, 2000)

What Panksepp is calling the "core human psyche" is perhaps comparable to Jung's "collective unconscious."[1] From another perspective, that of cognitive neuroscientists, we find the opinion that "human emotions are underpinned by specific but universal psychobiological mechanisms" (Stein, 2006: 766). Furthermore, "This fundamental point is at the heart of the evolutionary perspective, and concurs with a vast amount of neuropsychological research" (Gazzaniga *et al.*, 2002: 596).

Moreover, innate factors appear to profoundly influence behavior – animal researchers, for example, have shown many innate behavioral systems in animals:

> The existence of intrinsic but behaviorally flexible brain systems has been repeatedly demonstrated by investigators of animal behavior, in simple and elegant experiments. *For instance, most young birds do not learn to fly. They will fly at the appropriate age (i.e., maturational stage) even when deprived of the opportunity to exercise such skills . . .*
>
> (Panksepp, 1998: 37, emphasis added)

Such experiments would not be ethical if done on humans; I think this biases our explanations toward looking for developmental "causes" of behavior that may very well be innately driven. In any case, we do know that nearly all human behavioral tendency variations, as measured via cross-fostered identical twin studies, have been shown to be at least 50 percent genetic and often more (Turkheimer, 2000; Turkheimer and D'Onofrio, 2005) – combine this data with the success in animal breeding experiments:

> For many years, study after study of inbreeding has indicated that virtually any behavioral tendency in animals can be enhanced or diminished as successfully as bodily characteristics . . . it is now evident that similar processes contribute to psychological traits in humans and other animals.
>
> (Panksepp, 1998: 39)

We do not know how this is accomplished in humans with a "mere" 20,000 genes, but nevertheless it is. Thus the weight of converging evidence from multiple independent disciplines, then, supports some kind of universal psychological system that underscores human experience – a "collective unconscious," if you will – though researchers still debate what it is exactly. I am not the first to find a link between Jungian psychology and evolutionary psychology. The Jungian analyst Anthony Stevens (1993, 1995, 1998, 2002; Stevens and Price, 2000), who worked with the attachment theorist John Bowlby (1969) has already done a great deal of fascinating work toward this end,[2] particularly with respect to societal issues and the numerous analogies and comparisons to animal behavior. As I will show, however, a great deal of data has not yet been incorporated into a coherent whole. Why do we care? Because if the mind does in fact have a significant innate structure, and, as we will see, it does, it will certainly affect the way we construct recurrent symbols.

However, let me point out that domain-specific algorithms are *not* the same thing as archetypes. Rather, they are merely innate aspects of the mind that attend and process some aspect of experience, tag it with some kind of emotional significance and influence learning, judgment, cognition, motivation, and behavior. I think that the brain uses these things to make some symbols; if so, then calling them "archetypal" may be more appropriate. Furthermore, when I use the word "innate" I do not necessarily mean "genetic"; rather, I designate *innate processes* as those that *robustly manifest themselves in spite of large variations in environment*. Thus, *innate* factors are those that arise largely independently of personal history (see Goodwyn, 2010a, for more complete discussion).

Universals in anthropology

Returning to the concept of innately guided behavior, how might innate processes be observed? An obvious place to look would be at any behavior that is universal cross-culturally, since they might be reflective of innate tendencies that are largely resistant to environmental variation. The anthropologist Donald Brown, in his *Human Universals* (1991), reviews the results of decades of cross-cultural research, revealing a surprisingly large number of cultural universals. Far from being "empty" universals such as "all people feel pain and hunger," these observations are surprisingly specific. Regardless of culture, for example, all peoples

- have languages that include metaphor and express poetry in which lines are demarcated by pauses and are about 3 seconds in duration;
- express thoughts and inner states in terms of the same mental taxa, particularly with respect to animals;
- have easily recognizable "coyness" displays among females;
- make gender role differentiations, where men are always predominately in political and coalitional competitive roles and women in nurturing and social networking roles;
- personify external phenomena conceptually and linguistically;
- spontaneously make tools, always including ties, levers, and spears;
- spontaneously make drawings, dance and music, and all cultures have a separate category of music that is aimed at children;
- claim a certain territory as "home," even if they spend nearly their entire lives away from this homeland;
- are concerned with social rank and status, especially males;
- use fire, cook food, and make shelters;
- proscribe violence and rape, which are also universal;
- experience envy and engage in reciprocity and revenge;
- have religious beliefs in things beyond what is visible and palpable, practice divination and try to control the weather;
- engage in play in general, and always play-combat in particular, and always in males.

(Brown, 1991: 130–140)

This listing merely scratches the surface. There are scores of these universals, and the list continues to grow. Brown further points out the youth of the discipline, stating that: "Anthropology has scarcely begun to illuminate the architecture of human universals" (Brown, 1991: 141).

How are we to understand this growing list of universals of human behavior? One possibility is that they are the products of predispositions within the human mind that are universal, emotional, unconscious (in the sense that they are not consciously decided upon by cultural leaders), resistant to environment, and likely shaped via evolution. In other words, that they are reflective of instinctual or perhaps "archetypal" psychological processes as they interface with the environment.

The other possibility is that they are generated by repeated experiences impinging upon domain-general learning mechanisms in predictable ways (the belief that the sun is round, for example, is universal but is not necessarily innate). It remains to be seen, then, which of the universals such as the coyness display are innate and which are not. As I hope will become obvious, many are innate.

Innate neuroanatomy and the triune brain

The famous "triune brain" model originally developed by MacLean (1952, 1990; see also Panksepp, 1998; Ploog, 2003; Stevens and Price, 2000; Stevens, 1995) argues that evolution is visible in our brain anatomy. This model, based on extensive examinations of comparative neuroanatomy across a large variety of vertebrate species, proposes that the human brain has anatomical structure showing it to be the end product of a long evolutionary process of several "layers." The lowest layer contains the brain stem and basal ganglia, structures highly conserved across all vertebrates from reptiles to humans – known as the "reptile brain," containing basic instinctive tendencies and primitive survival plans. On top of this layer later evolved the "old mammalian brain," conserved in all mammals and found to a limited extend in birds, which contains the limbic system – the limbic system consists of functionally related brain structures; it is variably defined by neuroscientists, some of whom question its usefulness (see LeDoux, 1996); however it is generally agreed upon that the limbic system represents the "emotional brain."[3] This system processes information from the internal organs and senses and evaluates them for emotional significance. Then it responds with emotional states that influence blood pressure and hormone levels. The old mammalian brain and the reptile brain are therefore responsible for instinctive behaviors and emotions (Solms and Turnbull, 2002: 17–18, 29) in all mammals. Evolving still later upon these two layers is the "new mammalian brain," which consists of the cerebral cortex. The cortex is involved in our much vaunted logic and higher problem solving abilities. The triune brain, therefore (which I have grossly oversimplified here), is described by Panksepp as a highly useful model: "There appear to have been relatively long periods of stability in vertebrate brain evolution, followed by bursts of expansion. The three evolutionary strata of the mammalian brain reflect these progressions" (1998: 43). Note that I use it here primarily as an *anatomical* model, since its evolutionary history is somewhat controversial.

The basic idea is that the further "down" one goes from the newer to the older layers of the brain the more "closed" the processing systems get; by closed I mean resistant to environmental variation. Natural selection, it seems, does not like leaving some things to chance; these highly conserved areas of the brain are just such areas. It is highly likely, then, that the psychology of these older regions, when viewed from "the inside," is going to consist of archetypal images.

Consciousness in neuroanatomy

In the previous section I introduced the concept of *consciousness* as a property of certain brain regions. This is important because everything we remember about ourselves is due to consciousness, including our symbolic imaginings – however, most of what goes on in the brain is unconscious, though unconscious processes have a tremendous impact on what we know consciously about ourselves. As you might imagine, I think archetypal processes are a subset of these unconscious processes. A review of this research is necessary to show why.

The neurologist Antonio Damasio (1994, 1999b) has summarized a large body of work on consciousness that includes not only neurological studies but also detailed case reports of patients with rare neurological disorders. Working through the available evidence, Damasio has identified several brain regions that are implicated in conscious processing. A complete review of this fairly technical subject is beyond the scope of this book, but the bottom line is that what we perceive as "consciousness" is actually a complex system of many "layers" of consciousness – not unlike the triune brain model.

The usual state of things in a normally functioning human brain is what is called "extended" consciousness – that is, the "most" conscious level as opposed to slightly less conscious states such as dreaming, or states generated by certain types of brain damage. Damasio shows how extended consciousness is built up by simpler and more concretely measureable brain functions. Everything that does not fall under these mechanisms of consciousness is of course "unconscious." Damasio recognizes, however, that the term "unconscious" covers the vast majority of brain functioning that includes more than contents that were previously conscious – that is, contents that are "repressed":

> The unconscious, in the narrow meaning in which the word has been etched in our culture, is only a part of the vast amount of processes and contents that remain nonconscious, not known in . . . extended consciousness. In fact the list of the "not-known" is astounding [and includes] *all the hidden wisdom and know-how that nature embodied in innate, homeostatic dispositions.*
>
> (Damasio, 1999b: 228, emphasis added)

The "hidden wisdom" he describes here refers to a body of evidence that shows high-level complex decision making abilities (rather than mindless reflexes) that operate unconsciously (cf. for example Nelkin, 1993; Bauer and Vergaellie, 1988; Damasio, 1990; Damasio *et al.*, 1990; LeDoux, 1985). Damasio and many others have recognized that the unconscious is more than repressed autobiographical information; it also possesses a large store of innate "knowledge" or "wisdom" – the comparison with Jung's postulated "collective unconscious" is therefore obvious. Neuroscience has shown that the vast majority of our mental life occurs without conscious awareness. Support comes from LeDoux (2002):

> Consciousness . . . very likely developed in the brain recently in evolutionary history, layered on top of all the other processes that already existed. Unconscious operation of the brain is thus the rule rather than the exception throughout the evolutionary history of the animal kingdom . . . they include almost everything the brain does, from standard body maintenance like regulating heart rate, breathing rhythm, stomach contractions, and posture, to controlling many aspects of seeing, smelling, *behaving, feeling, speaking, thinking, evaluating, judging, believing, and imagining*.
>
> (11, emphasis added)

Consciousness therefore seems to rest upon a mighty edifice of many layers of unconscious processes that minimally depend upon it – meaning they act with relative autonomy. Though our understanding of the neural underpinnings of consciousness is far from complete, there are some broad agreements:

> A number of prominent neuroscience researchers (Damasio, 1999; Panksepp, 1998) have begun to argue that our higher cognitive processes rest on a primary or core form of consciousness. From this point of view, cognition is the latest evolutionary layer on the consciousness onion.
>
> (Watt and Pincus, 2004: 79)

Elsewhere they state: "This notion of consciousness as graded is consistent with basic distinctions made recently . . . between *primary, core, or affective consciousness* and more cognitive, semantically informed, or extended consciousness" (83, emphasis added).

This primary "emotional consciousness" is, at the deepest level, universal and innate; not only do we share it with all other humans, but, more deeply, we even share it with other animals. Panksepp (1998) has a similar model that divides consciousness into primary, secondary and tertiary layers that correlate with various regions in the brain. Thus a growing consensus appears to be that there are progressively deeper layers of consciousness that act with greater and greater autonomy and that these can be linked to the evidence of layers of processing in the brain, with the deepest layers being environmentally closed, affective, innate and universal.[4]

Panksepp's (1998, 2005) model differs from Damasio's in the details about what regions comprise what layers, but for our purposes these models are more alike than different (Watt and Pincus, 2004) – what is important here is the convergence of data on this issue of "layers," with the deeper layers being more progressively innate, affective, autonomous and *pregnant with meaning for the organism.*

I should point out that the topmost layer, or the so-called "neocortex," has been shown to be highly "plastic" or variable with regard to environmental variation (reviewed in Panksepp, 1998: 59–80; see also Braitenberg and Schulz, 1991). This conclusion comes as a result of experiments that show how brain regions can change their function in surprisingly flexible ways. This fact has caused some speculation as to how innately directed behavior can be (Buller and Hardcastle, 2000). However, no one is a free-floating cortex; a closer look at how the cortex is influenced by deeper structures appears to tell a different story. The neuroanatomists Llinas and Pare, for example, find the cortex tightly linked to a highly conserved area known as the thalamus. Accordingly, the brain has many "thalamo-cortical loops" that appear to be highly structured:

> since the brain did not appear suddenly, but rather was subjected to the vicissitudes of evolution, it may possess at birth as much of [a pre-existing] order to its organization as does the rest of our body. . . . the nervous system is primarily self-activating and capable of generating a cognitive representation of the external environment even in the absence of sensory input, for example in dreams . . .
>
> (Llinas and Pare, 1996: 3–4)

Cognition, or complex thought, they argue, is an *intrinsic property* of the brain that requires only a modest amount of experience to fine-tune; wakefulness "may be described as a dreamlike state modulated by sensory input" (Llinas and Pare, 1996: 6; see also Llinas and Ribary, 1992; Llinas *et al.*, 1998). In other words, their finding is that the brain appears intrinsically organized to represent the world, with preformed "templates" formed via evolution that sensory data modifies but only weakly (Llinas and Pare, 1996). The flexibility of the neocortex, then, does not necessarily imply a lack of innate functioning.

The structure of the brain/mind

With the above research in mind, I can make some rough correlations, outlined in *Table 1.*

Table 1 makes gross correlations between mind and brain activity. I also link these layers to types of "thinking" – meaning emotions, images, or language; more on this later. In any case, this model is very roughly hewn, as rigorous matching of neurobiology with precise descriptions of subjective

Table 1 Highly simplified comparison of brain regions and their proposed
corresponding mental activities

External/Brain		Internal/Mind
New mammal brain	Open language	Consciousness
Old mammal brain	Mixed images	Partially conscious
Reptile brain	Closed raw emotionality	Deeply unconscious

Note: The further "down" one goes in the central nervous system, the more closed the system is – meaning more resistant to environmental variation. For us, the activity of the neocortex corresponds (roughly) to conscious processing, whereas the older regions are less conscious, less verbal and more emotional. See text for additional comment.

Source: Adapted and expanded from Stevens and Price, 2000; Damasio, 1999b; Panksepp, 1998.

experience is still developing; the correlations at this point are therefore necessarily primitive. Panksepp further refines this outline by theorizing that a graded consciousness occurs through many levels in the brain, starting with reflexive behavior (reptiles) at the lowest "level," to affective awareness (lisencephalic mammals), to cognitive awareness (primates), to self-awareness (great apes) to awareness of awareness (humans) (1998: 35). Note especially that the lower "types" of consciousness (which are "unconscious" from the perspective the highest layer) are progressively more universal and hence "collective," not only to all humans, but to all mammals and finally all vertebrates. While these correlations are certainly in broad strokes and many complexities have yet to be worked out (Watt and Pincus, 2004), as a "big picture" sketch it shows how we might approach the question of innate core meanings.

For our purposes, I should note that Damasio has observed the similarity between Freud's notion of the unconscious and his own neuroscientific theory, stating that "we can say that Freud's insights on the nature of consciousness are consonant with the most advanced contemporary neuroscience views . . ." (Damasio, 1999b: 38). Of course, Jung's model includes not only repressed and developmental contents but innate, evolutionary elements. Notably, Panksepp has argued that Jung's theory of archetypal dream imagery has "potential credibility" from a neuroscientific perspective (Panksepp, 1998: 366). Central to the discussion, it seems, is the question of how innate emotions are – more on this in a moment.

In summary, neuroscience views a consciousness that rests upon a mighty edifice of unconscious processes which do not depend upon it, but without which it would be nonfunctional, a view so well supported by cognitive neuroscience that one may consider it a settled matter (cf. Damasio, 1994, 1999b; Gazzaniga, 1998, Gazzaniga *et al.*, 2002; Solms and Turnbull, 2002). These unconscious processes are very influential – the best estimates show that at most 5 percent of our actions are consciously determined (Bargh and Chartrand, 1999), leaving the other 95 percent to unconscious processing.

Conscious processing overlies multiple unconscious emotional processes

This cohering consciousness, however, is imperfect and fragile, as well as subject to disintegration via various processes such as trauma or drugs (Damasio, 1999b; LeDoux, 2002; Panksepp, 1998, 314–315). Furthermore, consciousness is a *unitary* phenomenon – there is only one at a time – but unconscious systems are multiple; this is shown from studies on memory. Cognitive scientists such as the memory expert Dan Schacter, as well as Graf (Schacter, 1996; Schacter and Graf 1986) and Squire and Cohen (1984; see also Solms and Turnbull, 2002: 80–84; Weiskrantz, 1986) have uncovered that the memory system can be primarily divided into explicit (conscious) and implicit (unconscious) memory systems. The explicit memory system, with its link to consciousness, is *a single system* based on the brain regions known as the temporal lobe, prefrontal cortex and the hippocampus, but there are *multiple implicit memory* systems, leading LeDoux to conclude that: "The brain clearly has multiple memory systems, each devoted to different kinds of learning and memory functions" (1996: 198). These unconscious systems have been suggested to extend beyond memory to include perception, judgment, learning and thinking (Kihlstrom, 1987) and operate in parallel distributed circuits rather than representing a unitary phenomenon (Spiegel, 1990; Spiegel and Li, 1997; Mesulam, 1998; McDonald *et al.*, 2004). Furthermore, they possess a "rudimentary kind of consciousness" (Weinberger and Weiss, 1997: 43) primarily concerned with emotions (Cloitre, 1997) and capable of social cognition (Stein and Young, 1997). These systems, it has been argued, are evolutionarily much older than the conscious system (Reber, 1993), and unconscious systems appear to act "without being linked to a conscious memory identified with self" (Spiegel and Li, 1997: 185).

Thus numerous studies point to *multiple unconscious* memory systems that are each focused on distinct and separate emotional evolutionary tasks that function independently from the conscious system in the brain (cf. also Damasio, 1999b; Gazzaniga *et al.*, 2002; Panksepp, 1998). Furthermore, extensive studies on neurologically impaired persons have shown that implicit memory systems are robust and perform well even in the presence of severe explicit memory deficits (Schacter, 1987, 1996); extended consciousness and the explicit memory system, then, are dependent upon many 'rudimentary consciousnesses', but *not the other way around*. Put another way, these more primitive types of consciousnesses can act on their own

Consciousness – single explicit memory system

↓↑↑↑↑↓

Multiple unconscious systems of perception, social judgment, cognition, and memory

Figure 1 Each task has its own "rudimentary consciousness" associated with it that is highly influential on consciousness (up arrows) but relatively autonomous otherwise (down arrows).

without the need for conscious processing, but conscious processing cannot function without the unconscious ones.

The above data on conscious/unconscious emotional processing systems can be diagrammed as in *Figure 1*.

Consciousness is a rare commodity in the brain, and the numerous unconscious systems compete with each other for access to it:

> Unconscious operations take place in the brain automatically, without the intervention or review of a central, integrated self. Each unconscious operation considers only the specific aspect of the self with which it is concerned, and not the entire person . . . Conscious operations, in contrast, require the synthesis of a complete self in time and space.
>
> (Viamontes and Beitman, 2007: 244)

This raises the question of how all these separate implicit emotional systems compete with each other to direct or dominate conscious attention. As it turns out, many times it *does not* lead to a coherent conscious experience – a phenomenon long since recognized and termed "dissociation" takes place. Dissociation has been observed in normal subjects as well as neurologically impaired subjects (Hintzman, 1988; Richardson-Klavehn and Bjork, 1988) and represents a clear indication of the way in which competing implicit systems can sometimes disrupt the normally coherent consciousness.

Unconscious systems should not be thought of as mindless reflex circuits; rather, research shows them to be quite sophisticated in their own right. In fact, the implicit systems of perception, recognition and memory have been shown to be capable of symbolic and interpretive thought (cf. Erdelyi, 1985; Safran and Greenberg, 1987). For example, reactions of implicit systems, as shown in physical measurements such as skin-conductance reactions to subliminally presented words associated with mild shocks, can even be elicited via words that *are only semantically related* to the shock-words (Corteen and Wood, 1972). This older data clearly shows the symbolic capacity of implicit affective systems. Implicit systems have been shown to be capable of learning and complex behavior (Van den Berg *et al.*, 1990; Klatzky *et al.*, 1989; Schacter, 1983); here Cloitre repeats the oft-found opinion that the implicit systems appear to represent "a more primitive, long-standing, and enduring form of memory" (1997: 73). Implicit memory systems are well developed in young children and remain intact among the elderly despite a rise and fall in explicit processing throughout the life span (Howard, 1992; Naito and Komatsu, 1993; Viamontes and Beitman, 2007), further supporting the idea of an explicit conscious system that develops slowly in children, reaches its peak in adulthood, then degenerates in senescence, but all the while dependent upon older and more robust emotional "primitive consciousnesses."

Unconscious systems are therefore capable of perception, symbolic processing, social judgment and motivated action, which becomes "activated" by the internal or external environment, and subsequently works to orient and bias *conscious processing* to "serve its own ends," so to speak. These different emotional systems process the same environmental stimuli in domain-specific ways and impinge, in neuroanatomical terms, on the "convergence zones" of conscious processing such as the hippocampus and the working memory system, where the information is winnowed out and selectively processed into a single conscious experience (LeDoux, 2002: 316–318). LeDoux (2002) summarizes this whole process:

> Through explicit systems, we try to willfully dictate who we are, and how we will behave. But we are only partially effective in doing so, since we have imperfect conscious access to emotional systems, which play such a crucial role in coordinating learning by other systems . . . because there are multiple independent emotion systems, the episodic influence of any one system is itself but a component of the total impact of emotions on self-development.
>
> (323)

As LeDoux and other researchers on emotional circuitry have noted, the older, domain-specific emotional memory can easily overwhelm the more domain-general (and newer) conscious processing, and frequently they are activated without conscious awareness at all (LeDoux, 2002: 206–234; Damasio, 1999b; Panksepp, 1998). This leads us to the neuroscience of emotions.

Affective neuroscience

Oddly, the emotional component of cognition has been long ignored in cognitive science (LeDoux, 1996; Panksepp, 1998; Damasio, 1994, 1999b). Jung argued that what he called the "feeling tone" (Jung, 1971 [2005]; Jung, 1997) is of paramount importance in the way we shape archetypal symbols, which are:

at the same time, both images and emotions. *One can speak of an archetype only when these two aspects are simultaneous.* When there is merely the image, then there is simply a word picture of little consequence. But by being charged with emotion, the image gains numinosity (or psychic energy); it becomes dynamic, and consequences of some kind must flow from it.

(1964: 87, emphasis added)

Similarly, the Jungian analyst Marie-Louise von Franz states that: "An archetypal image is not only a thought pattern . . . *it is also an emotional experience* – the emotional experience of an individual. Only if it has an emotional and feeling value for an individual is it alive and meaningful" (1996: 10, emphasis added). Emotion, then, is a required component of any symbol that is supposedly archetypal; without strong emotion behind it, an image is just an image and a cigar is just a cigar.

Jung insisted that archetypal symbols had a powerful emotional component, which is why he advocated their use in psychotherapy as tools for healing and why he insisted on describing the archetypes in poetic and colorful language:

because this is not only more expressive but also more exact than an abstract scientific terminology, which is wont to toy with the notion that its theoretic formulations may one fine day be resolved into algebraic equations.

(Jung, 1959a: para 25)

This insistence was probably detrimental to Jung because it made him appear "unscientific" and eccentric (the latter charge is certainly true). Nevertheless, his prediction was accurate: cognitive science did exactly as he predicted up to the last few decades. Time and empirical data, it seems, has vindicated his position. But in order for Jung's theory to make any sense, emotions must be largely innate also.

It seems they are; according to Panksepp:

Although some investigators still choose to believe that human emotions are unique and acquired through social learning, here we will proceed with the *data-based premise* that the ultimate sources of human feelings are *biological,* and that these foundations are essential for all of the many acquired complexities that characterize the detailed expressions of human emotions in the real world.

(1998: 20, emphasis added)

This is not to say that development cannot influence how these systems are expressed, but rather that their source is innate rather than cultural:

Even though our unique higher cortical abilities . . . may encourage us to pretend that we lack instincts – that we have no basic emotions – such opinions are not consistent with the available facts.

(Panksepp, 1998: 21)

Comparing the older emotional circuits with the newer cognitive circuits, "the evidence is overwhelming. The upward controls are more abundant and electro-physiologically more insistent; hence one might expect that they would prevail if push came to shove" (Panksepp, 1998: 319).

From a different perspective, the emotion theorist Ekman argues that emotions should not be thought of as some kind of nebulous global "affect," but that they are motivational programs that deal with fundamental evolutionary "life tasks" (Ekman, 1992); this sentiment is also shared by the affective neuroscientist Joseph LeDoux (1996). In other words, emotions are linked with universal evolutionary psychology. According to Ekman, emotions tell us what, out of the barrage of experience, is *important*. What we should attend to, what we should worry about, what we should seek out, what we should learn, is all dictated by our emotion systems in surprisingly subtle ways. Damasio elaborates:

> Well-targeted and well-deployed emotion seems to be a support system without which the edifice of reason cannot operate properly. These results and their interpretation [call into] question the idea of dismissing emotion as a luxury or a nuisance or a mere evolutionary vestige . . . evidence suggests that most, if not all, emotional responses are the result of a *long history of evolutionary fine-tuning*.
>
> (1999b: 42–53, emphasis added)

In his comprehensive review *Affective Neuroscience* (1998), Panksepp observes that at the most fundamental level, the universal vertebrate emotional circuitry appears to be divided into four primary modes: SEEKING, PANIC, FEAR, and RAGE. Added to these emotional circuits are slightly more specialized CARE, LUST, and rough-and-tumble PLAY circuitry, which we share with all mammals (and birds to a lesser extent). A full review of this theory is presented in the Appendix, but for now, regarding the innate structure of the brain/mind, he states that

> our brains resemble old museums that contain many of the archetypal markings of our evolutionary past, but we are able to keep much of that suppressed by our cortical lid. Our brains are full of ancestral memories and processes that guide our actions and dreams but rarely emerge unadulterated by [experience] during our everyday activities.
>
> (Panksepp, 1998: 75)

Elsewhere, Joseph LeDoux reviews that

> brain systems that generate emotional behaviors are highly conserved
> through many levels of evolutionary history . . . Emotions easily bump
> mundane events out of awareness, but nonemotional events (like
> thoughts) do not so easily displace emotions from the mental spotlight
> . . . While conscious control over emotions is weak, emotions can flood
> consciousness . . . Psychotherapy is interpreted as a process through
> which our neocortex learns to exercise control over evolutionarily old
> emotional systems . . . not simply by the dominance of neocortical
> cognitions over emotional systems, but by a more harmonious integra-
> tion of reason and passion . . .
>
> (1996: 17–21)

What Panksepp and LeDoux are emphasizing here is the innate biological
origin of intense affect. Jung proposed that the mind consists of "earlier
evolutionary stages of our conscious psyche . . . Just as the body has an
anatomical prehistory of millions of years, so also does the psychic system
. . ." (1961: 348). These and many other statements have been frequently
misconstrued as Lamarckianism (cf. Neher, 1996; reviewed in Haule, 2010
and Merchant, 2009).[5] However, in light of the well-confirmed functional
and anatomical layers that have been demonstrated to exist not only in the
brain (Llinas and Pare, 1996; Panksepp, 1998, 2005; MacLean, 1990) but
also in the mind (Buss, 2005; Tooby et al., 2005), and the recognition that
these two aspects are inextricably linked, this criticism seems baseless. It is
likely that Jung was intuiting these systems of layers when referring to "the
deposit of all human experience right back to its remotest beginnings"
(1919, para 339). This "deposit" is not due to any individual experiences,
but rather of the entire species within its environment of evolutionary
adaptation, and only in the sense that it could have been "deposited" via
natural selection.

I suggest that innate psychological activity correlates with activities of the
old mammal and reptile brain regions as they interface with the environment, no doubt in complex ways yet to be fully elucidated, as they qualify as
highly conserved and more resistant to psychological environment in all
humans, as opposed to the much more "plastic" regions of the neocortex.
Subjectively experienced imagery that correlates with activity of older more
closed regions would be expected to be emotionally charged because of their
well-demonstrated massive, nearly one-way input into regions that correspond to conscious processing, and their well-established and profound
effects on motivation, judgment, affect, and even perception (Panksepp,
1998, 2005).

Panksepp calls the activity of these layers of core, affective consciousness
our "ancestral memories" (1998: 75), which house even more profound

emotional foundations that, when experienced and described *subjectively*, emerge to speak with the authority of deep time; it is perhaps these experiences that Jung referred to when describing the archetypes.

To summarize, then, the findings of various neurosciences describe the mind as a large array of older unconscious emotional memory systems that are overlaid with a newer, more domain-general, highly differentiating but more fragile consciousness system. The older systems are more universal and "closed" with respect to environmental variations – they tend to respond to the environment in ways that do not vary much across the species, but they are able to dominate conscious processing, much more so than conscious processing can influence them. Furthermore, the older systems operate more or less autonomously, frequently without conscious participation, in response to various subliminal environmental stimuli. They possess a "rudimentary" type of consciousness capable of perception, social judgment, symbolic processing and autonomous activity – it is the symbolic processing that is crucial to the present work. They also are *intrinsically active*, rather than simple passive information processing mechanisms. Furthermore, these various systems tap into ancient emotional motivators that are describable in rigorous neurobiological terms, and, as we will see, are utilized by the human brain in a huge variety of ways.

I am *not* saying, however, that the archetypes are "in" the reptile or old mammal brain – subjective impressions are not "in" anything, no matter what brain regions they may be correlated with. Moreover, this is still only part of the puzzle, for an archetypal image is more than an emotional perception or an evolutionary instinct; it is also a subjective image – and a highly *symbolic* image at that (Jung, 1959b; von Franz, 1999). So far I still have yet to explore the details of mental imagery or symbolic thought.

Chapter 3

Mental images, symbolic images and "archetypal" images

The primary focus of this work is in symbolic *imagery* – how the brain constructs it, interacts with it, and imbues it with numinous significance (in the case of gods). Note that imagery scientists define an "image" as any internally derived sensory impression – not just a visual one. In any case, studying the direct processes that form mental images should provide still more evidence to consider with respect to our symbols, as the images that emerge in dreams, psychosis, myths and art are all derived from internally generated images, albeit under varying amounts of conscious control.

The study of mental imagery has actually endured a rocky course of development (Kosslyn *et al.*, 1995; Kosslyn *et al.*, 2001), surviving the dismissive (and ultimately unhelpful) ultra-positivist attitude of behaviorism to be studied in detail via neuroimaging techniques.[1] Mental imagery is an important intrinsic part of human life that underlies conscious reasoning; there is evidence that conscious reasoning is based largely on mental imagery as shown in subjects to whom are proposed logic problems while being imaged with fMRI (Knauff *et al.*, 2002). Human memory has been shown to improve if concepts are visualized as objects interacting in some way (Bower, 1972), and imagery is used spontaneously to understand and categorize verbal material, understand abstract concepts, or learn new skills (Kosslyn *et al.*, 1995).

A lot of literature supports the idea that visual imagery uses "like-modality perception"; in other words, we use the same brain region for imagining a tree as we do actually observing a tree. The brain's occipital, temporal, and parietal lobe activity is required for both activities, and deficits in perceptual ability coincide with deficits in imaging ability (Kosslyn, 1994; Kosslyn *et al.*, 1995). Thus *perceiving* and *conceiving* utilize almost the *exact same brain regions*.[2] This near equivalence has important implications as we consider the meaning behind the mental images reported in therapy, and furthermore the question of innately guided or "archetypal" imagery.

The perceptual/conceptual system goes beyond static images. There is also a large amount of evidence that *imagined motion* and action activate the same brain regions that actually carry out the actions (Kosslyn *et al.*, 1995), which shows how the motor system gets coopted for mental imagery generation in subjects. Children, who use more unconscious circuitry than conscious circuitry (Viamontes and Beitman, 2007; Foulkes, 1999), use imagery more often than adults to answer questions, and later during development appear to use more verbal descriptions as a function of increasing *conscious reflection* (reviewed in Kosslyn, 2005) – a theme that suggests older and more unconscious processing systems are more *visual and symbolic* than the "layer" of conscious explicit and *linguistic* systems overlying it. But image generation is not a matter of perceptual activity alone; rather it is an *active constructive process* (Kosslyn *et al.*, 2005).

Findings from the past two decades have shown that internally generated mental imagery recruits primarily the same cortical areas that image perception does, even down to the primary visual cortex in the case of visual mental imagery, and, moreover, these images evoke emotional responses in ways that are similar to perception. Kosslyn *et al.* summarize:

> researchers agree that most of the neural processes that underlie like-modality perception are also used in imagery; and imagery, in many ways, can "stand in" for . . . a perceptual stimulus or situation.
>
> (2001: 641; see also Kosslyn, 1994; Ganis *et al.*, 2004)

Thus we appear to have an innate image-generator built into the perceptual/conceptual system – this is the source of novel image generation.

Image schemata: Organizers of imagery

Image schemata – basic organizing concepts such as "object," "containment," "emergence," "force," and so on – are important cognitive structures that shape deep levels of our conceptual thought. Cognitive linguists (Lakoff and Johnson, 1980, 1999) have argued that they are also an important aspect of all conceptual metaphors that shape dream content (Lakoff, 1997) and are rooted in embodied functions (more on this below). The Jungian analyst Jean Knox (2003) has, using a large body of developmental psychology data, observed the fundamental importance of image schemata in shaping archetypal images.

Interestingly, these basic organizers and quite a bit more can emerge in the complete absence of visual input. Bertolo *et al.* (2003), for example, have shown that subjects born blind could sketch their dreams, which presumably consisted of touch, sound, and smell but not sight, onto a two-dimensional medium with such skill as to be indistinguishable from drawings by blindfolded subjects with a lifetime of visual experience. Such competence suggests strong variation-resistant emergence in the abilities of intuitive physics, object representation, two- and three-dimensional thinking, image schemata, force dynamics, and creative spatial representation/graphic capacities.

The blind understand distinctions between concealed and non-concealed objects as well as the sighted, and they can also produce drawings depicting three-dimensional scenes that have a "point of view" with spontaneous understanding and reproduction of perspective, depth and occlusion even in very young subjects (Kennedy, 1980). Marmor (1978) found that the congenitally blind also learn color relations with equal competence to the sighted, and both were able to reproduce indistinguishable color wheels. The blind moreover show ability at mental rotation equal to the sighted (Marmor and Zaback, 1976).

These studies suggest the brain is somehow set up to quickly acquire the ability, in a variation-resistant manner, to *spatially* (if not necessarily "visually") represent three-dimensional worlds of objects and agents moving about in it, complete with "point of view," depth, occlusion, color relation, rotation, and so on, irrespective of visual experience. This data also contrasts Lakoff and Johnson's (1999) theory that visual metaphors are acquired through repeat visual experiences and associations, and suggests a more innate origin for such metaphors since the brain generates spatial relationships without visual experience. Though blindness does produce some impairment in angle and distance estimation (see Arditi *et al.*, 1988; De Beni and Cornoldi, 1988), the differences are modest and far more specific compared to what one would expect with the more general "association" mechanism suggested by Lakoff and Johnson.

Furthermore, there is mounting neuroscientific data that the brain innately anticipates *conceptual* domain-specific organization such as faces, animals, eye-gaze, and objects, some of which have been *linked directly to genetic processes* (Atran *et al.*, 2001; Caramazza and Shelton, 1998; Duchaine *et al.*, 2007, 2009, 2010; Duchaine and Nakayama, 2005, 2006; Germine *et al.*, 2010; New *et al.*, 2007; Wilmer *et al.*, 2010). Further studies show that blind and sighted subjects show neural specialization between living and nonliving stimuli when viewed with MRI, leading Mahon *et al.* (2009) to argue that the brain is "innately disposed to handle information about different domains of objects" (p. 401).

The above data validates Knox's (2003) attribution of image schemata as archetypal, and suggests an innate and evolutionary origin for them. It further suggests that the mind is predisposed to create three-dimensional mental worlds in *independent* terms of animacy, faces, objects, and so on, even when that mind has no access to one of its typical sensory modalities.

How does this translate into symbolic/metaphorical thinking, much of which shapes dream/fantasy clinical material (Lakoff, 1997)? In Lakoff and Johnson's (1999) metaphor theory, which I will explore more fully below, this internally constructed, well-understood "inner world" of spaces, objects, faces, animate things, and so on, will be readily available for use as visuospatial metaphors of more nebulous or poorly understood experience. Given the finding (Zimler and Keenan, 1983) that both blind and sighted subjects recalled pairs of highly visual words *better than any other pairs* – even audio words in the blind – this further suggests that the brain is innately predisposed to make the kinds of *visuospatial* metaphors Lakoff and Johnson describe. The congenitally blind were not found to be impaired in learning words with visual referents compared to the sighted (on the contrary, sighted subjects showed impaired learning of auditory words when compared with the blind!), again suggesting vision is unnecessary to set up a visuospatially oriented brain innately primed to make visuospatial associations and metaphors.

Finally, all conscious reflection appears to involve mental image processing (Kosslyn, 2005). That is, whatever innate factors exist that orient and shape our perceptual system will also orient and shape our imaginal experiences, though very often in novel ways that go far beyond simple memory retrieval. This evidence finds its parallel in cognitive science (see Lakoff and Johnson, 1999: 38–39; Sperber, 1994; Tooby and Cosmides, 2005: 60–62).

The evidence for this link between perceptual systems and conceptual systems finds still further support from dream research and neuroanatomical studies (Solms 1997, 2000). Foulkes (1999) observed that the ability to dream is strongly correlated with visual cognitive perceptual ability (i.e. "visual IQ") in children along several different measures, and this is corroborated by others (Robertson, 1998). Further supporting this origin of dream images are a variety of independent studies that show that dream recall does not appear to be related to personality variables but to *basic visuospatial ability* (reviewed in Domhoff, 2003: 52).

There are also many neuroimaging studies that show that the dreaming brain is using sensory regions to a high degree – in this state the brain is furiously constructing imagery, while at the same time the language centers are relatively inactive (see Hobson, 1988, 1999, 2003; Hobson *et al.*, 2000; Kahan *et al.*, 1997; Pace-Schott *et al.*, 2001; Hobson and Kahn, 2007 for examples). In dream states the relative origin of the stimuli (i.e. external during waking versus internal during dreaming) and the relative conscious monitoring (i.e. high during waking versus low during dreaming) is different, and these differences are responsible for our experience of these images as being "self" generated, as in directed by the conscious ego, or "experienced," as in a dream, which is not under conscious control.[3] I hasten to add here, however, that the distinction between "internal" and "external" becomes quite blurry the deeper we go into the unconscious processors due to the fact that these universal unconscious circuits interact so closely with environments (Hogenson, 2009) and are far removed from the personal sense of "self."

In any case, now we're getting closer to the spirits and gods of religion and myth. Why? Because the perceptual/conceptual system is the system through which we experience these things – in whatever capacity they may "exist." That means if I perceive a mental image of a spirit, ghost or deity, it is through the actions of these brain regions.

Archetypal imagery: A subset of mental imagery

As Haule (2010) has pointed out, human thought and behavior can be organized into nested structures of affect, behavior, and subjectivity, in which the deeper, more universal and evolutionarily relevant "complexities within complexities" are considered more "archetypal," and I believe mental images fit into this paradigm as well. So in order to understand the subset of images presumed to be archetypal images, we must examine any images that emerge in the presence of heightened affect (to start). Further refinement requires us to seek images that are related to our evolutionary history (for reasons I explore below), and we can refine our search to include only affectively charged images that emerge when ancient, universal brain structures are relatively more active and conscious processing is relatively less active. Such an altered state of consciousness is well known and referred to as *dreaming*.

Dream imagery is emotional imagery

Dream imagery appears to be driven more by emotional concerns than conscious ratiocinations (for multiple examples, see reviews in Hartmann, 1998; Hobson, 1988, 1999; Hobson *et al.*, 2000; Kahn *et al.*, 2002; Kramer, 2007; Solms, 1997, 2000; Solms and Turnbull, 2002; Strauch and Meier, 1996). The neuroscientists Solms and Turnbull (2002), in fact, have proposed a model based on neurobiology, lesion case studies, functional imaging and neo-Freudian psychoanalysis that puts emotional brain processes at the forefront of dream generation:

> the parts of the forebrain involved in the construction of dreams are the entire *limbic system* . . . as well as most of the *visual system* . . . This implies, among other things, that the brain mechanisms of dreams are the same as for those for the basic emotions . . .
>
> (201, emphasis in original)

They argue that the particular emotional system responsible for this activity is the SEEKING system:

> Activation of the SEEKING system during sleep is commonly, but not exclusively, triggered by the REM state. A thought process occurring

during any stage of sleep can presumably also activate the SEEKING system . . . this would be enough to begin the dream process.

(212)

Dream imagery appears to be driven by activity of the limbic system and excludes the higher conscious processing regions (relatively) (Hobson *et al.*, 2000). SEEKING activity correlates with an intense sense of interest and exploratory urges, and in animals is correlated with exploratory behavior (see the Appendix for more detail).

Dream imagery is (partially) evolutionary imagery

Archetypal imagery should be more than simply emotional; it should also be somehow innate and "instinctive," as Jung proposed that archetypes were both "instinct and image." According to neuroscientists, the dreaming brain has a particular profile of activity wherein consciousness is "lowered" and unconscious circuits are enhanced (reviewed in Hobson *et al.*, 2000; see LeDoux, 2002; Damasio, 1999b; Panksepp, 1998; Viamontes and Beitmann, 2007).[4] Note that the active elements here are the more universal and older brain regions designated as the deeper "layers" of the old mammal and reptile brains that I suggested may correlate with the experience of archetypal images. If this is true, then the imagery experienced subjectively that correlates with this brain activity profile should reflect universal concerns that make sense given our biological history.

In fact, the dream scientists Hall and Nordby, in analyzing some 50,000 dreams from subjects all over the world, found repetitive universal themes that included conspecific aggression and status striving, predatory animals, flying, falling, being pursued, landscapes, sex, misfortune, marriage and children, being socially scrutinized, traveling, swimming, watching fires and being confined underground. These elements they called "universal constants of the human psyche" (1972: 35); this data has held up remarkably well over time (Domhoff, 2003; Hall *et al.*, 1982). Furthermore, when viewed cross-culturally, dreams "are more similar than they are different around the world" (Domhoff, 2003: 32), suggesting a common source of stock concerns that are resistant to cultural variation.[5]

The question of course is whether or not these universal concerns are driven at least in part by the innate structure of the brain, shaped by evolution to encounter typical ancestral life experiences (cf. Stevens, 1995). A closer inspection of dream content data is required. To further understand this question of whether dream content originates more from personal history or innate brain architecture, Hobson and Kahn (2007) examined dream reports removed of identifiers to see if judges could rigorously distinguish dream reports based on content analysis. The results showed that judges could not easily match dreams with dreamers, and they called into question the hypothesis that dreams are strictly individualized experiences, and stated the following:

> The inescapable implication is that this study does not lend support to the hypothesis of strong individuality in dream content. . . . This finding lends weight to the surprising hypothesis that dreams are at least as species specific as they are individual specific . . . dreams serve as much to reveal general characteristics of the human mind as they do to reveal specific characteristics of any one dreamer.
>
> (5–6)

This result is not "surprising" according to a biological theory of archetypal images; in fact it is expected. More evidence to consider comes from Foulkes (1999). In his *Children's Dreaming and the Development of Consciousness*, Foulkes reviews the largest available database on laboratory-based children's dream reports from both cross-sectional and longitudinal studies (the data of which agreed with one another). He found that growing data strongly suggests that dream imagery appears to come from the internal structure of the mind, that is, from the innate structure, rather than from everyday experience in the form of simple memory retrieval:

> The more general point is that, for children as for adults, dream stories do not depend on what the dreamers have done. . . . *Dreaming starts from the mind and its organization, not from the world and its organization.*
>
> (81, emphasis added)

The question of how much developmental versus innate content goes into dream imagery is still in debate, of course, and in fact both are likely prominent factors – but this is a far cry from saying that dream imagery has *no* innate guidance.

Random images?

I should note that some dream researchers feel that dream imagery is meaningless and random (Crick and Mitchison, 1983, 1986; Hobson 1988[6]). A large body of dream research suggests that dream content (measured in Hall–Van de Castle scales, see Hall and Van de Castle, 1966) is neither random noise nor merely reflective of the previous day's events. The dream researcher Milton Kramer (2007) has shown in a variety of studies that dream content compares with waking event report content with a correlation coefficient of approximately .43. If dream content were random, he argues, this coefficient would be 0; furthermore, if dream content were merely related to memory consolidation – that is, simply repeating what was experienced during the day – the coefficient should be closer to 1. That it is in the middle of these two extremes causes Kramer to argue that dream content is neither random nor mindless churning through memories (as suggested by Crick and Mitchison, 1983, 1986), but a creative process that selectively utilizes imagery from the past but in novel ways. Dream content (imagery) furthermore appears to be related to mood and tracks changes in mood – again linking dream imagery with affect; also it is nonrandom and according to Kramer reflects certain psychological differences, responds to emotional concerns of the dreamer and appears linked and continuous with waking life (Kramer, 2007: 129–131; see also Hartmann, 1998; Strauch and Meier, 1996).

Kramer's data that suggests dream content is reflective of individual differences contrasts with Hobson and Kahn's (2007) and Foulkes's (1999) data that dream content is more innate in origin. However, this apparent contradiction can be satisfied by assuming a combinatorial system that consists, as Hobson and Kahn suggest, of imagery that is composed of both innate and individual content – in fact, Kramer's coefficient of .43 may somehow be reflective of the proportion of these two contributors.

Dreams are autonomous and continuous with undirected fantasy

Furthermore, this idea that dream content is *both* developmental and innate finds support in the suggested "autonomous" nature of dream content. There are a number of studies showing that dream imagery is relatively unaffected by pre-sleep stimuli such as fear-arousing movies, sprays of water, sounds, the names of significant people, or blood pressure cuffs (Foulkes, 1985, 1996, 1999); in fact, most dream content has very few rigorously identifiable experiential antecedents (Fosse et al., 2003; Hobson, 2003), which would be expected in a system with spontaneously active innate predispositions but not in an architecture that was solely reactive to the personal experiences of the dreamer. More subtle effects, however, can be observed in the clinical case studies reviewed in later chapters.

Autonomously generated imagery is a hallmark of dreams and fantasy, and can be pathological, as in the intrusive images of posttraumatic stress disorder (Kosslyn, 2005), which is clearly emotionally driven and unconsciously directed. This has been clearly shown in brain imaging studies (Rauch et al., 1996; Orr et al., 2002; Bremner et al., 1997; McNally et al., 1995). Remember that repetitive nightmares are one of the hallmarks of posttraumatic stress disorder – perhaps now we are coming to see why: the emotional brain, disturbed by trauma, expresses itself through recurrent images in timeless ways.

Under conditions in which the conscious system is relaxed (but not eliminated), the unconscious systems become more prominent, leading some of the original theorists such as Jung to state as early as 1936 that "We are quite probably dreaming all the time, but consciousness makes so much noise that we no longer hear the dream when awake" (Jung, 2008: 3).

In fact, more recent data by multiple authors has shown that under the right conditions, dream *content* and waking mental imagery *content* are nearly indistinguishable, establishing a continuity between dreaming and waking (Cicogna and Bosinelli, 2001; Foulkes and Fleisher, 1975; Foulkes and Scott, 1973; Kahan *et al.*, 1997; Reinsel *et al.*, 1986; Reinsel *et al.*, 1992; Strauch and Meier, 1996), which supports Jung's above intuition. In these cases, the conditions appear to be those of sensory deprivation, like when subjects are calmly resting in a dark, quiet room; here electrical brain measurements (EEG) and rapid eye movement (REM) reports are compared in order to establish the link between relaxed reverie and actual REM dreaming (Foulkes and Fleisher, 1975; Reinsel *et al.*, 1986; Reinsel *et al.*, 1992; Strauch and Meier, 1996). Under these conditions, undirected fantasy reports are very similar to dream reports, and are driven by emotion (Strauch and Meier, 1996).[7] Haule (2010) and McNamara (2009) review several other altered states of consciousness in which such experiences are more prominent.

Are dream images symbolic?

Knowing that dream images are partially derived from spontaneously active evolutionary related concerns does not prove that they will be symbolic in nature as Jung, Freud and many other theorists suggest. Jung suggested that symbols visually represent something of emotional salience to the subject:

> One cannot *invent* symbols; wherever they occur, they have not been devised by conscious intention and willful selection, because, if such a procedure had been used, they would have been nothing but signs and abbreviations of conscious thoughts. Symbols occur to us spontaneously, as one can see in our dreams, which are not invented but which happen to us.
>
> (Jung, 1950: para 432, emphasis in original)

But even though the above literature supports the idea that dream images are partially derived from the processing of autonomous, unconscious, emotional systems guided by evolutionary concerns, Jung went further in suggesting that they can be understood as *symbols*. I will explore symbolism later on, but for the moment we should recall that mental imagery has been shown to be frequently utilized by subjects to understand *abstract concepts* (Kosslyn *et al.*, 1995). Furthermore, since dream imagery is mental imagery, it seems reasonable to speculate that the images derived from this activity *could* also be used similarly (i.e. in an abstract or metaphorical manner), though this would be difficult to test empirically. At any rate, the consideration of dream images as symbolic or metaphorical is supported by many dream researchers outside analytical psychology (though there are skeptics – see Kramer, 2007 for a complete review). Domhoff, who was dismissive of Jungian dream interpretation methods, nevertheless recognized the possibility of the symbolic nature of dream images and felt future research should focus on this quality by using content analysis scales (2003: 38; also 55–56, 130–131; this sentiment is echoed by Hartmann, 1998, who calls prominent metaphors "contextual images," and Nielsen and Levin, 2006). The dream researcher Robert Van de Castle (Hall and Van de Castle, 1966; see also Domhoff, 2003) has observed that Jung's contributions to dream analysis have been underappreciated (Van de Castle, 1994), primarily because of this issue of symbolism.

Further support for the idea that dream imagery is emotional *and* symbolic comes from Kramer, in his rigorous and comprehensive review of dream research over the past few decades:

> The linkage between waking and dreaming thought is *affective, thematic and figurative rather than concrete and literal* . . . and more open to associative connections built more on connotative rather than denotative meanings.
>
> (Kramer, 2007: 207, emphasis added)

He states elsewhere that "dreaming is probably more related to symbolic processing than to REM physiology" (2007: 79), and there is evidence that this attempt at symbolic emotional expression is what is behind the evolving nature of the nightmares of posttraumatic stress disorder, as the brain gradually expresses the trauma in progressively more integrative symbolic ways (Hartmann, 1998; Phelps *et al.*, 2007).

In summary, then, a variety of neurobiological, neurocognitive and dream research data suggests that internally generated imagery (under various levels of conscious control) utilizes virtually the same cortical regions and the same cognitive processes as perception, and therefore should be subject to the same innate organizing principles if any can be demonstrated. Dream imagery, fantasy, and directed imagery differ in their level of conscious control – it was the unconsciously generated imagery that Jung was concerned with and proposed to be organized by archetypal processes, with the more unconsciously directed imagery of dreams appearing to be less variable and more universal than consciously directed images, and often highly symbolic. Moreover, with the above data it appears that unconsciously directed imagery may be *more* constrained by innate organizing biological principles bequeathed to us by evolution as they interact with typical environments, which suggests a kind of abstract "innate imagery" system is in place. This raises some tough questions.

The tricky problem of "innate imagery"

Evolutionary psychologists argue that our emotion/motivational systems must be comprised of an irreducible set of programs that are innate, and further that they appear to be relatively large in number, content-rich, and domain-specific (Tooby *et al.*, 2005). Affective neuroscience, by comparison, has shown that emotional primitive consciousnesses lie within the deep, universal regions of the brain, forming a universal core human psyche (Panksepp, 1998, 2005) that represents our innate emotional motivations. Thus the question of how all this ties together remains a challenge to sort out; the evolutionary programs have not been rigorously correlated with neurobiological data so far, but nevertheless it seems reasonable to assume that these programs must use perceptual data (mental images) – in concert with highly conserved emotional brain regions – *which will be constrained by the same domain-specific programs that direct the perceptual system, and that they will be linked in some way with emotional predispositions.*

If this is true, then we have a sound neurobiological argument for "innate imagery" – this is because the perceptual cues present in the innate programs, and the innate emotional motivators they are linked to, will also be available for use by the conceptual system. This point of view is likely to draw some controversy; therefore I will need to explain some definitions here.

Jung himself was continually accused of saying that humans experience innate images, which at that time seemed so far-fetched that he continually denied it, stating instead that he felt the "predisposition" to create the same kinds of images, and not the images themselves, was inherited. Thus his archetypal theory posited *some kind* of instinctive basis for why we come up with the same kinds of images independently throughout the world, but stopped short at saying we inherit images. His defense (summarized nicely in Haule, 2010) was to argue that we inherit the "innate structure" which experience then "fills in," thus making a neat dichotomy. The archetype "in itself," Jung argued, is innate but devoid of "content," and the content consists of experience, which creates the *image*. This theoretical maneuver therefore preserves his archetypal theory without getting into the sticky business of innate imagery. Later Jungians have continued this structure–content dichotomy (Haule, 2010; Knox, 2003; Stevens, 2002) that Jung introduced, and for theoretical discussions it remains a useful paradigm that avoids many objections.

But whenever I see neat dichotomies like this, I become skeptical. What exactly is meant here by "content"? Does "content" exist "in itself" irrespective of a genetically directed brain to organize it? How does this play out exactly with respect to specific images – the primary focus of this book? I think the distinction between "structure" and "content" works in general, but a fine-grained analysis of it becomes troublesome, and this problem also shows itself in the "gene–environment" or "nature–nurture" dichotomies. In Jungian symbol analysis it carries over into the archetype–image dichotomy and creates problems when analyzing how the brain creates these images. This is because "cognitive content," "environment," "experience/ learning," or "image" is being used as if it is somehow a completely independent player in brain/mind functioning that is separate from "structure," "genes," "instinct," or "archetype"; a common metaphor used is a computer, with its "hardware" and "software." But development and gene–environment interaction are just not this simple. Brains self-organize, at all times embedded in a particular environment they interact with at every level; thus the computer analogy doesn't quite work because the brain is *never* independent of the environment or vice versa. Rather, a genome will orchestrate its surrounding environment to suit its needs – replication.

Indeed, many biologists, evolutionists and philosophers of science argue convincingly that "gene–environment" distinctions are very complex and that, for any particular organism, the "environment" can be viewed *only* in the context of the data acquiring and organizing structure (Buss, 2005; Carruthers *et al.*, 2005). The Darwinian philosopher Dr. Helena Cronin (2005) reviews these challenges by using the example of the indigo bunting, a bird with the scientific name *Passerine cyanea*. This bird navigates the environment using an evolved set of rules that direct the bird to pay special attention to the stars during night flights and in particular to their movement patterns, making a distinction over time between slow and fast circling stars. Further, the data processing program attends to the tightest circle of stars, estimates a point in the center of this circle and stores it. Using these rules, the indigo bunting can navigate using a fixed celestial point that will correspond with north – interestingly, this program is far superior to just learning to track onto the North Star, which would be simpler, but would lose accuracy every 27,000 years due to the procession of the earth's axis (a short blip in evolutionary time). The above learning program, rather, provides the species with an excellent compass designing program.

The essence of the problem is the question where in this whole process do "genes" or "innate structure" end and "environment" or "image" begin? One might argue that the "program" of gathering star location data is the "structure" and the stars are the "content" – but this dodges critical issues. The program already has content – it "knows," for example, what to look for, where to look for it, and when to look, and furthermore what distinctions to make. It not only knows how to recognize a "star," and what "location" is (which are deeper complexities within this one), but also *only* to worry about how the star moves. Why doesn't it also track the light spectrum of the star? Or make distinctions of intensity, or other things present in the star "in itself"? Indeed, the program knows to make distinctions between fast- and slow-moving stars, and that the "central point" is for some reason *important*, and then what to do about it. These same stars could have ten thousand other uses, but this particular usage is unique to this kind of behavior and represents a significant part of the bird's subjective world. Thus even the word "environment" is meaningful only from the point of view of the genetic structure interacting with it, and can have many definitions depending on how the genes "intend" to do so.

Cronin (2005) puts it humorously:

> In the beginning, natural selection created genes that could barely exploit the heavens or the earth; their adaptations were meager and their environments commensurately without form and void. But, down evolutionary time, genes have bootstrapped themselves from inchoate nakedness into magnificent dwellings, organisms of great sophistication . . . they have thereby been able to create and exploit ever richer environments in ever more ingenious ways.
>
> (21)

She goes on:

> Without genes to specify what constitutes an environment, environments would not exist. [They] are themselves the products of biology. Environment is . . . a biological issue, an adaptationist issue, a gene-centered issue. . . . Genes use environments for a purpose – self replication. Environments, however, have no purposes; so they do not use genes. Thus genes are machines for converting stars into more genes; but stars are not machines for converting genes into more stars.
>
> (21)

Each gene anticipates a particular environment from the start; the emphasis on the subjective world of the organism, here, is critical, because the environment is *defined* by the organism. Cronin finishes with this comment on the distinction between genes and environment by saying: "To unravel the confusion here, we need to parse 'learning' adaptively . . . learning from the environment is not an alternative to instinct; on the contrary, innate mechanisms are what make learning possible" (21).

The evolutionary psychologists Tooby and Cosmides (1992) put it thus:

> There is nothing in the logic of development to justify the idea that traits can be divided into genetically versus environmentally controlled sets or arranged along a spectrum that reflects the influence of genes versus the environment.
>
> (83)

Elsewhere, Tooby *et al.* (2005) tie this into motivation/emotion, stating that brain structure:

> operates jointly on values and [images] so that knowledge-representing cognitive processes *often cannot be intelligibly separated* from motivational processes . . .[8] Given data about which valuation problems humans solve, this is a method not only for demonstrating the general case for innate ideas but also for identifying specific sets of such computational elements.
>
> (337, emphasis added)

Tooby *et al.*'s 30-plus page argument is too involved to summarize adequately here, but essentially the argument is that innate "structure" already has "content," making the structure–content distinction dubious, and the brain/mind also intermingles motivation (and hence emotion) with sensory processing or *imagery*. Since external data is preferentially organized in specific ways and automatically tagged with motivational significance, the "content" obtained from the environment becomes so heavily colored and organized by the brain's structure, it can be said that the structure *imparts* a great deal of content of its own, a point often made by many evolutionary psychologists and behavioral ethologists (see Buss, 2005).

The Jungian analyst Warren Colman (2010) summarizes nicely that symbols are "the clothing of affect in image." I agree, and add that the choice of "clothing" can be traceable in part to evolutionary and neurobiological processes, leading me to ask: can we explain *why* the brain keeps picking the same kinds of images to represent various affects? Furthermore, these considerations show that archetypal processes, as "nested innate patterns within patterns" (Haule, 2010), may, then, not strictly be "images," but they do have very image-like characteristics.

Consider facial recognition development: the brain seems to innately anticipate *conceptual* organization of visual data such as faces, animals, eye-gaze, and objects, some of which have been linked directly to genetic processes (Duchaine *et al.*, 2006, 2007, 2009; New *et al.*, 2007; Wilmer *et al.*, 2010). Matsumoto and Willingham (2009), for example, reviewed the data on facial expressions in the congenitally blind and found that the blind spontaneously produce culture-independent expressions of smiling, laughing, crying, sadness, distress, surprise, disgust, shame, pride, anger, and contempt. These results suggest "that the universality in emotional expression . . . originates from evolved potentially genetic sources and that all humans, regardless of gender or culture, are born with this ability" (9; see also Tracy and Matsumoto, 2008).

The origin of these expressions would likely evolve in an environment where such displays were innately recognizable, which evidence *also* supports (Matsumoto and Ekman, 2004). So here we are seeing evidence of what I mean by "innate imagery": the innate ability of the brain to recognize and/or reliably and spontaneously organize facial data into these expressions and link it to specific affects perceptually, behaviorally, and, I argue, conceptually, *even when minimal environmental data are available*, such as in the case of the congenitally blind. *Specifically directed and attended* experience in which *particular details* are examined closely and *specific distinctions are made* while others are overlooked, even despite large variations in such "environment," like the blind, further refines this system, but it does not create it. Panksepp (1998) gives another example that hypothesizes why we constantly use the images of ice and cold to represent social isolation, since the neural systems for separation distress evolved from brain circuitry involved in pain and *thermal regulation*, both of which have been shown to be affected by manipulations in opioid systems:

> When we are lost, we feel cold – not only physically but also as a *neurosymbolic response* to social separation. . . . the roots of the social motivational system may be strongly linked to thermoregulatory systems of the brain . . . Thus, when we hear the sound of someone who is lost, especially if it is our child, we also feel cold. This may be nature's way of promoting reunion. In other words, the experience of separation establishes an internal feeling of thermoregulatory discomfort that can be alleviated by the warmth of reunion. . . . From the present perspective, it seems . . . likely that opioid blockade reduces chills because one no longer experiences the rapid decline in opioid activity that is produced during the perceptually induced affective experience of social loss, an experience that, in the human mind, is always combined with the possibility of redemption – being found and cared for when one is lost.
>
> (278–279, emphasis added)

These systems, universal in humans, therefore provide the neurological source and target domains for several kinds of ubiquitous symbols that will emerge reliably in a variation-resistant manner. Jungian analysts of course often equate the imagery of winter or cold as a metaphor for the lack of feeling a person is experiencing, whereas: "Fire and flame symbolize warmth and love, feeling and passion; they are qualities of the heart, found wherever human beings exist" (Jacoby, 1964). Now perhaps we can see why; it is something spontaneously evident to any intact human mind on an affect–image level. Certain emotions will conjure images of people with certain facial expressions, and disrupted attachments or social isolation will conjure "cold" imagery (with a distant warm hearth perhaps on the horizon) in a highly variation-resistant manner. This is but one example of many examples I will explore in this book.

The neurologist Antonio Damasio (1994) also observes that "we are wired to respond with an emotion" (131) when certain environmental features are perceived such as animals, snake-like motion, and growls, and these immediately trigger emotional reactions – further linking image to affect. As another example, consider the evolutionary data on human attractiveness. Here, Sugiyama (2005) reviews the evidence for an innate system responsible for emotional attribution of face and body characteristics that likely emerged for evolutionary reasons. For example, there is a great deal of agreement cross-culturally on facial attractiveness (Cunningham et al., 2002; Rubenstein et al., 2002; Zebrowitz, 1997), and attractiveness varies negatively with deviation from so-called "templates," which are modeled by amalgams of many faces averaged via computer morphing techniques (Langlois and Roggman, 1990). Why should this be? One clue is that facial attractiveness is correlated with low *fluctuating asymmetry* – a quality that is associated with greater developmental and reproductive success (Sugiyama, 2005: 312–313). Perception of attractiveness emerges early in life. This suggests genetic guidance; for example, a variety of studies showed that infants ranging from newborn to 25 months preferred faces that matched those rated as attractive by adults, regardless of whether they were Asian, African American, or Caucasian (reviewed in Sugiyama, 2005: 294–295). These above qualities apply equally to males and females.

This system appears more specific when it comes to sexual attractiveness. Generally speaking, Panksepp (1998) observes that: "Male brains appear to be instinctively prepared to respond to certain features of human femaleness, including facial and bodily characteristics, voice intonations, as well as ways of being" (233), providing our first clue that more than just visual cues are present in the perceptual/conceptual system in question that trigger the prespecified valuation systems.

Evolutionary psychologists like Sugiyama (2005: 308–326) review the universal cross-cultural preferences in female appearance that men report as attractive; not surprisingly, *all of them correlate with reproductive fitness*. Among the qualities reported as attractive across all cultures studied are smooth skin (which correlates with low pathogen load or disease), shiny, long hair (which correlates with age of peak fertility in women and also reflects health and reproductive status), a waist-to-hip circumference ratio of approximately 0.7 (also positively correlated with increased health and reproductive success[9]), long legs (associated with fertility), and developed, firm, high breasts that point slightly up and out, with small areolae and low fluctuating asymmetry (strongly cueing nubility, age, parity, pregnancy status, and/or reproductive success – the sheer level of detail here explains the human preoccupation with breast imagery). Even movement patterns have been assessed in terms of attractiveness – masked or pixilated images of dancers were found to be more sexually attractive the larger and more sweeping their movements were. Grammer et al. (2004) suggest that such movements are a predictor of underlying genetic quality and fecundity, which accounts for their attractiveness. This system even goes beyond visual images; men have been shown to prefer the scent of females during mid-cycle to those outside their fertile period when blinded (Singh and Bronstad, 2001). All of these strongly suggest innate, universal image systems in the male brain that are primed to respond emotionally to these patterns. Furthermore, the research in this field is still growing; there are likely many more aspects of this system that have yet to be shown. The frequent emphasis on dental beauty and foot appearance cross-culturally, for example, is another probable perceptual/conceptual cue yet to be studied.

That men place high emotional significance on this kind of imagery is obvious. But these "fertility detection" principles are not unique to men; they apply to women as well, though not as measures of mate choice but as *mechanisms to identify the competitive power of other females*. The difference, then, is the kind of emotional significance that is attributed to the imagery. Culture and learning can modify this system quite a bit, of course, but they must work within the biological constraints that natural selection has created.

Is it so strange that men and women should have innate imagery detectors designed to identify highly fertile females?[10] Not really; animals certainly do, so why should humans be any different? Overall, the system is argued (Sugiyama, 2005) to have evolved to orient men toward fertile females who have a high probability of producing healthy offspring, and automatically invests them with a significant amount of sex-drive and attachment-related emotions; developmentally, interest in this imagery correlates with surges in testosterone levels in males during adolescence, at just the time when it should become useful and it is used in females as a way to orient toward potential mate-stealing (and hence offspring resource-stealing) females; also it is used in women as a self-ideal with which to measure one's own physical competitiveness (men do this, too, of course).

This system works not only to *recognize* a sexually and/or romantically attractive female, but also to *generate* novel internal imagery of such a person never met before – an "ideal" mate that exists in the mind innately (more on this in later chapters); these images can therefore emerge spontaneously in dreams and undirected fantasy at any given time, particularly when emotion is present.

The sexual selection data provides evidence of a highly detailed, yet innate, value assigning system that can *generate* imagery *and* meaning – or at least a strong attentional cue into which meaning will be quickly and easily added during development. This is, therefore, evidence of innate (though abstract) affectively meaningful imagery which generates universal preferences that "just so happen" to correlate with high reproductive value.

In summary, a considerable body of evidence suggests that thinking in images is "older" than thinking in terms of language (Haule, 2010), and that imagery is an important foundation to rational thought. Furthermore, the conceptual system is constrained by the perceptual system, and hence any innate principles that order the perceptual system will likely order the conceptual system as well. Some imagery has been shown to have innate affective, value-assigning prespecification and provides evidence of abstract, highly meaningful "innate imagery" prototypes that experience colors and which the mind can generate at any time in anyone. Furthermore, imagery of dream content has been shown to be at least partially focused on evolutionary concerns that are as much universal as they are unique to the dreamer.

Thus mental imagery has multiple sources; the images of dreams and fantasy are likely to correlate with the activity of deeper, more universal brain activity. They can also take advantage of innate abstract image prototypes such as those used to detect high reproductive value females (and males, reviewed in Sugiyama, 2005), and many other types of meaningful imagery I will explore later. But an innate image prototype *is not an archetype or an archetypal image*. Archetypal images are more than innate programs – what is missing is the key element of *symbolism.*

Symbolism and metaphor theory

Symbolism is perhaps the most important aspect of the archetypal image. Jung felt that there was a fundamental difference between a *sign*, which is an arbitrary place holder devoid of inherent significance – like algebraic variables – and a *symbol*, which is according to Jung (1959b) a concept that the mind uses to attempt to understand something relatively unknown; it is the "best possible formulation of a relatively unknown thing" (Jung, 1971 [1976]: 474).

In his early work, Jung describes his intuition on the supreme importance of metaphor and symbol in human thinking in general:

> It seems as if this process of analogy-making had gradually altered and added to the common stock of ideas and names, with the result that man's picture of the world was considerably broadened . . . a positively overwhelming importance attaches to the little word "like" in the history of human thought [and] was responsible for some of the most important discoveries ever made by primitive man.
>
> (Jung, 1956: para 203)

Jung felt archetypal images were infused with emotion, so therefore the archetypal image is not only an image with a strong innately directed structure/content, but one that emerges in correlation with heightened activity of emotional brain processes, and is used in a metaphorical way to represent something "relatively unknown" to the subject. Without this key factor, it is merely a sign and not a symbol. In order to make a model of archetypal images that accounts for this we must explore the data of metaphor theory.

Cognitive linguistics and metaphor theory

In the last few decades, a theory on metaphorical thought has emerged that has synthesized a number of fields into a coherent model. The cognitive linguist George Lakoff (1997) outlines his findings on the functions of metaphor in unconscious thinking: metaphors, he argues, are not arbitrary mappings from one literal domain to another (like algebraic variables), but rather deeply embedded patterns of thinking based on our brain structure. He outlines three basic findings from the field:

1   Humans constantly use metaphors to explain and understand things.
2   The metaphorical mappings are *not* purely abstract and arbitrary.
3   Very little everyday language is literal: most of it is metaphorical.

Lakoff and Johnson (1999), drawing from numerous lines of evidence in systematic polysemy, inference pattern generalization, extensions to poetic and novel cases (Lakoff and Turner, 1989), priming studies (Boroditzky, 2000), gesture studies (McNeill, 1992), semantic change research (Sweetser, 1990), sign language analysis (Taub, 2001), and language acquisition (Johnson, 1997a, 1997b), argue that the vast majority of thought and reasoning is built upon a system of "primary metaphors," for example the SEEING IS KNOWING metaphor.[11] This metaphor is at the heart of such common phrases as "I *see* what you mean," "let's shed some *light* on the subject," "I didn't understand his *point of view*," and so on. Of crucial importance to these primary metaphors, however, is that they are *embodied*, that is, rooted in *physical biological experience*, in this case visuospatial form – which, remember, is readily created even in brains that have no visual experience. This primary metaphor then gives rise to all the commonly used SEEING IS KNOWING expressions that are easily recognized by everyone (even the born blind), even when used in novel ways. Other examples of primary metaphors are MORE IS UP ("prices are *high* today"), CHANGE IS MOTION ("I don't know where these ideas are *leading* us"), CAUSES ARE FORCES ("he *pushed* me into doing something bad"), and many others (Lakoff and Johnson, 1999: 45–59), which are the building blocks of more complex metaphors such as LOVE IS A JOURNEY ("this relationship is *heading in different directions*, the marriage is *off track*, we may have to *bail out*, we're *in this together*," etc.). These metaphors are grounded in our physical experience, such as physical movement, sensory data, motion, and spatial relationships, but are mapped from more conceptually nebulous domains such as time, mind, self, morality and virtually everything else. Some examples of Primary Metaphors are given below (adapted from Lakoff and Johnson, 1999: 50–54; see also Grady, 1997).

Visuospatial metaphors

Important is Big: "we have a *big* problem here."
Happy is Up and Sad is Down: "my moods have been *up and down* lately."
More is Up and Less is Down: "the price of gas has *risen and fallen* today."
Understanding is Grasping: "he could not *get hold of* the concepts being taught."
Intimacy is Closeness: "we are getting *closer* as a couple."
Similarity is Closeness: "he was so *close* to the right answer."
Categories are Containers: "I think you are *in* the wrong."
Measurements are Paths: "her running speed *surpassed* his."
Time is Motion: "winter *passed* by us slowly."
Change is Motion: "his views are *moving* from Republican to Democrat."
Mental states are Locations: "suddenly he *flew into* a rage."
Purposes are Destinations: "she is working hard to *reach* her goals in life."
Purposes are Objects: "you should *take* any opportunity you have to improve."
Relationships are Containers: "we have been *in* this marriage together for years."

Somatic primary metaphors

Affection is Warmth: "*warm* wishes to you all."
Difficulties are Burdens: "this assignment is *weighing* me down."
Causes are Forces: "stop *pushing* her to leave."

Metaphors are "mappings" that translate data from one domain, say the emotional domain, and "map" it into another domain, say "traveling," to create things like the LOVE IS A JOURNEY metaphor, and this mapping is used by the brain to make nebulous concepts more concrete and understandable. Metaphors are therefore based on our biology; metaphors for anger, for example, cross-culturally emerge from the physiology of anger (Kövecses, 1986, 1990). Rather than a trick of language or airy poetic invention, metaphors are a healthy type of thinking, wherein sensory information or internal states are perceived as visual (or other) phenomena that help us to understand and construct the mysterious aspects of our mental world.

Metaphors are crucial to the way we understand the world as humans, well beyond simple primary metaphors. Complex metaphors are the source of imagination, since they allow us to map things we know well cognitively from our neurobiology, such as the visuospatial system, to things we are trying to understand, like the universe, the mind, and emotions. But the key insight is that this foundation – an unconscious metaphor-generating system – is not random, but founded in the physical makeup of our brains and primary experience of the world; it is *embodied*. This system is therefore grounded in neurobiology, is unconscious, and underlies most of our waking thought and language, including the highest expressions of art, philosophy, and poetry. According to Lakoff and Johnson, "Metaphorical maps are part of our brains, [and] we will think and speak metaphorically whether we want to or not" (Lakoff and Johnson, 2003: 257).

Elsewhere the authors describe metaphors as

> a natural phenomenon. Conceptual metaphor is a natural part of human thought, and linguistic metaphor is a natural part of human language. Moreover, which metaphors we have and what they mean depend on the nature of our bodies, our interactions in the physical environment, and our social and cultural practices . . . [furthermore] metaphor is a *neural phenomenon*. . . . They constitute the neural mechanism that naturally, and inevitably, recruits sensory-motor inference for use in abstract thought. Primary metaphors arise spontaneously and automatically without our being aware of them.
>
> (Lakoff and Johnson, 2003: 247–256, emphasis added)

Lakoff explores the creativity of this system:

> because of the wide range of possibilities permitted by the metaphor system, one person's dreams can have powerful meanings for other people. Other people's dreams hold for us the same fascination as myth and literature – a potential vehicle for finding meaning in our own lives. It is the operation of our metaphor systems that allows such a possibility.
>
> (Lakoff 1997: 108)

The metaphors cited by Lakoff should be familiar to Jungian dream analysts: LOVE IS A JOURNEY, ANGER IS HEAT, INSTINCTS ARE ANIMALS, or THE MIND IS A HOUSE (Lakoff, 1997: 117; Lakoff and Turner, 1989; Lakoff and Johnson, 1999). The dream researcher G. Domhoff (2003) criticized Jungian dream interpretation by stating that the archetype is more easily explained as "merely" a shared cultural metaphor, citing that the same metaphors can be found cross culturally (Lakoff and Johnson, 1999; Yu, 1999). But an archetypal image is not simply a metaphor; it is a *special kind* of metaphor that comprises the innate, the affective, and the instinctual. It impresses strongly upon our conscious subjective experience, and feels powerful and moving – more on this below.

Metaphors are relational structures; that is, they represent relationships between things. In one series of experiments, subjects were asked to provide metaphors that supported each side of a debate over whether the federal budget should be balanced at the cost of cutting social programs. Most subjects were able to provide over ten metaphors in just a few minutes, over 80 percent of them having nothing to do with economics or politics. This pattern of novel metaphor generation held when hundreds of newspaper clippings discussing politics were analyzed (Blanchette and Dunbar, 2000, 2001). Here we can see this "symbol generator" in action – a mechanism we all share (provided the proper neural structures are intact) for recognizing and symbolizing *relational patterns* in the world. Note that in comparison, the Jungian analyst Brooke (1991) has also argued that archetypal images are relational structures.

In summary, cognitive linguists have determined that the mind constantly uses metaphors, which are defined as mappings that redescribe ephemeral concepts as concrete concepts – with the implicit understanding that they are not *literally* equivalent but equivalent by *analogy*. Anger is "like" fire, for example, but anger is not literally fire. The constant use of metaphor is universal and, since we all have the same physiology, we tend to use the same kinds of metaphors. In other words, all brains are better at comprehending visuospatial data than deeply felt emotions, so we frequently describe love as a journey, sadness as a descent ("falling into despair"), elation as an ascent ("with head in the clouds"), and so on.

Lakoff and Johnson (1999) draw from decades of research in cognitive neuroscience, discourse coherence studies, historical semantic change studies, and language acquisition studies; sign language and spontaneous gesture studies have shown that humans come to conceptualize the world in terms of a large collection of metaphors that are ubiquitous and grounded in physical experience. What distinguishes humans is that somewhere along the primate line we developed the ability to represent other things *as if* they were objects moving in space. So now we can take things that are difficult to understand by our limited brains, like time, emotions, or death, and say "time is like a river," "love is like a journey," or "death is like a window." But are such statements "true"? Yes and no – it depends on what you mean by "true": since these metaphors are accurate portrayals of subjective experience, they are quite true in a subjective "big picture" way, which is extremely important for us as human beings. But as literal statements, they are not – it is this dichotomy, I think, that befuddles so many debates about science and religion.

Meet Mr. Literal

The findings of metaphor theory are striking in their simplicity – but they are easy to underestimate. In order to illustrate just how much of our thinking is metaphorical, and hence *symbolic*, let me introduce you to Mr. Literal. Mr. Literal takes everything we say absolutely literally. He's a funny guy that way. Problem is, you can't have a conversation with him, because normal people just don't think this way. Here's an example of a conversation I had with him just the other day:

Me: "So, Mr. Literal, do you see what I'm trying to say?"

Mr. Literal: "No . . . because you can't *see* what people say. Words can't be seen."

Me: "Ugh . . . I mean do you understand what I'm saying?"

Mr. Literal: "Huh? How can you stand under a word?"

Me: "Oh good grief! Look, I'm going to show you what I mean."

Mr. Literal: "How can you *show* me what you *mean*? Oh, and also you can't *go to* a statement."

Me: "Are you saying I can barely go through a single sentence without using a metaphor?"

Mr. Literal: "Excuse me, Dr. Goodwyn, but you cannot go *through* a sentence, and you cannot *use* a metaphor as if it were an object."

Me: [pulls out gun and shoots Mr. Literal]. "There. That solves it."

Mr. Literal: [in death throes] "But a problem isn't a liquid that has a *solution* . . ." [choke, die]

Thus the only way we "understand" the world, cognitive linguists have "shown," is "through" the "use" of metaphor, even to the "level" of our preverbal thoughts. See how this works? Slowly, it seems, through the course of evolution, our primate ancestors evolved the ability to think of experiences "as if" they were objects moving around in space. This ability predates language, which allows us to further specify the details of these more vague visual "thoughts." But the preverbal language underlies the verbal one, and directs most of how we think – except, that is, for the most banal facts of existence.

Dream symbols and metaphor theory

Earlier I showed that dream scientists largely agree that the dreaming state differs significantly from the waking state in the origin of the mental imagery – with waking imagery more consciously directed, and dream imagery emerging from the deeper "layers" of the brain/mind and directed by more "outside" influences – outside the singular conscious self, that is. Lakoff (1997) illustrates how the metaphor system is apparently used during this state:

> What Freud called *symbolization, displacement, condensation,* and *reversal* appear to be the same mechanisms that cognitive scientists refer to as *conceptual metaphor, conceptual metonymy, conceptual blending,* and *irony*. But whereas Freud saw these mechanisms as irrational modes of primary-process thinking, cognitive scientists have found these modes to be an indispensable part of ordinary, rational thought, which is largely unconscious.
>
> (90, emphasis in original)

Lakoff goes on to state:

> The metaphor system plays a generative role in dreaming. . . . That is, the metaphor system, which is in place for waking thought and expression, is also available during sleep and provides a natural mechanism for relating concrete images to abstract meanings. Of course, upon waking, the dreamer may well not be aware of the meaning of the dream, since he or she did not consciously direct the choice of dream imagery to metaphorically express the meaning of the dream. . . . [however] The system of metaphors, though unconscious, is not "repressed." . . . dreams are [not] just the weird and meaningless product of random neural firings, but rather a natural way by which emotionally charged fears, desires, and descriptions of difficulties in life are expressed.
>
> (1997: 104–107)

Regarding dream metaphors, at one point Lakoff even states that: "When I read books on dream analysis by psychotherapists, I rarely find much attention accorded to those aspects of the meanings of dreams that depend on the everyday metaphor system" (1997: 119) – a sentiment that shows an apparent unfamiliarity with Jung's writings on dreams. Jung understood the symbol to be a powerful shaper of dream and fantasy imagery, arguing that it should not be taken literally but rather metaphorically (numerous examples can be found in Jung, 1984, 2008) and regarded for its symbolic and subjective (not literal) truth. Jung understood the symbol as "the best possible formulation of a relatively unknown thing, which for that reason cannot be more clearly or characteristically represented, [and] is symbolic" (Jung, 1971 [2005]: para 815).

Therefore Jung's concept of the *symbol* shares some similarity with Lakoff and Johnson's concept of the metaphor. Both concepts are defined not as arbitrary signs devoid of inherent meaning but as meaningful mappings that analogize something difficult to comprehend with something easy to comprehend. In the case of Lakoff and Johnson, the "easy to comprehend" is a well-defined sensorimotor experience and the "difficult to comprehend" is an aspect of experience that is vague, abstract, or otherwise difficult to describe concretely, that is, to understand the experience of "knowing" in terms of visual experience ("seeing"). In the case of Jung, the easy to comprehend is the dream or mythic image (visuospatial data) at face value, and the difficult to comprehend is the emotional meaning or otherwise ineffable concept that this visual image is inferred to *mean* to the subject. Both formulations, then, appear to be exploring the same phenomenon, though Jung went further in describing a set of symbols that he postulated were "archetypal," that is, loaded with emotion, "primordial" with respect to consciousness, numinous, and "instinctual."

Thus the metaphor system is deep rooted and works the same during dreaming as it does during waking, with the exception being that what is being mapped into a symbolic image is consciously directed during the waking state, whereas during dreaming or other altered states, it is nonconsciously directed. This becomes important in later chapters where I give a detailed example of this system at work. Presently, what metaphor theory tells us is that when we dream, the unconscious layers of the mind are stating: "The current situation I am in *is like* this collection of images."

An example of novel complex metaphor construction

This metaphor-generating process is capable of tremendous creativity in human thought, dreaming or not, since it provides us with a method for building complex metaphors from primary ones. As Lakoff and Johnson (2003) point out, this happens via known psychological mechanisms:

> Innovation and novelty are not miraculous; they do not come out of nowhere. They are built using the tools of everyday metaphorical thought, as well as other commonplace conceptual mechanisms.
>
> (251)

The authors give the example of the "Grim Reaper" symbol made popular in the Middle Ages during the prevalence of the Black Death. The Grim Reaper is of course a complex metaphor using the People are Plants and Death is a Departure metaphors and the Death is a Skeleton metaphor, combined with the Cowls = Monks' Robes = Funerals metonymies.[12] The combination of these metaphors formed an emotionally powerful symbol of death at a time when death was unavoidably common and gruesome. Note that the conceptual power of this system lies in its combinatorial capacity to generate new metaphors with new implied meanings from more basic parts, and the imagery is easily understood even without verbal explanation.

What becomes evident through this process is that the *mapping is what creates meaning* from the metaphor. Even primary metaphors contain this additional meaning generator within them. Time is not literally "passing by" anyone, yet when conceptualized this way new meaning is found and new understanding generated. The meanings, however, are elusive to specific explication; there is really no better way to express the combination of despair, inevitability, and perhaps solemnity of the Grim Reaper symbol except as it is. Reducing it to the simple one-to-one sign Grim Reaper = Death erases the more subtle points utilized in the image such as the monk's robe, the scythe, and the agricultural symbolism of people as dying but playing a part in the life–death cycle. *The only way to explain metaphors, then, is through other metaphors.* This, I propose, is the *ineffable core of meaning* that is contained in the metaphor. It is ineffable since there is really no other way to explain it except in metaphorical terms, and the reason for this limitation is merely the fact that our brains are not infinite (despite our frequent delusions to the contrary). If our brains understood everything as well as we understand objects, creatures, and movement, we wouldn't need to use metaphors of moving objects and creatures to symbolize.

Though psycholinguists disagree on primary metaphor acquisition (Pinker, 2007), they agree that the use of metaphor is an innate capacity in humans, and we constantly use metaphors of things we perceive with great clarity, like objects moving in space, to represent things we perceive more nebulously, like feelings, time, society, the universe, death, and many other things. Metaphors, and hence symbols ("archetypal" or not), therefore represent patterns: patterns of the world, patterns of our feelings, patterns of relationship, that, being metaphors, contain an ineffable core of meaning that cannot be described except in terms of other metaphors; nevertheless, they are of paramount importance to the way we understand things. But a symbol of a god or spirit is quite a bit more than simply a pattern, and this is because of the aspect of *interaction*, that is, praying or communing with a god consists of more than simple pattern recognition; on this subject I elaborate in later sections.

How this relates to the concept of archetypal images and analytical psychology

Recall that above I showed the evidence for an "ideal mate" image according to evolutionary psychology. This innate image prototype is *not* a symbol. It is a straightforward image that orients humans toward high-genetic-quality others (either as potential mates or as sexual rivals), and, due to decoupled cognition, allows for such imagery to be conjured up spontaneously, particularly in dreaming or fantasy states when deeper "layers" of the brain/mind have freer reign regarding what is perceived subjectively. What metaphor theory shows is that the brain/mind *also* has the ability to use this imagery in an *as if* manner. Thus the image can become more than just an image: it can become a symbol; as such it can be used to symbolize many different things. Furthermore, this frequently occurs during dreaming and other altered states of consciousness.

Since symbols are mappings that metaphorically equate something the brain/mind understands well to something it does not understand as well, this means that the ideal mate images could be used in the same way that objects moving in space are – that is, they can be ubiquitously used as metaphors. This is because ideal mate imagery is something well known to every intact human brain. Thus it can be used to symbolize something relatively unknown – meaning appreciated with relatively less clarity. Anything that can be shown to be well "understood" by the brain as a consequence of its evolutionary history can be used to generate symbols of things less well understood. As Lakoff (1997) pointed out, this appears to happen frequently in dreaming, and moreover, the data on mental imagery, affective neuroscience and evolutionary psychology appears to argue that ancient affective concerns are more prominent in dream imagery – hence dream symbols are more likely to be innately ordered, "instinctual" and affective, which suggests they can be archetypal.

This puts us in a position to understand archetypal images from these many perspectives. Accordingly, it appears that an archetypal image is as follows:

1   It is a symbol that represents something difficult to grasp by means of using something easily comprehended.
2   The imagery used is easily comprehended because it is "innate" in the sense that the brain/mind naturally resorts to images that are "hard-wired" to the process or are learned quickly and with great clarity and differentiation, such as objects moving in space, "ideal" mates, and many other concepts I will describe in later chapters.
3   This imagery is furthermore linked to our emotional experience – an ideal mate, for example, is not a dry emotionless calculation but one fraught with specific motivational significance (subjectively felt as emotion) because of our evolutionary history. This aspect of the symbol differentiates the archetypal image from an intellectual symbol devoid of such emotional meaning.
4   The image, *as a holistic symbol*, is ultimately *ineffable* and remains a stand-alone mental construct that cannot be described in other terms without resorting to using other metaphors.
5   Finally, the image is experienced when the brain/mind is in a state that is weighted toward the deeper, more universal, layers, such as dreaming, reverie, or other altered states of consciousness such as trance or ritual, and is therefore less consciously directed – such sources can be

either implicit layers related to personal history or deeper layers related to species history.

6 From the previous point we can also conclude that such symbols are derived much less from our personal history than from other symbols, and will therefore feel "external" from the point of view of consciousness.

Haule (2010) has a further insight that the archetypal patterns that give rise to such images are *nested* within each other and can be observed in our primate relatives and inferred from what we know about our extinct predecessor species. Thus archetypal patterns in the human mind emerge spontaneously in development from more fundamental patterns, which themselves emerge from even more fundamental patterns. They are "complexities within complexities" (Haule, 2010: 31). These patterns result in similar images appearing across world cultures that have the same basic structure but with many local variations.

The description of the archetypal image as it is experienced consciously can therefore be broken down into two components, the image and the environment/intrapsychic pattern that the image is being used to represent. The *image* is an innate brain product derived from domain-specific programs that use prespecified emotional attribution and data recognizing/generating mechanisms (described by Tooby *et al.*, 2005), such as mate recognition, mother, father, predator, and so on. This skeleton of an image/meaning system is colored in by experience to generate more detailed imagery.

Since archetypal images are defined as symbols (Jung, 1959b, 2008), however, these are more than just images. Rather, they represent *something difficult to formulate* that is only equivalent to the image by analogy. Furthermore, since it is produced by unconscious processes rather than consciously, what the image symbolizes is not explicitly known – rather, it is known only implicitly. Last, we must remember that the mind is using a symbol here because what it represents is not easily comprehended; it is a symbol for a reason. Love, for example, is something we *feel* deeply but cannot easily *describe* in concrete linguistic terms without resorting to metaphor (it is perhaps impossible), and this is presumably because our brains are not hardwired to process "love" in the same way that they are hardwired to process visuospatial data such as moving objects. But obviously love *exists*,[13] and so we are forced to describe this nebulous entity with metaphors – in fact we can never escape doing so. Archetypal symbols, with their presumed correlation with activity in the deepest layers of the mind, likely describe perceptions or environmental patterns that are even more difficult to quantify and process – hence they can be highly ineffable expressions that are frequently paradoxical and/or baffling, but nonetheless *real*. It is no coincidence that so many religious/mystical concepts fall into this category.

This leads us to conclude that any images that are archetypal will be images that are inherently mysterious to our limited brain/minds (1) because of this ineffability and (2) because it is generated in deeper layers that impose on our consciousness as if from "outside." The imagery itself is derived from innately acquired programs we all share, colored by early developmental experiences, and in the context of current environmental happenings, but *what it means,* or rather what environment and/or unconscious dynamic the image metaphorically *represents*, originates from the deepest layers of our highly conserved emotional consciousness as it interacts with the chaotic patterns of the environment. Remember, at this level the division between "internal" and "external" starts to become very blurry, and so we must simply regard such symbols as general aspects of experience that cannot be easily resolved into internal/external or subjective/objective. As Haule puts it, "the archetype may not quite be 'in' the brain, rather it *uses* the brain" (2010: 21).

Such a symbol can be something as simple as a static dream image or it can be an entire narrative in complexity, as stories can be metaphors just as static images can. In the case of gods or spirits, such a symbol is a personality, complete with motivations, intent, purpose (all of which I explore in the next chapter), and so on, and because of this it can be an important "player" in our lives. A particularly emotional image or image sequence may therefore be a *symbol* of an important process relevant not only to personal history but to *species* history; the latter of these two would arguably be the most emotionally moving.

Searching for gods

Now that I have reviewed some of the normal ways in which our brains formulate our subjective experience, I intend to show that this same system is involved in the experiencing of gods and/or other so-called supernatural beings. In fact, the evidence I review in this book suggests that gods, spirits, and so forth are a normal part of brain functioning and subjective experience (two aspects of the same phenomenon), involving self and non-self, conscious and unconscious, internal and external. Therefore we should probably discard the "supernatural" moniker from them since they are entirely natural due to their neurobiological, if highly complex, origin – though this does *not* mean they are not mysterious or monumentally moving. Nor does it suggest that these things are "all in our heads," since subjective impressions are not "in" anything, but simply another aspect of the brain interacting with the environment, in which it is inextricably embedded. But there is no need to call them "supernatural" on that account, unless we should need to redefine what "supernatural" means. I suspect this word is more often used to mean "amazing," "mystifying," or "arresting" rather than "outside nature" (whatever that means) anyway, which is entirely appropriate. Life experience does not need to be outside nature to be miraculous; life is in itself miraculous (sometimes).

Part 2

Individual symbols

Chapter 4

Human and animal spirits

So far I have explored the view that the archetypal symbol is a symbol that is charged with affect and uses innate imagery acquisition programs to represent things unconsciously perceived or that the brain/mind is ill-equipped to process with great clarity due to its limited nature. Now I can provide some examples of how this may work, using the case of "animate" symbols – that is, images of creatures moving through space. Since we are dealing with symbols, however, we will by necessity be limited by the fact that all symbols have an *ineffable core of meaning* that cannot be explicitly defined. This is because if it could be so defined, the brain/mind would not need a symbol to represent it. This requires a certain humility, since metaphors can be described only in terms of other metaphors (Lakoff and Johnson, 1999, 2003), which means we are essentially trying to describe something that really cannot be described concretely.

Other minds: Agency, intent, mentality

In order to understand the neurobiology of animal symbols (which include humans and theriomorphic symbols[1]), we need to explore the way in which the mind comprehends *intentionality*, as this will be the key to under-standing the peculiar qualities of anthropomorphic symbols that the brain creates. As I will show, other minds are one of those things the brain "gets," and so we symbolize many things with them.

Anything that has the qualities of intentionality and self-generated movement calls into play our ability as humans to divine other people's intentions. In other words, when presented with an object in the sensory domain, there are mental tasks that are unconsciously carried out that determine whether or not the object is animate or inanimate, and if animate, what its "intentions" are, that is, what it "wants." This ability is known as "theory of mind" (TOM), and allows us to sense and guess at another's beliefs, desires, and intentions, and helps us to navigate the social environment as humans. According to evolutionary psychologists (Atran, 2005), anthropologists (Brown, 1991; Dunbar, 2003), and neuroscientists

(Brüne and Brüne-Cohrs, 2006), this ability has been shown to be an evolved psychological skill to infer others' mental states and emotions; TOM is in fact an *entrenched neural system* that comprises the social brain in humans and other primates.

TOM likely evolved as a result of an "evolutionary arms race" wherein increasingly social animals needed brains that could infer another's intentions (Byrne, 2003). This developed into a TOM *faculty* in humans. The psychologists Brüne and Brüne-Cohrs state that "almost certainly there is an innate 'hard-wired' foundation of the theory of mind faculty . . ." (2006: 440). This faculty develops according to predictable stages.

Human infants, for example, can distinguish between the movement of animate and inanimate objects by as early as six months (Golinkoff *et al.*, 1984). At 12 months, the skill improves, and infants can form a triad consisting of the infant's perception, the perception of another agent such as her mother, and another object. At 14–18 months, infants can turn their heads to follow the gaze of others and can understand desire, intention, and causal relations between internal states and goals (Saxe *et al.*, 2004). 18-month-old toddlers can differentiate between reality and pretense, recognize themselves in mirrors and engage in pretend play. By three years of age, children can express self-propelled versus caused motion (Karmiloff-Smith, 1992: 81), and TOM improves still more, in that children of this age can distinguish between their own and others' *beliefs* (Perner and Wimmer, 1985). By age four, children have an intact TOM, which ascribes belief, intentionality, pretense, humor, and discrimination between mental and nonmental phenomena (Karmiloff-Smith, 1992: 132–133). By six years of age, children can comprehend metaphor and irony (Ackerman, 1981). These developmental stages appear to constitute a human universal, meaning they are observed cross-culturally (Avis and Harris, 1991); also they codevelop with language acquisition (Frith and Frith, 2003) and, importantly, with progressively more symbolic dream imagery (Foulkes, 1999). This ability even works with pictures of *implied* motion (Gallese and Goldman, 1998; Kourtzi and Kanwisher, 2000; Ruby and Decety, 2001; Paus, 2001). The TOM ability also appears to be malfunctioning in a variety of psychiatric disorders, including autism and, to a lesser degree, schizophrenia (for a review, see Brüne and Brüne-Cohrs, 2006; see also Burns, 2006).

The ability to conceptualize "intent" and "agency" even emerges in the complete absence of visual experience (Bedny *et al.*, 2009) – just like image visuospatial reasoning. Here, the development of the neural mechanisms of TOM are argued to depend "on innate factors and on experiences represented at an abstract level, amodally" (Bedny *et al.*, 2009: 11312) rather than arising from simulation or imitation:

> having seen is not necessary for the development of normal neural representations of another person's experiences of seeing. . . . Our

results therefore suggest that reasoning about beliefs does not involve simulating the sensory experiences that gave rise to those beliefs . . .

(11315)

The brain appears to have multiple avenues through which it develops TOM, as shown in studies comparing language development and TOM ability in the deaf (Moeller and Schick, 2006). Bedny *et al.* (2009) conclude that TOM is a sophisticated and resilient trait that is facilitated by the visual, auditory, linguistic, and social environment but is not dependent upon them to develop. Recall also the innate facial recognition ability discussed in previous chapters, which likely plays a part here.

What all of this research points to are the mechanisms that give perceived objects the qualities of animate versus inanimate, intentionality, expression, belief, gaze, pretense, desire, and irony; all of this reliably emerges universally despite wide differences in culture. In the following sections I explore a lot of detail about the way the mind generates animal and human symbols – but don't lose sight of the main goal, which is to understand how this system as a whole creates symbols that come to be understood as spiritual entities.

Animal symbolism

At the neurobiological level, we share a tremendous emotional heritage with animals, particularly mammals (Panksepp, 1998), including neurobiological circuitry for FEAR, RAGE, PANIC, SEEKING, as well as higher-order emotional systems of CARE, LUST, and rough-and-tumble PLAY; Panksepp calls these areas "deep functional homologies in mammalian brains which arise from a massively shared genetic heritage" (Panksepp, 2005: 60). This statement refers to the way in which we conceptualize brain activity, but as we will see it applies to symbols also. But there is abundant evidence that animals share many if not all of these same basic emotional states with humans, particularly all mammals as attested to by their striking similarity in structure and function (reviewed at length in Panksepp, 2005). This common heritage is shared in the deeper emotional systems of every human; thus these structures remain very "animal-like."

There are also specific animal recognition systems; much of the available data comes from infants and cross-cultural studies as well as neurobiology. For example, animal versus nonanimal distinctions develop precociously in infants (Gopnik and Meltzoff, 1987; Mandler and McDonough, 1998; Quinn and Eimas, 1996). Infants can discriminate complex information about goal-directed behavior, such as pursuit and evasion in experimental objects (Abell *et al.*, 2000; Castelli *et al.*, 2000), and discriminate animal from nonanimal on basis of shape, even when shapes have considerable overlap (such as birds and airplanes) (Mandler and McDonough, 1998).

This capacity develops quite early; three-month-old infants, for example, become upset if faces go still, but not if an object suddenly stops moving (Gelman *et al.*, 1995).

The animal perceptual/conceptual system not only makes TOM distinctions and animal versus nonanimal distinctions, but further delineates animals on the basis of their *behavior type*. Toddlers as young as three years old in two very different cultures consistently show evidence of an intact "predator-prey inference system" (reviewed in Barrett, 2005), have a precocious ability to acquire animal information and have animal-specialized memory systems that are functionally and neuronally separate from non-animal information systems (Caramazza and Shelton, 1998). Humans are preferentially adept at discriminating pursuit and evasion from other types of motion (Abell *et al.*, 2000), are more sensitive to changes in scenes involving animals than nonanimals (New *et al.*, 2003), and are sensitive to animal images over other images in peripheral vision fields (Thorpe *et al.*, 2001). Furthermore, humans are highly sensitive to gaze direction, which in turn causes autonomic (heart rate and breathing) arousal (Coss and Goldthwaite, 1995). The tendency of humans to anthropomorphize animals from an early age is well known and likely associated with the brain regions involved in TOM processing. There appears to be good reason for this personifying: there is evidence that this tendency leads to accurate predictions of animal behavior among hunter-gatherers in cultures as distinct as the Amazon and the Kalahari desert, even in children as young as three years old; this and other data suggest that this activity is part of an evolved system for intentional inference – in other words, attributing human emotional states to animals is an evolved psychological adaptation (Barrett, 2005: 214–215).

This innate animal

The perception/conception system is known in cognitive science as "folk biology" (Atran, 2005). Converging evidence from ethology, cross-cultural studies, developmental psychology, cognitive psychology, pathology, social and educational studies, and cognitive anthropology show that folk biology conceptualizations are innate, domain-specific, and may actually be evolutionary adaptations (reviewed in Atran, 2005: 143–149; see also Atran, 2002a). Note that specifying something as innate is not as strong as saying it is domain-specific, which in turn is not as strong as saying it is an adaptation. The folk biology system, the evolutionary psychologist Scott Atran argues, appears by all accounts to be an adaptation – remember that Atran was the person who theorized that religion is an evolutionary by-product of the predator–prey detection system, but more on that later.

Finally, Atran (2005) shows that this system is *essentialist*: that is, each taxa is innately recognized as having a characteristic intuitive "essence," for example, a tadpole and a frog, though vastly different in appearance and behavior, are automatically placed in the same category as being "the same thing" even though there is little evidence to suggest why children should come to this conclusion except via an innate ordering structure (see also Ahn *et al.*, 2001; Gelman *et al.*, 1994). This concept therefore allows for shape-changing creatures to have the same "essence" – this is starting to sound like notions of the "spirit," isn't it? This essentialism is cross-culturally present in preschoolers and is only utilized in relation to animal objects; children do not apply essentialism to artifacts (i.e. tools) (Ahn *et al.*, 2001: 61), and the notion of essence is frequently applied to metaphors throughout adult life to describe things such as the "essence of being" or the "essence of the universe" (Lakoff and Johnson, 1999).

To summarize, then, research shows that humans have an innate system for recognizing, categorizing, and organizing animal data in distinct, essentialist categories. It commands attention, leads to precocious acquisition of knowledge in informationally impoverished psychological environments, gives animals a special place in the mind, attributes to them an immutable "essence," invests them with human-like thoughts and behaviors, and (recalling dream research on children) tends to identify them with the subject, at least in part. Note that even a system that is already this complex and rich would be even richer if humans had any innate predispositions toward specific classes of animals. As it turns out, we do.

Snakes and spiders

Humans and other higher primates have innate mechanisms to specifically recognize spiders and snakes that require minimal environmental input compared to other mechanisms (Hagan, 2005). Using a variety of research methods such as interviews, field observations, and laboratory studies, evidence has accumulated that suggests humans have an evolved capacity that is responsive to snakes and spiders in particular; for example, in humans and other primates, fear of snake-like objects is preferentially acquired and retained over innocuous stimuli regardless of environmental variation. Humans are more likely to make illusory associations with snakes and negative stimuli (compared to non-snake associations), even when no such association is actually present, and even when stimuli are backward masked – meaning subliminal, which circumvents conscious awareness (above data reviewed in Simpson and Campbell, 2005: 138; see also Barrett, 2005: 207). This and other evidence leads Tooby and Cosmides (2005) to conclude that this data:

> not only establishes the necessity of evolved motivational elements but also resurrects the argument for the necessity of [Immanuel Kant's] "innate ideas," that is, evolved conceptual procedures within the cognitive architecture that embody knowledge about the world

and are triggered by stimuli with certain features (however abstractly described).

(50)

Elsewhere, Tooby *et al.* (2005) conclude:

> For natural selection to cause safe distances from snakes to be pre-ferred over closeness to snakes, it must build the recognition of snake-like entities into our neurocomputational architecture. This system of recognition and tagging operations is computationally a snake concept, albeit a skeletally specified one . . .
>
> (321)

Spiders appear to have the same effect. Human subjects, for example, can rapidly pick out pictures of snakes and spiders from arrays of fear-irrelevant objects such as flowers and mushrooms much more quickly than they can do the opposite task (Öhman *et al.*, 2001a); furthermore, snake and spider images are detected *prior to attending them* and spontaneously emerge into consciousness as a "pop out" effect. The effects of snakes and spiders cannot be accounted for by statistical learning or content-free inductive inferences, which would predict modern urban people to reliably develop fears of, say, electric sockets and cars rather than snakes (Cosmides and Tooby, 2005: 619) – on the contrary, urban schoolchildren state they most fear lions, tigers, "monsters," spiders and snakes, often reflecting dangers they have never experienced (Marks, 1987).

Animal images

The brain appears well primed to organize experience into *animal-related* categories, with special information about predator–prey, gaze, essentialist and anthropomorphic TOM-related and snake- or spider-related detail – further detail is likely present here; more studies need to be done. What we do know is that the brain innately learns very quickly to understand animals! This makes animals prime targets for use as symbols. So then the question becomes: *how* does the brain typically use them?

The first clues come from dream-content research, since it provides us with a variety of non-consciously-directed images. Children more often than adults dream of animals (Domhoff, 2003; Van de Castle, 1994), and children represent themselves as animals in dreams up to the age of eight (Foulkes, 1999), where, superimposing upon this tendency and paralleling development in visuospatial ability (Robertson, 1998) and metaphor construction, they dream about multiple selves, which coincides with the ability to see other points of view; in other words, the fully developed TOM capacity is coopted and comes "online" by this time, and is incorporated into the dream content.

Foulkes suggests "that animal characters stand in for the dreamer before the dreamer can be directly and actively represented in dreams" (Foulkes, 1999: 87) – a hint at the symbolic character of these images. By age seven to eight, self-representation develops in dream imagery as a reliably developing phenomenon that parallels the child's visuospatial skill in waking life; in other words, self-characters in dreams emerge as a consequence of normal brain development by age seven, and are correlated to the child's ability to differentiate herself as knower and as a concept (this is called "meta-cognition"), a capacity obviously related to the growing TOM ability. By age 13, children develop dream character "double self-reference" (Foulkes, 1999: 112), that is, characters representing the child but seen as external characters, and this occurrence was also correlated with visuospatial ability.

Here we see dream images of the dreamer in various guises acting things out in the dream, correlated with visuospatial skill (i.e. the neurobiological ability to generate mental imagery). Jung postulated that dream characters represented "complexes" (Jung, 1919, 1953a, 1959b, 1974, 1984, 2008; Hall, 1983; Haule, 2010), or unconscious aspects of the dreamer's personality, or perhaps potential personalities,[2] rather than simply recalling or reviewing people encountered during waking life. This is an important point, so let me reiterate – all this data suggests that dream characters act out various potential parts of the dreamer's personality, and at deeper levels they play out universal (i.e. innate) aspects of experience relatively unrelated to personal history.

There is still a further distinction in the imagery between common animals such as dogs and cats and so-called "wild animals" like bears, lions, tigers, gorillas, elephants, bulls, dinosaurs, dragons and monsters, which account for 27 percent of animal characters in children's dreams as opposed to 7 percent in adult dreams (Van de Castle, 1994: 305–308), recalling the theme of the more implicit-processing-dominated brain of youth as being more concerned with wild animals and other more "primitive" concerns than the adult.

Note that in most of these studies the children *had never encountered* any of the wild animals dreamt about (Revonsuo, 2000). Furthermore, "wild" animals (as opposed to dogs, cats, or goldfish) are dreamt about more often by boys than girls, and, interestingly, women dream of more mammals than non-mammals, which is reversed in men. Finally, dreams with aggression increase as the presence of animal figures increases, and increased animal figures in dream content also coincides with more misfortune, apprehension, and disorientation, and efforts to cope with challenges posed within the dream as well as unfamiliar settings; all of these findings point to more of the symbolic meaning behind animal images. Interestingly, bird figures in dreams are a cultural universal (Van de Castle, 1994: 310), as are dreams involving snakes or snake-like creatures such as eels (Hall and Nordby, 1972). As we will see, snakes and birds are well represented in somewhat more consciously influenced symbolism such as that of mythology, religion, and the quasi-religious symbolism of medieval European, Middle Eastern, and Chinese alchemy.

An exploration of animal symbols

This data suggests that our brains have a thorough understanding of animals – perhaps as much as we do for objects and motion in space (this is an example of an archetypal pattern within a pattern). Here, the mind takes something experienced, and creates an image that has an essence, a predator–prey dimension, an anthropomorphic set of beliefs and intentions, and likely a host of other aspects yet to be uncovered by empirical research. The mind then says "this situation/feeling/impression *is like* this animal." In other words, the brain uses animals to create symbols. But symbols of what? This is a tough question, since because they are symbols they have an ineffable core of meaning; this keeps us from explaining things as precisely as we like to do in science. But that's just too bad: we can't escape our brains. Literally speaking, emotions are not fire nor is fire anger. Fire is a chemical reaction. Anger correlates with the stimulation of the RAGE circuit. They are not the same – but then again, symbolically they *are* the same, and everyone knows it! Metaphors are "lies that tell the truth," but try to explain why, though, and you will find yourself just using more metaphors. To proceed from here all we can really do is look at what animals have been used to symbolize in the past and see if there is some commonality; if it is truly arbitrary, then animals should be used to symbolize pretty much anything. As we will see, however, this is *not* the case. Humans use animals in particular ways to symbolize difficult-to-describe things that have a lot to do with not only our emotions but also the mysteries that lie beyond our brain's limited capacities.

Scholars of symbolism have noted that many symbols recur throughout history and cross-culturally. This evidence supports Jung's idea of a "collective unconscious" that is highly creative, emotionally moving, and firmly anchored in evolutionary history, which, however, forces us to recognize that the symbolic images of such a system must have some kind of common meaning throughout the human condition that is not dependent upon the vagaries of culture and upbringing alone, but also rooted in our deeper experience as *Homo sapiens*. This is the meaning that cross-cultural and panhistorical studies of symbols are trying to approach.

Animal symbols in myth, religion and folk tales

Animal drawings have been found that date back to at least 60,000 BC, and indigenous religions worldwide imbue members with "totem" animals or animal "spirits" (Jaffé, 1964) – more on this below; furthermore, there is good evidence that the animal images were symbolic rather than simple representations (Campbell, 1959) and that they are related to inducing altered states of consciousness (Haule, 2010). When it comes to animal symbols, one common motif in fairy tales observed by the world expert in comparative fairy tale lore Marie-Louise von Franz is that: "Anyone who earns the gratitude of animals, or whom they help for any reason, invariably wins out. This is the only unfailing rule that I have been able to find" (1999: 89). Moreover, so-called shamanistic practitioners all over the world, when in trace states, describe "animal spirit" behavior in strikingly similar ways (Eliade, 1964).

In general, animal symbols appear to have an ambivalent nature, which makes sense considering how animals can frequently harm as well as help humans; the important thing is that they are never *irrelevant*. Not only that, but most symbols have an ambivalent nature anyway, which comes not from the symbol necessarily, but our inability to comprehend it in simple black/white clarity. Animal symbols appear to command attention and imply deep significance, probably because they provide an important function that natural selection deemed important since time immemorial; whether it be in the form of helpful animals, animal gods, or therimorphic gods, humans throughout history have naturally thought that animals share a close "link" with humans and hold some kind of wisdom we do not have access to, wisdom that is vital for our survival and well-being. Considering the advantage such thinking has on survival and hunting, for instance, it is likely that there is a good reason why we do this, despite the fact that it may be accused of being "primitive" or "superstitious."

Struggles between heroic warriors and wild or fabulous animals are very frequent in mythological and religious symbolism, and usually seem to represent the struggle between good and evil, or order and chaos (Tresidder, 2005). Furthermore, animals throughout the world are often considered to be more timeless and constant in their behavior than humans – a plausible belief. Echoing the TOM attribution to animals, speech abilities are attributed to animals in ancient Greek, Hebrew, and Islamic traditions, as well as Disney movies.

Snakes

Given the empirical research on the peculiar way snakes activate our perceptual/conceptual systems, it should be no surprise that the image of the snake finds (or slithers) its way into myths and religious symbolism worldwide. But understanding the way the snake is used metaphorically as a means of understanding the world and the self requires a careful phenomenological approach; simply stating that snakes trigger sensitized fear circuits is not enough to help us understand the way in which the mind generates novel metaphors and uses snakes to symbolize them.

As a result of his own studies on snake symbolism, Jung felt that "the snake always means the cerebrospinal nervous system . . . the lower instincts or functions" (Jung, 2008: 211–249), to which I would add, "when they interface with the current environment." Throughout history, the snake has been used as a so-called chthonic (grown from the earth) symbol, such as representing the fundamental "essence" of the material world (Gnostic myth), which can mean evil in dualistic religions such as Persian Zoroastrianism or Christianity, where the snake is the primitive enemy of the human-like gods/heroes. This theme of the snake being the earth-derived, material enemy of the high-minded heroic gods finds its way into many symbol systems: the Midgard serpent (Norse myth), Vritra (Indian myth), the "rainbow snake" (African myth), Apep (Egyptian myth), Echidna and Chronos (Greek myth), Tieholtsodi (Navajo myth), Ouroboros (Greek alchemy) the Leviathan and the snake of Eden (Old Testament), the serpent of Mithraism, the snake of the Krater (the alchemy of Zosimos), the snake racial enemy of the eagles (Indian myth), and the serpent/dragon enemies of St. George, Heracles, Siegfried, Beowulf, Thor, and Apollo, and the serpent-form of Seth, enemy of the sun-hero Re (Egyptian myth). The kernel of meaning in all these metaphors appears to be that the snake symbolizes instinctive primitive drives and darker stirrings, or represents a principle of the "inherent evil" in the material world (Cirlot, 1971). The snake is recognized by symbologists as "the most significant and complex of all animal symbols, and perhaps the oldest" (Tresidder, 2005: 445), and they note its association with the phallus and the umbilical cord, noting its metaphorical equation with "primeval life force." This terminology recalls Panksepp's description of SEEKING activity, which originates in the reptile brain (ironically?), and guides basic exploratory behavior in its most primordial form.

This link with SEEKING appears to give the snake image a highly complex character. The snake has also been depicted as a symbol of healing and salvation, representing the highest god of Phrygian myth, the union with deity (Greek mysticism), the staff of Asklepios. Snakes are a common healing element in fairy tales, and the staff of the caduceus, the well-known symbol of a staff with two snakes intertwined around, frequently used in modern medical symbolism, was owned by various gods of wisdom such as Hermes, Anubis, Ba'al, Isis, and Ishtar (Stevens, 1998: 239), and has its place among even more ancient Indian, Buddhist, and Sumerian symbolism (Cirlot, 1971: 36). The snake has been depicted as the possessor of the "herb of life" (Indian myth, Greek and Babylonian sagas). The healing *serpens mercurii*, which is metaphorically equated with the water of life and contains the philosopher's stone or a diamond (alchemy and Indian myth), shows similarity with the symbol of the snake as the keeper of divine wisdom (Gnostic mysticism), the "wisest of creatures" (West African myth), keeper of fire and other technological knowledge, as well as eternal life (neolithic myths). The snake has been used as a symbol of Christ (Gospel of John) or the apostle John (medieval art), holder of undifferentiated phallic power capable of fertilization or destruction (Polynesian, Greek and Egyptian myth, Kundalini Yoga), and as a bearer of culture and savior (Aztec myth). The snake has also been depicted as an evil creature that is nonetheless capable of transforming into a being of higher knowledge (Buddist myth; cf. Zimmer, 1972), or of a synthesis of opposing powers, like the "plumed serpent" of Aztec myth who combines earth and sky as well as male and female, or the twin snakes of the caduceus (staff of Mercurius of medieval alchemy representing equilibrium), of good and evil (Gnostic *agathodaemon* and *Kakodaemon*), and of creation and destruction, container of the "water of life" (Indian myth) (Campbell, 1959; Cirlot, 1971; Tresidder, 2005), or the winner of poetic inspiration (as when Odin transforms himself into a snake to win the "mead of poetry" in Norse myth). The snake has been depicted as guardian of the springs of life and immortality, or of "spiritual riches" as metaphorically represented by hidden treasure (Eliade, 1958), as keeper of "deep wisdom" (Bayley, 1951) or knowledge of the gods. The snake has also been depicted as symbolizing the most primitive level of life, composed of demonic matter with a hidden core of spiritual sublimation (Egyptian myth). Finally, the amphisbaena, a two-headed snake, is a frequent European heraldric image, found also in ancient Greece, proposed to represent ambivalent feelings (Cirlot, 1971) – here again the snake seems to represent strong emotional engagement with life.

Jung associates the snake as representing salvation or renewal, citing these types of parallels, where the serpent is a symbol of the "soul" or essence of the earth, matter, metal, but also man. It is also seen as a helpful animal (recall the helpful animals of folklore) containing secret wisdom. As mentioned, these symbols recall the SEEKING activity described in the last chapter and in the Appendix. SEEKING, remember, is the innate emotional system that enlivens the world and brings intense interest to our activities. It is possible to feel this as redemption or a "saving" if one previously felt despondent and depressed; neuroscience has shown that depression is associated with reduced activity in the SEEKING system (Panksepp, 1998).

Jung argued that the snake is

> the most spiritual of all creatures; it is of a fiery nature, and its swiftness is terrible. It has a long life and sloughs off old age with its skin. . . . It is both toxic and prophylactic, equally a symbol of the good and bad daemon (the Agathodaemon), of Christ and the devil . . . an emblem of the brain-stem and spinal cord. . . . It is an excellent symbol for the unconscious, perfectly expressing the latter's sudden and unexpected manifestations, its painful and dangerous intervention in our affairs, and its frightening effects.
>
> (1956: para 580)

Related to the snake is the symbol of the dragon, a universal symbol throughout the world that appears to stand "for 'things animal' *par excellence*" (Cirlot, 1971: 86), that is, for primal instinct and primitive adversarial qualities internally and externally. Like all animal symbols it has an ambivalent quality to it: not only is the dragon ferocious and fantastic but it also frequently guards treasure. Perhaps this refers to universal FEAR versus SEEKING systems, diametrically opposed as they are and driving all vertebrate organisms from their deepest levels either toward potentially resource-gaining stimuli or away from noxious stimuli.

Lions and tigers

There are more animals in the world than snakes, of course, and the previously cited research on dream content shows that all sorts of wild animal imagery is created spontaneously in children who have never encountered such beasts. Given the innate folk-biology system, this should come as no surprise. Jung (2008: 225–231) describes how animal symbols are often depicted as transforming into each other, such as that of the Mithraic image of the *Aion lentocephalus*, or the unity of the lion and snake – obviously a metaphorical unity – which speaks to both animals having a common "essence." The lion, Jung observes (2008), has been depicted as a "transformation" symbol in medieval alchemy and Persian myth, as "attacking" substance, a personification of "wild desire," containing a "tincture" of sun and moon and a symbol that unites the "essences" of male and female, and of "earth containing the seed of light." Medieval and Biblical Christian symbolism depicts Christ as both lion (as king) and lamb (as victim of the lion) and a paradoxical figure that represents wild desire and also the love of understanding hidden within it. Buddha is symbolized by a lion also, as has been Ashoka (Indian culture hero) and Vishnu (as Narashimha, a half lion), and the lion is used to signify protection in Chinese and Japanese temple architecture.

In alchemy, the metaphors transform from serpent to a lion, then to an eagle, which is "something psychical and spiritual . . . the eagle is the meridian where [life] reaches the highest heights" (Jung, 2008: 231). Note here again the connotation of a gradual "elevation" – a visuospatial relation – that rises from lowly subterranean reptile, to the mighty terrestrial lion to the soaring eagle in the ubiquitous tripartite cosmos that Haule (2010) argues is "hard-wired." I agree and explore this concept in depth elsewhere (2010b).

The lion is associated with instinctive forces, like the snake and many other aggressive animal symbols (Gnostic mysticism) and is sometimes depicted as "linked" with fire (which is also linked metaphorically with passion). The ravenous lioness Kali (Indian myth) appears to be associated with potentially dangerous feminine instinct, an idea also found in Chinese and Egyptian myth, and English folklore. The lion has been traditionally used to represent royalty, dominance, strength, courage, but also ferocity and destruction (Tresidder, 2005). Finally, as a tiger, this symbol has been depicted as representing animal kinship to humankind (Naga myth).

Birds

Bird symbols are found in every culture and always seem to represent higher spiritual knowledge, often encountered during trance-like altered states (indigenous societies worldwide; cf Eliade, 1964; also Haule, 2010), images of immortal or sky-god beings (Chinese myth), knights of unearthly purity (Germanic legend), messengers or servants of supreme gods (like the dove that visited Mary in the New Testament, angels, or the ravens of Odin), begetters of great beauty (Greek myth of Helen of Troy), symbols of Zeus (Greek myth), or gods of wisdom (Egyptian gods with bird-heads). Birds have alternately been described as messengers of Heaven or carriers of the soul, and are associated with the "cosmic tree" (Stevens, 1998: 360; Campbell, 1959). Birds are also creators, such as the thunder bird of Native American myth, or the lightning bird of southern Africa (Tresidder, 2005).

Birds and winged beings are very frequently symbols of "spiritualization," thoughts of fancy, supernatural aid, thought, imagination and swiftness; birds are used to represent the soul in folklore worldwide, as well as Hindu, Egyptian, Greek, Roman, Babylonian, and Biblical mythologies. The giant bird is always symbolic of creator gods in mythology, and is frequently opposed to the snake (Cirlot, 1971; Tresidder, 2005). Eagles are frequently depicted as symbols of nobility, masculinity, warfare (European, Sarmatian, and Oriental symbolism), cosmic messengers (Vedic lore, Norse and Celtic myth, Christian symbolism), and carriers of thunderbolts (Greek, pre-Columbian American, and Mesopotamian symbolism). Furthermore, birds are universally used to symbolize celestial messages and amorous yearnings, and their motions of swooping and soaring are used to symbolize various metaphorical meanings related to motion – we have encountered this kind of symbolism (using moving objects to represent hard-to-verbalize concepts) already. Birds have also been implicated as symbols of release or liberation (Henderson, 1964). Finally, throughout the world of iconography, images of gods and angels are often depicted with wings from the fourth millennium BC onward (Cirlot, 1971: 9).

Spiders

The above data on snake symbols could be equally applicable to spiders, as spiders appear to activate innate perceptual/conceptual mechanisms in similar ways. The spider symbol is described by the Jungian analyst Anthony Stevens (1998) as representing a weaver of the web [who] has always encouraged cosmogonic fantasies, especially as the web is made in the form of a mandala, with its creator sitting at the center. The spider's life of weaving and killing, creating and destroying, is an allegory of the opposing forces on which the existence of the cosmos depends . . . [it] is a creature of fate, weaving the thread of destiny on which it hangs. It is also sinister, a dangerous, mindless beast of prey, sometimes an object of fear, in many instances amounting to frank phobia, which is probably phylogenetically induced.

(351)

The spider also carries the symbolic meanings of creativity, aggressiveness, and convergence on a central point; also the moon is depicted as a giant spider in many myths, perhaps reflecting on qualities of rhythmicity and life/death symbolism (Cirlot, 1971: 304)

Experiencing animal symbols

Animal images could be used theoretically to represent nearly anything. But the fact is that humans do not appear to experience them randomly. We seem to use animals in recurrent ways to represent the same kinds of metaphorical "truths." Getting at this process is not easy, but we do have some clues. An important aspect of all animal symbols is the anatomical considerations reviewed in Chapter 2, especially with respect to the triune brain and the shared emotional systems of FEAR, RAGE, CARE, LUST, PANIC, PLAY, and SEEKING. The reptile brain, recall, is named such because of its highly homologous structure with reptiles – it "thinks like" a reptile, though integrated with our more complex mammalian brain regions. The higher emotional systems of the old mammal brain also think in "animal-like" ways, just not like reptiles per se. Since these systems and layers are more resistant to environmental variation and are therefore less dependent upon personal history, they feel and act more "separately" from the conscious ego. They feel and in some ways *are* "external" in this fashion.

Thus what all this suggests is that any particular animal or human image that spontaneously appears in dream or reverie may be a symbol of our more universal, less conscious, mind operating in the context of the current environment. A possible self, or a past self, may be represented by an animal. As we traverse into the deeper, less historical, layers of the mind, the animal imagery will become more and more "archetypal" and will seem "external" from the point of view of consciousness. Note that these images can and will be combined in highly unique ways in each subject to generate complex metaphors. An emotional process operating relatively independently of consciousness may be mapped onto the image of an animal; however, the particular animal still makes a big difference. Bird symbols, for example, carry connotations of elevation, wind, and flight, all of which utilize different neurobiological systems for metaphor mapping that I explore in later chapters.

Understanding animal symbols neurobiologically

As one can see from the previous paragraphs, figuring out what a metaphor "really means" is no easy task – this should be no surprise, since we are dealing with things like primordial emotions and vague patterns in the environment; the brain is not wired to understand these things very well. But it rapidly acquires the ability to understand objects and creatures moving about in space (among other things), so the only way we can really explain these mysterious things is through metaphors. But there is more to this: flies have lived with humans probably as long as snakes have; why don't we use flies to symbolize all this stuff? I think the answer lies in the fact that the brain does not generate metaphors randomly or arbitrarily, but rather comes to use animals to symbolize similar ineffable things.

So far, the snake *image* (not the symbol) appears to represent "something important" to man for the evolutionary reason that ancient hominids needed to be able to quickly recognize snakes and attend to them to ensure survival, and natural selection favored just such a psychological mechanism in almost all primates, including humans. The kernel of all these symbols that *use the snake image* is therefore the folk-biology system/snake recognition evolutionary adaptation that *natural selection has built into* our perceptual/conceptual system. Jung hypothesized that "the snake [symbol] touches on the deepest instincts of man, so that from time immemorial one thought it to be in possession of great secrets" (Jung, 2008: 251) – in the parlance of neuroscience, the snake may therefore partially map the SEEKING and FEAR system in the brain, and this emotional inertia will drive the metaphors created.

So, the mind is hardwired to recognize snakes and think "Hey – here is something important!" and emotional parts of our innate brain wiring get primed for action. The same can be said of other animals, as the research on folk biology shows. Since this system is in place in every human mind, whenever the brain needs a metaphor to try to understand something, these images are readily accessible for use, and they are already loaded with emotional significance.

Interpreting symbols

When it comes to determining the meaning of dream imagery, of course there are no simple answers. Despite this limitation, we do know that it appears that everyone with an intact brain has the capacity to generate a mental image of a previously never encountered animal or human due to the innate properties of TOM, our innate emotional propensities and the innate folk-biology adaptation. Add to this our natural tendency to create visuospatial metaphors to conceptualize ineffable or abstract intuitions, environmental patterns and/or feelings as objects and creatures moving around in space.

The evidence, then, seems to point to a brain that in various altered states like dreaming grapples with primarily emotional (and hence evolutionarily important) concerns, equal parts universal and specific (at least on average; see Hobson and Kahn, 2007), which further emphasizes how such experiences cannot be easily resolved into "in our heads" and "out there." These concerns are perhaps often formulated into preverbal visuospatial metaphors that, though they appear to have repeated themes throughout history and cross-culturally, can be challenging to interpret individually. Dream images seem to originate from the nascent symbolic thoughts of the subject when the topmost "layers" of their conscious autobiographical self have been temporarily peeled away by altered conscious states. What drives this, however, is much more robust and resistant to experience (Viamontes and Beitman, 2007; Panksepp, 1998).

What information, then, does the mind use to create these symbols? The first clue comes from a number of experiments which have shown that the unconscious "emotional mind seems to be particularly susceptible to stimuli that its conscious counterpart does not have access to [but are recoverable in dreams, fantasy and free-association]" (reviewed in LeDoux, 1996: 61). In other words, the older implicit multiple emotional systems appear to "know" more about the internal and external environment than the conscious system does, merely as a matter of processing limits. The conscious system is powerful in its ability to process information in a deeply recursive and highly differentiating manner, and has access to personal autobiographical memory for comparison. This makes consciousness a very powerful differentiating device to modulate behavior. However, the abilities of consciousness make it come with a price – it is slower and also unable to process large amounts of information this way (Viamontes and Beitman, 2007; Watt and Pincus, 2004); it therefore is limited in a way implicit systems, which are relatively more "crude," domain-specific, and ahistorical, are not. Consciousness has a high "filter" and cannot fully process everything impinging on the various implicit systems, but when the conscious system is relaxed, as in various altered states, the implicit systems reveal what they know and "think" (in rudimentary terms) about the current state of the organism and its surrounds. These systems generally have less access to personal history and are therefore more "nonself" than consciousness is.

It is probably this information that is being formulated into visuospatial metaphors by the dreaming brain and its deeper, more autonomous emotional consciousness*es* – hence the conscious self, when the filter is "lowered," gets a glimpse at these prelinguistic and affective "thoughts" of the multiple implicit systems in the deeper layers of the brain/mind as they push what they want forward and attempt to find their way into consciousness; often times such systems are at odds with each other, creating internal conflict.

During dreaming, language is ramped down and imagery ramped up (Hobson *et al.*, 2000), and the primarily internally focused "default network" (Buckner *et al.*, 2008) is more active. As metaphorical thought appears to structure dream narratives (Lakoff, 1997), the people and animals active in them may be *symbols* of unconscious parts of the mind as they – at the deepest level – merge with the current environment.

I should point out here that *animate* symbols associated with activities of the deepest layers of the brain/mind will have a number of important characteristics according to the above research. First, they will "behave" with a rudimentary type of consciousness, that is, have an ability to judge, think, and perceive on their own terms outside conscious circuitry (Viamontes and Beitman, 2007). They will furthermore seem relatively "timeless" because of their origin in highly conserved brain/mind systems, giving the conscious self the impression they have existed from time immemorial. Because of their affective momentum, they will appear "powerful," and possessing of sensory information that is "secret knowledge" from the point of view of consciousness, and because they derive from *species-conserved* brain activity they will also appear omnipresent. Finally, these human or animal-*like* symbols can take many forms (i.e. they can be symbolized by many images with the same "essence"). Hence these symbols appear relatively timeless, expansively present, protean, powerful, and relatively omniscient. In this respect, therefore, these symbols can appear like recurrent descriptions of gods or spirits. Symbols experienced by certain evocative environments will be "gods" of those environments (i.e. demons, elves, ghosts, fairies, etc.).

Archetypal animate symbols and gods

Let's think about the EMOTION IS A PERSON mapping for a second. Let's say we're talking about RAGE. In this case, something vague, ineffable, and very subjective, that is, the feeling of rage/anger/revenge, and so on, is being represented as a person. Remember that rage is innate in all animals – so it's ubiquitous, although you can't *see* it anywhere in particular. It's also always there in the deep, highly robust brain regions – so it's *timeless*, existing before we (our conscious autobiographical selves) did and lasting long after we're gone. It's very powerful, in that primitive emotional activity has the ability to overwhelm our conscious thinking much more so than the other way around; all we can do is *react* to rage, as it takes a lot of effort to control it, but it controls us quite easily. Finally, rage-driven implicit systems also possess a rudimentary type of consciousness, ability to judge, think, and perceive on their own terms outside conscious circuitry, and they have access to information that normally does not reach consciousness; this makes them more knowledgeable in some ways than the conscious self is. Because of our metaphorical brains and TOM capacity, we can perceive this system consciously. Now, let's ask ourselves what the qualities of a god or "spirit" are. As I mentioned above, gods are immortal (timeless), much stronger than we are (powerful), process unconscious sensory information that frequently does not reach consciousness (know secrets) and their effects can be guessed at but not directly seen anywhere (ubiquitous but immaterial). Not only that, but they are human-*like* (have an independent consciousness, judgment, and cognition) and can change shape or take many forms (can be symbolized by many images).

Regarding the cognitive science of religion and ritual, McCauley and Lawson (2002) call gods the scientifically precise but terribly dull term "culturally postulated supernatural agents" (or CPS agents). I largely agree with their model – though I strongly dislike the word "supernatural," since it is hopelessly vague, dependent upon whatever the word "natural" is supposed to mean, and further layered with "super," which assumes something "beyond" or "outside" this nebulous adjective – this arbitrary dichotomy assumes we at some point in history arrogated the knowledge of what *could* happen naturally and what *must* be "outside" that set of assumptions and hence "supernatural." I doubt we are so clever; hence I find the term scientifically dubious at best and of limited usefulness. In any case, their research explains a lot about the functions and intuitive "rules" of rituals derived from universal mental processes; only my model expands theirs, that is, a CPS agent is a special type of (animate) archetypal symbol. Importantly, I postulate that there is a psychological reality beyond the "culturally postulated" aspect of the god, and rituals are real interactions with these "symbolic beings," when performed by sincere adherents to the symbolic system in question. Furthermore, the qualities I attribute to gods are essentially my own definitions. A more complete review of the many attempts to define the squirrely concept of a "god" can be found in Pyysiäinen (2009), but the bottom line is that it is a largely intuitive idea that defies easy definition. The one I provide here, then, seems appropriate, but others could certainly be devised.

In any case, from the point of view of consciousness – which is the only point of view we have, by the way – if an unconscious animal/person image emerges that is a symbol of this strong emotional activity, the symbol will be very "godlike" (or demonic) indeed. Is it any wonder that every culture has a war god? And RAGE is only one of innumerable other systems and *combinations* of systems capable of influencing consciousness similarly. So in fact gods *are* real, in this metaphorical sense, and we would do well to heed their utterances, whether it be by placating them, obeying, or fleeing their presence – in fact that is what dreams and rituals do. And as I will show in the final chapters, and indeed in future work, rituals appear to work quite well toward this purpose – and I include psychotherapy as a type of ritual (as does Moerman, 2002; and Benedetti, 2009). These characters therefore meet the criteria we have set out for gods, perhaps "symbolic beings" if you like, roaming the dreamlike Otherworld environment conjured up by the perceptual/conceptual system (more on environment symbols in later chapters).

Method actors trying to feel anger are essentially "summoning up the war god." Obsessives trying to flee their own aggression enact rituals to placate the war god. Hunters of indigenous cultures engage in a war dance to obtain the war god's favor. Athletes channel the aggression of the war god. Yes, I am speaking metaphorically here, but remember Mr. Literal? He would look at the image and state that there's no such person as a war god. Indeed, he is correct – on a concrete level. But on a symbolic level he's dead wrong (and not just because I shot him in Chapter 3). There are many complexities and subtleties at work in generating this being, and those are not imaginary.

Further compounding the issue is the fact that the source domain is unconscious, so unconscious symbols or interactions with these "symbolic beings" can be experiences of great mystery and emotional significance on top of everything else;[3] it's not just rage, but any emotion, intuition, environmental pattern, or who knows what. Only *by way of* the symbol *itself* can we even try to understand it, and this is not because of some hazy "supernatural" property, but simply a consequence of having limited brains. Dream, fantasy, and consciously created symbols are likely going to be much more complex and nuanced, jammed with subtleties from many domains besides emotions or animals, and on top of that they will have been created in response to something going on in the subject's internal or external environment. Moreover, since metaphorical mappings and hence symbols are in essence ineffable, and also frequently unconsciously generated, all we can hope to do is "close in" on their meaning (to use another metaphor) by approaching them cautiously from many angles.

Finally, there does not have to be a simple one-to-one relationship between symbols and mappings. Any one symbol is usually an amalgamation of *many* mappings; the reason for this is that they are consciously perceived, and we know from neurobiology that anything that is consciously appraised has to make it through a "high threshold" filter. Only about 5 percent of what we do is consciously directed; due to the high volume of information handled by the implicit systems and the limitations in processing speed and information capacity, only the most "loaded" representations are going to make it through the "filter" into consciousness.[4] Multiple meanings, then, are probably the rule rather than the exception. As you continue through the rest of the book, note how mappings build on each other and link with each other in multiple ways.

In the end, subjective images that are highly emotional, autonomous, and correlated with the activities of deeper, more universal systems – like those that appear in a dream or dreamlike state – can be thought of as a subset of the symbol-producing aspects of the brain/mind. These symbols move and act with a certain autonomy relative to consciousness, simply due to the fact that the brain operates via multiple parallel processors, and hence so does the mind, since the brain and mind are two aspects of the same (only indirectly observable) phenomenon (Solms and Turnbull, 2002). These experiences are, on closer inspection, virtually indistinguishable from mythological or folkloric descriptions of encounters with gods or spirits of many varieties. And their reality is as firmly established as any other subjective experience such as love, pain, or fear, which are also linked to neurobiology but not reducible to it.

Clinical example: The bear spirit

Since in the previous sections I have spent a lot of time discussing things in the abstract, I will provide a concrete example from my own observations that will hopefully draw things into focus. Here I analyze the subjective reports of a Ms. Green,[5] a 44-year-old female who had suffered years of sexual molestation until she turned 14. At the same time, for as long as she can remember, Ms. Green dreamt about a large bear. The earliest versions of this dream involved the bear trying to break into her house and harm her loved ones – notably she was never being threatened by the bear (lest one jump to the conclusion that the bear "represents" the abusers only). Other dreams involved being concerned about the bear that was not present but was "out there." Years later, in her late 30s, while interacting with me, she reported that in the context of a major conflict within her family, she had the dream:

> I am at the home of my childhood, and the bear is trying to break into my house and harm my pet animals. My son is with me, helping me block the door and preventing the bear from coming in.

In the subsequent analysis of this dream, we came to the conclusion that the bear emerged whenever she felt threatened or – particularly – when she felt like she was being taken advantage of. This bear would appear in her dreams in such circumstances and threaten the other more care-related animals, as in this example. Notably, as before when she was a child, the bear was scary, but never threatening to her directly; rather, the bear always threatened her loved ones or her pet animals. Interestingly, her first memory of the bear dream was at age nine, which was also the same time she remembered starting her period and being noticed by boys at school, and, significantly, when she began to feel shame over being molested (before this she reports not understanding what was happening). While she related that she felt she had to "put up with" the molestation at home, both because it had gone on so long and because it was family members perpetuating it, at school if boys teased her in sexually inappropriate ways she would lash out at them, defending herself violently from anything resembling unwanted contact. She recalled one time when a boy touched her inappropriately and she turned around and kneed him in the groin, and another instance when a boy kissed her and she punched him in the face. Given her description of the scenes, we both remarked upon how fiercely and courageously she was able to defend herself from unwanted advances. Furthermore, she noted that despite the abuse, she luckily had been able to protect her virginity.

As a freshman in high school, she was able to avoid any further molestation and became "wild" in school, dating numerous boys but always avoiding intercourse with them, and she remembered that the bear dream occurred at this time with multiple variations, particularly in the summer prior to her senior year. At this time she had gotten serious with a boy and mused that the bear had been "stirred up" because she had contemplated sleeping with this boy. Eventually she did, and quickly afterward panicked, broke up with the boy and swore off all dating. That year, in which she felt "free" and got excellent grades, she remembered fondly. Interestingly, she did not remember having the bear dream during that year.

Thus this "bear spirit," for lack of a better word, was powerful and emerged at an early age, but to label it as "positive" or "negative" is to oversimplify. Furthermore, the bear seemed to find its way into waking life (recall the boundary between sleep and waking is fluid and not rigid), and even in my interaction with her, if she felt threatened or disregarded, there was a visible change in her mannerisms and voice, and she would become very defensive and nearly fearless, as if this bear was "taking over" the conscious self.

Merely the act of analyzing this dream, and trying to understand it produced an interesting change: she began to feel emotionally attached to bears, and her dream content changed. She began to have dreams of resting comfortably in her bed with the bear curled up and asleep with her. She also became unable to watch nature shows in which bears were threatened or their habitats harmed, due to the overwhelming sadness she felt; she once watched a nature show where a bear was shown starving and stranded, and was unable to continue watching the show, and this had not happened before. She stated that watching this made her feel desperate, as if a loved one was dying and she could not help them. As we continued to explore these dream images over time, she began to note waking impressions of the bear, and came to see the bear as a strong protective "spirit" that was tremendously powerful and often overprotective of her, with "collateral damage" sometimes being caused to loved ones when aroused. Normally describing herself as a "pleaser," the bear spirit would emerge suddenly if she felt threatened, and she would react ferociously in her defense, only later to feel like she had overreacted. Later, however, as she came to regard this image *as is*, meaning as a "spirit bear," and she felt comforted by this and better able to handle the intense affects that sometimes arose from it. Rather than try to explain it away or run from it, she said she felt lucky to have "her" bear, even though it sometimes threatened to run amok.

Animal spirits culturally – comparison material

Since the human brain/mind has not undergone much change in the last 50,000 years (Haule, 2010), it is likely that Ms. Green's experience is not unique. In fact, the concept of a "guardian animal spirit" is widespread, particularly in indigenous cultures. Eliade (1964), in his globe-spanning review of so-called "shamanistic" practices, recounts numerous tales told by local magicians or folk healers of traversing the spirit world and having an animal guide and/or help them, and often these relationships would be lifelong. A closer view of particular ideas about animal spirits, however, yields some interesting parallels to our case above. The Icelandic sagas were written around the thirteenth century, and are a large repository of tales and folk beliefs of the European north up to the ninth to tenth century, but likely contain a great deal of material that is very ancient. Among the ancient Norsemen, a concept very similar to the above case of the "guardian bear spirit" was known as a *fylgja* ("fetch," or "follower"), which was said to be a spirit animal that is tied to particular persons and follows them throughout their life. In many sagas (sources include Turville-Petre, 1972; Waggoner, 2009),[6] *fylgjur* (plural of *fylgja*) were reported as appearing in dreams, but also to those with "second sight," which perhaps means to individuals who were intuitive and perceived "spirit" animal imagery in the context of a person, much like dream characters but during waking or altered states of consciousness. Like Ms. Green's bear, these animal spirits do not normally talk, and many animals are reported, such as wolves, bears, lions, stags, foxes, and so forth, with the animal matching the cultural impression of the animal (wolves and bears were warlike, stags and lions "noble," and so forth). In the saga *Sögubrot*, the bear *fylgja* of a woman named Aud appears in King Hraerek's dream and protects him from harm, and in *the Saga of Hrolf Gautreksson*, a great bear appears in a man's dream, and this bear is interpreted as the *fylgja* of the foster brother to King Hrolf Gautreksson.

As mentioned, sometimes *fylgja* were said to be visible to those with "second sight," such as in *The Tale of Thorstein Bull's-Leg*, where a man reports seeing the bear-cub *fylgja* of a young boy as he walks into his hall. Scholars in Germanic mythology and folklore describe the *fylgja* as protective spirits which "attach themselves to individuals, often at birth, and remain with them right through to death, when they may transfer their powers to another family member" (Orchard, 2002: 122; Simek, 2007). Such beings were said to appear during times of crisis, both during waking and dreaming, and were often in animal form, or (in men) appeared as fierce warrior-women (a concept that shares many similarities with the *valkyries*, but is not identical). In Oddr Snorrason's *Saga of Olaf Tryggvason*, Olaf's *fylgjur* are even described as "gods" – interesting terminology, considering the Christian context of the saga.[7] Finally, many sagas describe people who were able to assume the "skin" of their *fylgja* or other animals, meaning they take on the "aspect" of the animal, which allows them to perform feats of skill or insight normally not available to them, such as the "shapeshifters" of *Egil's Saga* (Smiley, 2001), who take on the "skin" of the bear or wolf in battle, making them ferocious combatants. These descriptions remind one of the "taking over of consciousness" observed in the above case study; only the ancient practitioners appear to have been more skilled at the altered states of consciousness that were likely involved in such practices.

The bear spirit – analysis

The modern supposedly scientific approach to such experiences tends to dismiss them as poetic fancy or delusional thinking, or perhaps condescendingly as "primitive" or "wishful" thinking. For some reason, we arbitrarily privilege "ordinary" waking consciousness above all other states, even though the ability to use such states is innate and has been used by humans for somewhere between 60,000 and 200,000 years – perhaps more. Apparently we're much too clever now for such "superstition." Another problem is that this ability is likely an evolutionary adaptation (reviewed in Haule, 2010 and McNamara, 2009), which further calls into question the validity of dismissing such states as pathological, illusionary, or erroneous.

A more valid approach, returning to the research review of earlier chapters, can shed some light on what scientifically may be going on here, to which we can compare the cultural theories of animal "spirits" above and see how they agree or disagree. According to Ms. Green, the earliest she remembers the bear dream is age nine, which, according to children's dreaming studies (Foulkes, 1999), is precisely the age we would expect a child to be able to have a dream in which animal figures act like "personalities" that are perhaps "linked" with the dreamer (more on this part below), with the dreamer participating in a fairly complex narrative. Evolutionary psychologists show that the human brain quickly and easily acquires animal-related data, and as such the propensity to think in animal terms, and to see animals in the environment is an innate capacity. Anthropology reveals that personification and metaphor-creation are absolute universals, further suggesting the same thing, and the neuroanatomy triune brain model shows how at the deeper levels of the brain, and hence the psyche, we all share the same neural machinery, and these conserved layers are also shared with other animals such as the old mammal brain and the reptile brain (though the structures are not identical, they are broadly similar in function). These layers "think like" animals and are only partially tied to our personal history. From affective neuroscience we know that basic emotional instinctual programs and motivations emerge from these deeper layers, transcend individual differences and have progressively less to do with personal history; however, the *particular way* in which these systems behave can be heavily modulated by personal history. These emotional motivating systems are relatively autonomous and can strongly influence consciousness, whereas consciousness has a much weaker influence on them. From the study of mental imagery we know that strong emotions can conjure imagery (and vice versa), and heavily involve the sensory processing portions of the brain, thus mimicking actual perception, and this is an actively constructive process that is symbolic and pre-linguistic. Autonomous imagery occurs especially in dream and reverie states – states in which the conscious self is more "fluid."

From dream research we learn that these images are non-random and are usually non-literal and symbolic, and can occur during waking as well as dreaming (though at differing frequency and intensity) at different levels of conscious control. Those outside conscious control therefore are likely to be associated with more autonomous unconscious systems forcefully acting upon consciousness rather than being directed by it. Further data from evolutionary psychology suggests that imagery and meaning are inextricably bound, and such meanings are often – at the basic level – fairly universal in form, such as the "ideal mate" imagery or "predator–prey" imagery discussed in this chapter. Metaphor theory explains just how the brain uses such metaphors: using what it knows well, animals, for example, as shown by the evolutionary psychology data, to depict what it does not – the mysterious pattern of sensory data that triggers the conception/perception of the symbol. Furthermore, like all symbols, there is an ineffable core of meaning that evades simple concrete explication, and can only be experienced *as it appears*, containing a subjective truth that is independent of whatever parts make the whole. From folk biology and TOM research we learn that some symbols are labeled with mentality, personality, intentionality, purposefulness, and so on, and even though they may lack physical form they still behave like independent personalities.

What all this points to, then, is the subjective experience of an image that has a mentality that is separate from the conscious self's point of view and identity, which is associated with activation of the perceptual/conceptual areas of the brain, which appears to have its origin *associated with* (not caused by) activity in the deeper, more universal layers of the brain *as they interface and blend with the environment*, since the internal/external boundary is so blurry at this level and likely associated with unconscious systems that act with relative autonomy.[8] The bear itself contains an ineffable core of meaning and is therefore best regarded in an "as is" manner, that is, as a bear, dangerous, powerful, apparently protective (in this case) and with a mind of its own. In Ms. Green's case, just as in the saga lore, the bear appears throughout life and appears to react to the life experiences of the dreamer, both in dreams and in waking life. It behaves with a personality, intent, and purpose that is independent of the conscious self and has a clearly defined, if somewhat mysterious, animal-like personality. This bear therefore differs very little from any other bear, with the exception of its unusual behavior, in that it can only be detected while in certain brain states such as dreaming or reverie, or in someone with "second sight." Ms. Green's bear thus matches most of the basic criteria that define the *fylgjur* of the ancient north people.

Objections

Comparing "religious" or "mythical" ideas to science always runs the risk of reductionism – that is, pointing to what causes such and such, and then making the triumphant statement "That's all it is!" after which (poof!) the thing disappears. In this case one might make several such mistakes. The first would be to say that the bear is "all in your head," or that because so much of the science involves neurobiological evidence, such experiences are not "real" because they involve only perception without any physical bear lumbering across the environment. But there is nothing unreal about the brain activity in the perceptual/conceptual areas of the brain, or the emotional centers associated with vivid imagery, or with the brain regions that designate such bears as "outside" the conscious ego of the perceiver. There is nothing about the experience of such a being that does not utilize the same old brain regions involved in the experience of other, perhaps more "conventional," bears. Thus if it is not "real," then what is it? Moreover, these brain regions do not operate in a vacuum: they are intimately tied to the environment in a variety of ways, and many of the unconscious systems at the deeper levels are independent of the conscious self; thus the line between "out there" and "in your head" becomes very blurry if not unresolvable; hence the objection approaches meaninglessness. In any case the only way to assess the "reality" – perhaps better labeled as overall relevance or behavior – of such experiences is subsequent experience (known in science as "predictive validity"). A being that appears and reappears later, and is only visible to some and not others, is simply one kind of experience of mentality and personality among many, with a variety of interpretations that may lead one to a variety of impressions as to their relevance and meaning. Ms. Green came to the conclusion that the bear was a very significant being that she needed to understand more fully, and this act in itself subsequently changed the behavior of the bear.

Another reductionism is the one that claims that perception of agency or mentality in the absence of a physical being is a "cognitive error" – that is, it's an example of our animal detection machinery gone awry. The evidence for such a claim is normally that the innate capacity to detect animals in the environment, which evolved to alert us to potential predators, for example, operates "in error" sometimes and leads to delusional beliefs in spirit animals. The neuroscientist Patrick McNamara (2009), in his excellent review *The Neuroscience of Religious Experience*, makes the point that such a claim cannot itself be directly tested. This is because it presupposes that when a person perceives a spirit being subjectively, since there is nothing "really" to perceive in the environment, it must be working in error. But this argument is circular; how do we know there's nothing (animal-like or not) to be detected in the first place without assuming the very thing we're trying to prove?

Furthermore, his own research on dream characters shows that they appear to have a mentality that is separate from the conscious self in ways that are virtually indistinguishable from other mentalities we encounter during waking life. In other words, McNamara observes that dream characters are not merely conscious inventions of the dreamer. They have a will of their own and appear to exist independently of the conscious self. In his own studies, he showed that when examining dreams of subjects in series, some dream characters reappeared, and seemed to "remember" previous interactions with the dreamer, changing their behavior accordingly. McNamara (2009) explains:

> In short, dream characters . . . appear to satisfy some of the most stringent criteria philosophers have produced for "personhood." It should not be surprising, therefore, to find that our ancestors treated dream characters as spirit persons and accorded special and sometimes divine status to characters in dreams.
>
> (198)

Ms. Green's bear displayed this quality, and changed its behavior after an interaction with it in waking life – dream analysis. This fact might seem startling to the modern reader, that a dream character can be logically afforded the same ontological status as a person encountered in waking life. The fact that such a character can disappear and reappear, for example, might be used to argue for its "unreality" – however, even a toddler will tell you that just because a ball rolled behind the couch doesn't mean it's gone. It's still there; you just can't see it.

Through all this we should remember that the very qualities of mentality, purposefulness, volition, and so on are also dependent upon proper brain functioning and are therefore entirely subjective or "all in our head" as well. That is, no matter what the causal origin for spirits, gods, or guardian bears may be, the attribution of mentality is a subjective appraisal, and if we dismiss that out of hand, we must also dismiss the same subjective appraisal for everyone else we encounter. After all, your best friend is "merely" a collection of biomolecules moving about in accordance with chemical and physical laws. Is the attribution of mentality and intent to him or her also a "cognitive error"? Without some criteria to differentiate, dismissing so-called spirit beings is just being arbitrary and we are better off assessing each experience at face value and taking such perceptions seriously rather than reciting something vaguely scientific about molecules and pretending they don't "exist." Put another way, science is to trees as myth is to forest – they appraise different levels of analysis but are not separate from one another or necessarily contradictory.

Chapter 5

The anima/feminine symbols

In the last chapter I discussed how the brain uses animals to symbolize emotions, intuitions, environmental patterns, or vague sensations and ineffable feelings, and some of these behave with personalities and are virtually indistinguishable from so-called "physical" beings. In the next few chapters I will explore more specific types of these "spirit" beings, continuing with the same type of scientific and comparative mythology approach. One *type* of these beings was defined by Jung as the "anima." In his own words, Jung describes this enigmatic character:

> she stands for the loyalty which in the interests of life he must sometimes forgo; she is the much needed compensation for the risks, struggles, sacrifices that all end in disappointment; she is the solace for all the bitterness of life. And, at the same time, she is the great illusionist, the seductress, who draws him into life . . . not only into life's reasonable and useful aspects, but into its frightful paradoxes and ambivalences where good and evil, success and ruin, hope and despair, counterbalance one another. Because she is his greatest danger she demands from a man his greatest, and if he has it in him she will receive it . . . the factor she embodies possesses all the outstanding characteristics of a feminine being.
>
> (Jung, 1959a: paras 24–26)

It is evident that what Jung is describing is a highly potent symbol – the metaphorical language he uses highlights its symbolic nature. This symbol is experienced to varying degrees by all men and appears as a woman (and sometimes other images). Jung further described the anima and animus as exhibiting

> feeling qualities [that are mostly] fascinating or numinous. They are surrounded by an atmosphere of sensitivity, touchy reserve, secretiveness, painful intimacy, and even absoluteness. The relative autonomy of the anima- and animus-figures expresses itself in these qualities.
>
> (Jung, 1959a: para 53)

This character therefore represents vague concepts of "femininity" as men come to understand it through their development into adulthood; nature provides men with a way of recognizing and understanding "feminine beings" through the anima, and she symbolizes all sorts of entanglements and heartaches, but also the promise of bliss and redemption. As described, the anima comes in many forms; conceptualizations of the anima are varied and sometimes apparently contradictory, so much so that some authors argue that it is an unhelpful construct (von Raffay, 2000).

Whether or not it is "helpful" is beyond the scope of this book: I am concerned only with exploring whether or not it is a consistently generated symbolic image in light of recent research. In other words, I am essentially reexamining Jung's idea from a fresh perspective. The only way this can be accomplished is to start with a basic question: are there aspects of a man's perceptual/conceptual system that are innate, unconscious, affectively charged, domain-specific, universal, resistant to environmental variation and rich with *feminine-specific* content such as that proposed by Jung?[1] If this is the case, then it follows that it should reliably give rise to autonomous agents like we saw in the last chapter.

Earlier I reviewed the data that strongly suggests everyone has an "ideal female" innate image prototype, and I argued that this imagery could be used symbolically. As we will see, more detail on this system consists of the ability to recognize what potential mates are kin or not, with an additional subsystem that devalues kin as potential mates. This system evolved in an ancestral environment in which toddlers raised with a high degree of familiarity would almost always be kin, and so provided natural selection with a method for differentiating kin versus non-kin in potential mates, which then subsequently preferentially invests non-kin with sexual and love attractiveness. This theory has found a great deal of support; for example, children reared together *like* siblings, such as in Taiwanese minor marriages, later have an adult aversion to mating – this effect is postulated to be an adaptation to avoid inbreeding (Burnstein, 2005: 533). This effect applies even when subjects *know* that they are unrelated, such as in Israeli kibbutzim, implying that male–female familiarity primes a subjective sense of genetic relatedness and fear of mating that *overrides conscious knowledge to the contrary*.

Such imagery does not merely motivate short-term sexual behavior but long-term mate bonding as well, the result being a successful pair bond. Pair bonding has a neurobiological basis that has been characterized to some degree; it is associated with high levels of the brain hormone oxytocin between mother and infant as well as romantic partners (Carter, 1992; Carter, 1998). Pair bonding in men and women is associated with lower incidence of depression and better ability to cope with stress (Myers, 1999), suggesting that humans have evolved to respond positively when a long-term relationship is secure and enduring (Campbell and Ellis, 2005).

To summarize, both men and women have innate "fertile, high-genetic-quality female" detection mechanisms in their brains, which involve not only physical appearance but also scent, motion, and likely a host of other factors not yet characterized. This system attributes very high emotional significance in both sexual (LUST) and romantic (CARE) bonding systems to such images in heterosexual men, and is used to assess competitiveness in women. If all this is used to create an animate *symbol* in a dream or fantasy brain/mind state of a male, then I argue that what is experienced may be definable as an "anima" symbol.

Mythological descriptions of "the anima"

In mythology, female symbols appear all over the place; obviously all goddesses are female symbols, and all kinds of things are related to "the female," though technically many are goddesses, which are more archetypal and less related to the subject, and thus not quite the same thing as the anima, which Jung described as tied into a person's individual history more than a purely archetypal figure is (more on this below). Anyway, just to examine how experiences are symbolized as female beings, one can see that rivers, the earth, the sun, and the moon have all been represented by a goddess, and goddesses have been said to "take the form of" various animals and images that are usually packed with characteristics that are innately recognized as "high-fertility female," if they are fertility or love goddesses, or they are conspicuously absent in the case of child or "old crone" type images. Evil magical female creatures who entice, seduce, and destroy men, such as the Lorelei (Germanic myth), the Sirens (Greek myth), the banshee and various evil female fairies (Irish myth), appear throughout mythology. Germanic folklore describes numerous *disir* "female spirits" which, significantly, are often described as *appearing in dreams* and inhabiting various places (Turville-Petre, 1975); folk customs here often involved making offerings to such beings at yearly festivals or at sacred places.

Such characters in folklore can lead the hero to his doom or aid him in his goals. Recurrent "maiden" figures, such as those found in many medieval tales where a knight rescues a "damsel in distress," seem to represent psychological redemption for male protagonists (Cirlot, 1971). That two such apparently contradictory mappings could find themselves using the same target domain is what probably causes the confusion as to the meaning behind the anima symbol; this should not be a surprise, however, since anything so emotionally charged could potentially spell weal or woe for the subject, much like the snake. The important thing, however, is that, like animal symbols, the anima is never *irrelevant*. Her appearance always symbolizes some sort of highly emotional, and hence likely at least partially archetypal, process that is otherwise very difficult to express concretely.

Not surprisingly, "anima" images are also depicted along with animal symbols, such as the swan-woman (Celtic and German myth), the goat-woman (Hispanic folklore), the lion-goddess Sekhmet (Egyptian myth), or the lamia (Talmudic myth), just to name a few. These symbols are basically co-opting animal symbolism and incorporating it into the image in order to jam more meaning into already rich symbolism, and are good examples of *polysemy* (multiple meanings) in action.

Neurobiological substrates of the anima and animus symbols

Since mate-finding is a major biological tendency ingrained into the central nervous system of all vertebrate animals, including humans, it should be no surprise that a tremendous amount of emotional energy should be devoted toward such activity, since emotions are what drive our behavior. As a consequence, the symbol-making mechanism that operates in *Homo sapiens* has plenty of innate material to work with as it attempts to understand the world by metaphor creation. All of these mappings are therefore more specific versions of the animal symbols outlined previously. Like animals, humans do not appear to use female imagery to symbolize just anything, but rather a collection of vaguely intuitive and difficult-to-describe feelings and unconscious rumblings. In order to qualify as an "anima" symbol, Jung argued, however, it should be more personal than a goddess.

Metaphorical mappings of anima symbols

The innate drive toward attachments (in a heterosexual man) could be symbolized, among other things, by a female symbol. In such a mapping, it is the psychological motivation for relationship or intimacy *in the subject* that is being symbolized by the anima image. An exception to this might be when *the memory* of such behavior in someone else is being symbolized. For example, a man may dream of an unknown young woman encouraging him to get more involved with his friends. What she symbolizes, possibly, are partly unconscious tendencies toward intimacy, and these are becoming embodied by her behavior and appearance. The fact that the image does not refer to anyone in particular, then, suggests that the mapping of intimacy, or the activity of the LUST and/or CARE systems *in a particular context*, may be an appropriate interpretation for this image – being careful to remember that "interpretation" cannot magically dispel the ineffable core of meaning in the symbol. If he dreams of his wife doing this, however, it may be derived from something specific that the patient has stored in memory about her, but even then the colorations derived from the subject should not be disregarded because of the highly personal and subjective way we construct memories. In those cases it is the "spirit" of that person as she appears to the dreamer, and not fully equivalent to the person in herself, or even resolvable to "inner" and "outer" components.

Related to the above mappings is one in which lonely feelings, which derive from activity of the PANIC system that evolved to promote social attachments, provide the impersonal source domain. That is, the emotional consequences of isolation or separation result in predictable activity of the PANIC system, which in animals evokes separation calls and in humans evokes crying behaviors (Panksepp, 1998). The subjective experience of this activity is essentially feelings of loneliness, that is, of being "incomplete" or "empty" (to use two common visuospatial metaphors). Thus the subject may generate an image of a female that personifies his need for "completion" or relief from attachment separation. Similarly, a source domain that consists of any unconscious circuits that for whatever reason are ignored by the very information-limited conscious processing system will provide the neurobiological basis that symbolizes the desired unknown as an anima character.

LUST obviously plays a part in anima symbolism, and will be tied into it as well, particularly if unsatisfied or more activated for whatever reason, and can provide a source domain for this mapping. Since in a heterosexual masculinized brain the aforementioned "fertile young female" recognition system of the brain evokes a great deal of sexual significance, this will be a ubiquitous potential mapping. Another possibility is one that uses longings for family, and all the biological motivators involved in attachment and mating might be symbolized. The specific behavior of the anima symbol in a dream has to be attended to if we are to understand what the symbol is supposed to be representing; hence a dream of a seductive unknown female who disappears after sex might be symbolizing mating instincts (and we should never underestimate their complexity!), whereas a female who through the course of the dream becomes pregnant or "gives" the dreamer a child (another symbol) or leads him to a house where they "dwell together" may be associated with love motivations (aka CARE circuits). Of course *both* might be in use at the same time – this is one of the challenges of symbol interpretation. The generation of new life is the end result of all the mate-seeking affective motivational systems that are present in all vertebrates; this is not likely to be perceived by the unconscious systems, however, since emotions motivate behavior without there necessarily being any awareness of the outcome: the appearance of forethought is derived from the fact that the end result is selected for during the course of evolution. Interestingly, this gives these archetypal processes an appearance of "timelessness" because the end appears to be prefigured. In any case, the rather nebulous concepts of productivity, fertility, or creativity are likely very often going to be a part of anima symbolism, and other emotions such as RAGE and FEAR can get tied up into this imagery as well.

If you will notice, the way in which a person interacts with the anima image is essentially a metaphor for the "dialogue" or interaction between two parts of the mind: on one hand is the conscious self, and on the other is the various unconscious systems as they interface with the world. The way these two entities interact with each other provides a clue as to how the subject is dealing with these aspects of his subjective experience in waking life and other states of consciousness.

Communing with feminine spirits

So now we see how the brain can generate all sorts of female images innately, and by "images" I mean *all* the stuff that goes with it, such as "ways of being," scent, movement, behavior, and so on. When this imagery is experienced, she can have all the qualities of a goddess or spirit: she is powerful, timeless, ubiquitous, and protean. She likely will be experienced in the context of strong SEEKING activity (though it may not be very conscious). Why? Because what better subjective symbol could one make to represent intense exploratory interest in a heterosexual male than to utilize all the innate imagery of an attractive female? Indeed, a return to Jung's initial description of the anima reveals a very apt description of how SEEKING activity in humans feels subjectively. But since we usually don't know what she is symbolizing, caution is best advised, since many times what we want doesn't always end well ("be careful what you wish for"). Not only that, but, as with animal symbols, the anima is also unconscious in origin, and not entirely "self" in origin either, and so what she is symbolizing is frequently going to be difficult to figure out. But understanding her goes a long way toward understanding our various unconscious motivations and environmental subtleties as they go about their business "under the radar."

But throughout the exploration of the anima, we should remember that she has the characteristics of other "spirit beings": she has autonomy, timelessness, and emotional muscle relative to consciousness, and is capable of judgment and symbolic expression – she's not just a mindless reflex, or a regurgitated or hobbled together memory trace or primitive drive. She has a personality and intention, and as such will behave much like the mythical descriptions of *disir*, for example. Jung often hypothesized that the anima sometimes represented the "voice of the unconscious" (Jung, 1959a, 1959b, 1961, 1974, 1984) and advised "listening" to her with this in mind; like the bear spirit, she lives and responds to the current context and situation the person is in.

In any case, in dreams we can be visited by such a "spirit" and learn what she wants and feels; her actions can therefore tell us quite a bit about our subjective world that we might be unconscious of. Since we are typically unconscious of a lot, we would do well to heed her. Moreover, since dreaming is barely distinguishable from waking reverie, it is likely that we can encounter this being and whatever it is she symbolizes (which, remember, is ineffable anyway) when engaging in religious rituals, trance, and other altered states, or any other state where we are mentally prepared and "open."

I should add here that my own formulation of "the anima" differs a bit from Jung's, in that I really see no good reason why we should call feminine symbols "the" anima, as if there could be only one that is constantly changing shape. Perhaps this is merely a matter of semantics or preference. In any case, to fully acknowledge each symbolic image in itself would be to not assume it is *anything* right away, but to inquire into its meaning based on its qualities and the context in which it has arisen; hence I tend toward a "polytheistic" interpretation of the anima since it avoids overhasty interpretation. Since the evidence suggests that all sorts of subjective beings can appear at any time, it may be merely a matter of classification to call one an "anima" figure. Jung felt that anima figures were only "partly" archetypal, meaning that a good portion of anima activities were tied to the dreamer's own self-systems – that is, systems involved with the subjective sense of identity and personal history. If we are to define the anima image as one that is associated with the activity of mate-seeking systems, which are very complex and personal-history dependent, then this makes sense, and suggests a classification scheme whereby we might organize such beings. Those unknown humanlike figures that seem to be mainly related to SEEKING, LUST, or CARE type behavior, and that change considerably with time and/or therapy, would seem to fit this description and therefore qualify as "anima" symbols. Others, however, which seem immune to personal history and appear with a greater level of numinosity or awe-inspiring power, would more precisely be characterized as "god/desses," since they match the typical cultural description of such beings. The experience of such beings would likely be associated with more universal and emotional brain functions, since these are more innate and non-autobiographical. Three dreams reported in psychotherapy are illustrative:

> I am walking along a narrow tunnel that is fraught with traps and spikes, accompanied by a beautiful, voluptuous young woman. I immediately stop her and begin to rape her, and she fights me but then complies. I awaken horrified and disgusted with myself.

This dream was reported in the context of a high degree of neuroticism and conflict toward intimacy. And we later discussed the likelihood that the behavior of the dreamer toward this being paralleled the problems he had with female relationships and sexuality. Engaging in a dialogue with this figure over time was associated with improvements in some of the conflicts and a later dream was reported:

I am in Greece and I see a woman who resembled the one in the tunnel. She told me she had something to teach me – a new language – and that I would be able to "break concrete" after a certain time.

This character had changed following a long-standing dialogue with her from the earlier session, and she clearly represents a less conflicted relationship. Thus one might label this figure as an anima figure, given the subjective data. Contrast this with another dream:

I am sitting at a picnic table next to a woman who is beautiful, but more than that. Her gaze is utterly entrancing, and being with her is like a thousand lazy summer days free of care. Tremendous power and majesty emanates from her, and I feel to leave her presence would be like death itself. I remember thinking in the dream, "I would gladly kill someone just to spend another day with her." I have a suit of armor and it is melting away and I sense that it was her will that I should allow it.

This being seems much less personal and more "eternal" than an anima character – the experience of this woman was likely correlated with intense activity in a variety of very old brain structures that are less subject to personal history. Ultimately, the experience in itself cannot be reduced to anything except what it is at face value without "cheating," but the science at least gives us an idea of how these experiences can occur given our knowledge of how the brain interacts with the environment – sometimes brain states occur in the absence of clear environmental variations; hence these changes run along trajectories that can be considered innate (cf. Goodwyn, 2010a, where I explore this concept in more depth). In any case, this woman carries the power and intense feeling of a goddess. Could we attribute the label "anima" to her? I think it would be less precise but perhaps still defendable. Unfortunately, Jung was not terribly precise in his definitions, but this is likely due to his intuition that such precision might be detrimental to the thing he was trying to describe.

Chapter 6

The animus/masculine symbols

Much as a man has an innate "internal image of woman" as part of his perceptual/conceptual system surrounding mate-seeking (typically), women have an innate "internal image of man." Like the anima, animus images are associated with much more than sexuality; the animus can create heartache and complications for women, as well as the promise of salvation or contentment. But what are the specific characteristics of the perceptual/conceptual system at work in the generation of male figures in the female brain?

Cross-culturally, a man's mate value as adjudicated by females is typically determined by his status, prestige, current resource holdings, long-term ambition, intelligence, interpersonal dominance, social popularity, sense of humor, reputation for kindness, maturity, height, "v-shaped" body, strength, and athleticism (Barber, 1995; Buss and Schmitt, 1993; Smuts, 1995). Furthermore, nonverbal indicators of *dominance* increase a man's attractiveness to women, but not women's attractiveness to men (cf. Sadalla *et al.*, 1987). These are, of course, broad averages and subject to wide variation. And there are fluctuations in which of these characteristics is emphasized in women that depend on certain variables. In contrast to the male mating strategy that is largely a function of relatively consistent testosterone levels, female mating strategy fluctuates somewhat with hormone levels throughout each cycle.

For instance, as men age, their age preferences change relative to their own age – but at the same time, men retain a constant attraction toward women in the years of peak fertility; women, on the other hand, are attracted to men who are slightly older than them and are usually not fixated on a narrow range of fertility, presumably because male resource-gathering potential (the female imperative in mate selection in animals and probably ancient humans) increases with age until senescence, but female peak fertility (the male imperative on mate selection) stays within the range of the ages of approximately 20–40 (Kenrick *et al.*, 2005: 809).

According to sexual selection theory, males with high levels of testosterone and social rank, more masculinized features, low fluctuating asymmetry (markers of genetic quality), and who display high resource-acquiring potential are more likely to choose short-term mating strategies, likely because from their point of view they are more likely to "get away with it" because of their attractiveness. This is a reflection of the fact that, overall, male mating strategy is also associated with testosterone levels, in which higher testosterone levels are associated with more short-term mating strategies (Putz et al., 2004; extensive review in Schmitt, 2005).

The female counter-adaptation to this imbalance in men's mating strategy choice is to be attracted to less competitive men in some circumstances, and more competitive men in others. Men, by contrast, pursue mates based on two age ranges as well as the aforementioned physical characteristics (all else being equal, of course – more data needs to be gathered on behavioral qualities universally sought after in females). The evidence of this fluctuation in attraction comes from a variety of sources. Studies of the perceptual/conceptual system show that during the late follicular phase, right when a female is most likely to be impregnated, women prefer more symmetrical faces with more masculine features, higher dominance and testosterone-related attributes such as prominent brows, large chins and deeper voices, and more competitive and arrogant behaviors "precisely as though women are shifting to a short-term mating strategy" (Schmitt, 2005: 275) during this time. Furthermore, women, when they are ovulating, report stronger sexual attraction to and fantasies about extra-pair partners, and this pattern does not hold for current partners (Simpson and Campbell, 2005: 139). Ovulating women also prefer the scent of T-shirts worn by more symmetrical men, but this effect was not found in non-ovulating women (Gangestad and Thornhill, 1998). They also have more frequent and intense orgasms, and dress more provocatively (while at the same time reducing behaviors that may put them at risk for rape) during this part of their menstrual cycle (Gangestad and Thornhill, 1997; Gangestad and Thornhill, 1998; Grammer et al., 2004).

Women report finding high-testosterone and high-symmetry (and hence low mutation load) characteristics such as musculature, height, broad shoulders, high shoulder-to-hip ratio (no such association with attractiveness exists for females with this measurement; Hughes and Gallup, 2002), masculine facial features, and high intrasexual competitiveness desirable in short-term mates and extra-pair sex partners (Buss and Schmitt, 1993) and are more likely to copulate with men exhibiting these "masculine" traits during ovulation. Note that, like women, men recognize these features as well, yet not as attractive mates but rather as rivals. In fact, the above physical features are more likely to invoke jealous feelings in other males (Dijkstra and Buunk, 2001), suggesting that the perceptual/conceptual system has this recognition ability in both sexes.

Women are more likely to have extra-pair affairs when they are ovulating, but are not more prone to have sex with their long-term partners during this time (Baker and Bellis, 1995). Women actually show a prefer-ence for masculine features, as listed above, peaking near ovulation but *only* for evaluation of short-term partners, not for a long-term investing partners (Penton-Voak *et al.*, 1999). Gangestad *et al.* (2004; also Gangestad *et al.*, 2005: 356) showed that women rate men as high on potential for short-term partners when they are arrogant, competitive with other men, muscular, physically attractive, and socially influential. They did not show a prefer-ence for kindness, intelligence, a tendency to be a good father or sexual faithfulness when mid-cycle. These latter qualities were valued in long-term partners and did not vary with ovulation cycle. Women also preferred more creative men for short-term but not long-term partners (Haselton and Miller, 2002). The cues that orient the perceptual/conceptual system apply even to hands. For example, if a male's ring fingers are longer than his index fingers, caused by high testosterone exposure during development, he is more likely to have more children, engage in more short-term mating strategies, have higher sperm motility, be more competitive and assertive, and be perceived as more attractive (Manning, 2002). Finally, more symmetrical men are more likely to engage in extra-pair sex and are more prone to be selected by women as extra-pair partners (Gangestad and Thornhill, 1997).

Women appear to have adaptations that orient them toward long-term partners as well; women have been shown to prefer the scent of men who are either dissimilar to themselves at the so-called MHC genetic loci (a collection of genes used by the immune system to combat infections; Wedekind and Füri, 1997). Specifically, women prefer the scent of men who are genetically compatible,[1] but this effect does *not* increase during ovulation (Thornhill *et al.*, 2001).

So how does all this help us to understand dream or "spirit" beings? As it happens, the above universal aspects of the perceptual/conceptual system are reflected in dream imagery (Van de Castle, 1994) wherein women show an increase in imagery associated with sexual situations near ovulation, and retreat afterward, which verifies the mental imagery data that shows how universal emotional systems correlate with subjective images. All of this data points to unconscious tendencies that orient women toward two essentially different types of men – the more aggressive, "dominant," creative, high-testosterone male, more desirable as a short-term partner, especially during mid-cycle, and the less aggressive, less dominant, more investing, "kinder, gentler" partner who is "long-term compatible" genetically. Contrast this with the strategies of males that orient toward youth and fertility, and also to a similar-age partner, fluctuating not with ovulation (since men don't ovulate) but with overall age and testosterone levels.

Since mating behavior involves not only LUST circuits but PANIC/CARE attachment circuits, all of this will affect more than just sexual activity, in fact all the *subjective* emotional turmoil from bliss to despair that accompanies relations with men. The important point here is that all of the characteristics of the perceptual/conceptual system outlined above affect symbol making (as shown in part by the dream imagery studies) in a variety of ways.

Animus symbols

All of the above data strongly suggests that just as men and women have "fertile and/or bonding female" recognition systems, they also have "dominant or investing male" recognition circuits, and, like the female symbols, male symbols will be used similarly for the same reasons. LUST activity may be somewhat more complex for women than men, largely because of the above shifts in mating strategy. Here the objects of desire vary from genetically compatible long-term mates to high-testosterone, high-genetic-quality short-term mates. This creates a shifting dynamic in terms of which image (in terms not only of physical features but also of behavior) will be most emotionally charged. What this has to say about symbol making is that a variety of different types of animus images will likely be used to symbolize different ideas or feelings or whatever.

The animi may represent a motivation to understand the unknown, to explore the unknown, as in SEEKING activity, both in the environment and within the mind. Here we see symbols like the "mysterious other," which may carry connotations of SEEKING and/or LUST. The afore-mentioned relationship of ring-finger length to testosterone exposure, and its correlation with dominance, creativity, and fecundity, because they are part of the innate perceptual/conceptual system, can all play into the meaning behind a symbol of the hand, since the neurobiology here suggests a ubiquitous, easily acquired and innately directed semantic link between hands and virility. Symbols that use hands may be correlated with the mate-seeking systems that recognize and label hands as "attractive" or not. Consequently, it is not surprising that the fourth digit is the "ring" finger, that is, the finger utilized to symbolize marriage, though this is not a universal. Another example is the idea among the ancient Anglo-Saxons that this finger has special "magical" power (Storms, 1948) – which prob-ably means it attracts attention due to these universal recognition systems, since it is the innate propensity to recognize this as a cue of mate quality that is universal. The hand, then, can be utilized by either gender to rep-resent masculine categorizations or tendencies. Other body-part-recognition mechanisms likely exist but have not been studied.

Like the anima for men, these entities behave with timeless emotional power and autonomy, and represent a subtle distinction between a being who more properly would be described as a "god," that is, perhaps embodying many attractive (or unattractive by negation) characteristics but also intense "awe inspiring" subjectivity, and a being that is more closely related to the woman's own experience of relationships. Ms. Green, for example, dreamt the following:

> A soldier with severed hands has captured me. He uses prosthetics on his hands, and demands revenge on me for my husband's behavior. He orders me to shave my head and says he will kill me.

This character seemed to be a very personal one, unlike the bear, who was more impersonal and powerful, and appearing somehow older and more "primordial." During analysis of this dream we quickly came upon the issue of Ms. Green's sexual abuse and the various complexities it created in relationship with her husband. The hands in particular are an interesting feature not only because of the above universal associations between "masculine" hands and attractiveness/virility (which suggests Ms. Green's husband had somehow been responsible for this being's virility), but also because of the rage behind this animus figure's behavior. As we analyzed this figure she experienced a curious physical response in that she felt a drop in desire for intimacy, but it seemed to overlay a continued physical arousal that seemed immune to this effect – the overall experience of these two conflicting intrapsychic forces she reported as very odd, and we interpreted them as a conflict between two independent unconscious activities: the sex drive appeared overtaken by an opposing force that feared and loathed intimacy, likely due to abuse experiences. This interpretation "felt right" according to Ms. Green. By contrast, the bear spirit was never identified as male or female, and thus furthermore does not appear to fit the criteria for an animus figure or "spirit," though she often reported that it seemed these various complexes were conflicting with each other as much as with her. Interestingly, Northern European folklore (Turville-Petre, 1975; Davidson, 1993) describes many beliefs in elves, dwarves, or trolls that dwell in sacred places and – more importantly for my purposes here – appear in dreams to communicate with the dreamer and sometimes get intensely entangled with the dreamer's life. Some even describe people having had sexual relations with such beings, and other characters are described as having "elf" or "troll" in their ancestry. The descriptions of such beings, which are basically nonphysical, masculine, unknown characters that appear in dreams or other altered states, therefore nicely match up with the above characteristics of various partially personal dream characters as understood using recent evidence.

Thus, if we were to make a sliding scale of "personal" to "impersonal" figures, one could argue that the soldier was more personal than the bear, just as folkloric descriptions of elves or spirits are more personal and local than gods. All of these are, however, less personal than, say, the husband or someone encountered daily in waking consciousness. More on this in later chapters.

Chapter 7

The mother

Not only does the brain recognize males and females to a high degree, it also recognizes and orients strongly to mothers. Available evidence suggests that humans reliably acquire a set of rapidly and spontaneously emergent concepts concerned specifically with mothering that are unconscious, universal, affectively charged, resistant to environmental variation, and shaped by evolution, and upon this considerable substrate much idiosyncratic development can of course occur.

Infants can discriminate their mothers by voice within 24 hours, via scent by two days, and via face by two weeks (reviewed in Burnstein, 2005). This mother–infant bond acquisition process appears to be mediated by highly conserved circuitry in the deep brain involving the neurotransmitters oxytocin and arginine-vasopressin (AVP) in mammals, including humans (Lim *et al.*, 2004; Young and Insel, 2002). Fluctuations in oxytocin are associated with proportional fluctuations in maternal attachment behavior in many animals (Carter, 1998, 2002), suggesting a highly instinctive component to the mother–child bond. Neuroimaging studies of attachment in humans show that reward centers with high density oxytocin and AVP receptor activity are activated during bonding (Fisher, 2004) – these are centers that are situated in the deeper environmentally resistant "layers" of the brain/mind, though this is certainly not immune to personal history; many cases of disrupted maternal attachments have been observed clinically to produce a host of problems later in life; my primary point is that we retain a "polytheistic" approach and not collapse all attachment-related imagery onto the personal mother. Not all goddesses have heard of one's mother, nor do they care. In any case, there is a link between mother–infant bonding and mate bonding; falling in love with a *mate or offspring* may involve temporarily deactivating regions associated with social mistrust (Flinn *et al.*, 2005: 561) and encourage beliefs that the subject's mother (or mate) is "the best ever."

The problems with children who experience poor maternal bonding are legion – much has been written about this from nearly every theoretical school of psychotherapy; this fact alone points to a strongly innate system that orients the child toward his mother very early on. Furthermore, the mother–child bond has a variety of behavioral consequences in both parent and child; it is not merely a mindless reflex. It has implications in a variety of motivations and settings involving parenting. For example, both human and rat mothers display intense "nesting" preparations immediately prior to birth, and this behavior is more pronounced with subsequent births – this is associated with marked increases in oxytocin production in the deep brain. Furthermore, oxytocin levels increase in response to suckling infants, and this coincides with increased nurturant behaviors in mammalian mothers and increases in milk production (Panksepp, 1998: 250–251).

Mother symbols

The mother "image" appears to comprise a particular class of *subjective feelings* rather than specific imagery – all likely correlated with highly conserved deep brain activity involving oxytocin, AVP, opiod, and likely many other systems yet to be identified. As we have seen, female recognition systems already exist within the perceptual/conceptual system and are likely present from a very early age. What makes these images *mothers*, then, are that they are female images imbued with the intense feelings of the mother bond. The point, however, is that these feelings are strong, phylogenetically stable and specific toward mother–child bonding, which was so important to mammalian survival during the course of evolution. All of the mappings, then, are further differentiations of the human symbols described before. In this case the mother is a female image that is imbued with mother–infant "significance," which may be correlated with activity of the oxytocin and opiod systems in the child, and perhaps in the mother as an "ideal mother," which she is trying to aspire to.

Mythical expressions of mother symbols

One of the most ancient anthropomorphic symbols is the Great Mother – should this be a surprise? Images such as Gaia (Greek myth), Mut (Egyptian myth), Nerthus (Germanic myth), Erde or Jord (Norse myth), Erce (Anglo-Saxon), Mahimata, Mother Mary (Christian iconography – called the "mother of God"), or Eje (Mongolian myth) abound through the comparative literature. She is felt to be present in the fertile earth, the cornucopia, and was felt to be a protective and enclosing, embodying "containment" (see Knox, 2003 for an excellent discussion of this concept), and is associated with vessels such as cups, vases, the ocean, and all that comes from the water such as fish, pearls, shells, and dolphins. The mother has been metaphorically linked with nature, the earth, fertility, warmth, nourishment, but also stifling love, mortal destiny, and the grave (Tresidder, 2005: 326). Bird symbols given a mother significance include the dove, swan, and, as mentioned previously, the lily, rose, lotus, and fruit tree are also associated with the great mother. The earth is very often attributed a "motherly" aspect, as the sky is very often attributed a masculine aspect. Burial ceremony has been viewed as a "return to the great in many cultures mother" (Stevens, 1998: 188–189).

The darker aspect of the mother is typically portrayed as the "devouring" mother, like Kali and Durga (Indian myth), Lilith (Talmudic myth), the Morrigan (Celtic myth), Hecate (Greek myth), and Coatlicue (Aztec myth), and rituals designed to appease her involved bloody ritual sacrifice to fertilize the earth, which Stevens feels may be related to the ubiquitous observation of menstruation and its relationship to fertility – when menstruation stops, blood is "conserved" and life is gestated (1998: 191). The "devouring" mother seems to represent an overattached parent figure who does not allow one to grow and separate.

Another aspect of mother symbolism is the association with death and rebirth; throughout the world the mother is used as a symbol of life and the world, but also as death, which appears to always be equated with regeneration and rebirth (Cirlot, 1971); thus the mysterious idea of death is symbolized as a "return to the great mother" in many cultures. Perhaps the concept of rebirth is created by this metaphor, in that returning to the mother easily associates origins with mothers. Note also that essentialist thinking, inherent in the brain, would equate death as merely a change of form – essences are immutable (Ahn et al., 2001) – and thus providing another link between death and new life.

Metaphorical mappings of mother symbols

Nurturant feelings are correlated with the ubiquitous CARE circuitry; other variations on this theme could be intimacy or kin-bonding, or the safe feelings of being in an enclosed shelter, frequently referred to by dream interpreters. Environmental symbols such as trees, landscapes, and lakes have innate aspects as well, a point to which I will return in later chapters. For now, suffice it to say that there is evidence that abstract tree symbolism is a part of the innate perceptual/conceptual system and therefore can also be used to create a lot of metaphors, one of which views trees or The Great Tree as an aspect of an image embodying the ineffable essence of "mother." The fact that fruits come from trees and plants and feeding on these foods is a lasting part of our primate heritage is perhaps why this symbolic expression comes so naturally to the human mind.

The concept of "origination" is essentially a cause–effect relationship, which is an innate part of our processing system that we share with many mammals, especially primates. Thus the concept of "cause" can easily be linked with mother symbols. Furthering this link is the fact that the innate folk-biology system allows young children to understand that zebras, for example, which are raised by cows will still behave like zebras and have "zebra innards" (Atran, 2005); in other words, a key component of the "essentialist" thinking with respect to biological objects in the perceptual/ conceptual system is that what makes an animal what it is depends upon its parents, which obviously includes the mother, and this "essence" carries on to offspring. Thus the origin–mother link is quite strong and spontaneous, which provides the basis for this universal symbol.

The most important part of this analysis is to remember that these are all symbols working in exactly the same way every other metaphorical mapping works: that is, they take something emotional, difficult to describe, or intuitive and map it onto something we can all easily understand due to our evolutionary makeup. Hence our tendency to symbolize the universe or "nature" as a mother. What drives the *particular* equation with a mother, rather than say a rock or a hand – both of which are also easy to understand – is its particular aptness. The world is definitely "like" a mother in many ineffable metaphoric ways. But in order for this to be more than poetic flourish, the subject must have a genuine sense that such a mother, even if obscure (like other people can be), has a real personality and purposefulness.

The mother goddess

Mother *images* probably have their origin in the universal attachment systems we all share. Therefore, when they are experienced as *symbols*, they import a great deal of emotional and ultimately ineffable connotations with them. Further, because she is an unconscious, universal creation, she has the "godlike" qualities of other personified symbols that originate in our deep emotional intuitions; she demands our attention and also wants our love, but, like all primitive, ancient implicit systems, she can be overwhelming to consciousness. How she is perceived by consciousness will likely be influenced by personal experience and the attitude of consciousness toward *her*.

The large number of mythological expressions that have an earth mother goddess is in itself fascinating; apparently the propensity to conceive of the physical world and its mysterious origins as somehow embodying or related to a great mother is universally evident. One report from a schizophrenic patient involved the great mother:

> I was at a party before I came to the hospital. I was with the Earth Mother, the moon goddess, and the sun god.

When consciousness was hindered by her disease, it seemed the mother goddess was a natural intuition. It is often observed that dreams can have a similar quality to psychosis, and it appears that our native propensities lean more toward a "polytheistic" way of thinking when in states of reverie, dreaming, or psychosis, even among subjects who are consciously monotheistic or atheistic.

In any case, experiences of mother goddesses likely correlate with the same innate systems that orient us toward our own mothers initially. But such systems do not seem to depend upon much specific input in order to function.[1] Like the subjects in the unusual dream study (Bertolo et al., 2003), who though born blind were able to draw pictures of their dreams that were indistinguishable from those of blindfolded sighted subjects, the human mind is probably able to construct a "mother" concept in the absence of a physical mother – though this would be difficult and unethical to study directly. In any case, this variation resistance suggests innateness, and may explain the clinically oft-observed motivation behind adoptees to find their "real" mothers. Many times the fantasies such people have about these never-before-met mothers speak with the voice of the Great Mother, as I observed once in a child case; in this case, the child had been separated from her biological mother from a very early age and raised in an orphanage in Eastern Europe. This child was adopted later and suffered from severe attachment and behavior problems. The whole time she maintained that she did not have to behave for her adopted mother because her "real mother" lived across the sea and loved her very much. This perception did not match the patient's biological mother at all, which suggests she was experiencing an archetypal mother image generated in the context of her very difficult situation.

What all the data suggests, then, is that the mother image acts with the concept of agency, purpose, motivation, and personification, and a "mother" can be sensed and subjectively felt outside the context of a human parent – in other words, like the bear spirit, we can sense that somehow "behind" the activity of the fertile earth, death–rebirth cycles, abundant life, and so on, is a Great Mother; and on a more personal level we can sense a mother figure acting in our lives that is independent of our physical mother, though initially they are usually merged. These mother goddesses have mentality and personality as well, unrelated to personal history, and appear external to the conscious self. The same concerns about "cognitive errors" and "all in your head" apply here as they did to the fylgja concept, and in this case the Great Mother transcends personal experience and even species history.

During development, the human mother interacts with and activates or "resonates" with this innate "ideal" mother in the child, and the resultant complex of feelings toward her mother is dependent upon both components, but what the above evidence seems to show is that the deeper, more innate component can act independently to give the subject the impression of a Great Mother spontaneously that may not always have to do with the actual mother per se. While it is true that this mother symbol is entirely "subjective," the experience of such a mother is likely correlated with the activity of very real and intense emotional circuits in the brain (and in later chapters I will show how symbols can affect mind/body physiology); hence her "utterances" should not be taken lightly, though the particulars of how and when these experiences are or are not present will depend a lot on cultural variation, and the subject's personal attitude toward her.

Chapter 8

The father

What about correlates of father symbols? Here, the neurobiological data we have is less clear than with mothering, which shows infants in development discriminate between "mother" and "non-mother" very quickly. But some data is available. Physiologically and socially, having a strong father bond appears to enhance a child's well-being and success in many areas that appear to be distinct from the benefits gained from a strong mother bond. Fathering provides clear benefits to children in both social and physical effects (otherwise it would not have evolved in humans). In fact, human paternal investment has been shown to contribute to children's well-being and health, as well as lower infant and child mortality risks in foraging societies (Hill and Hurtado, 1996). Fathering improves social competitiveness in industrial societies (Cleveland *et al.*, 2000) and upward social mobility even when maternal characteristics are controlled for (cf. Kaplan *et al.*, 1998) – note the importance of fathering on *non-kin-related social navigation* in these studies.

Conversely, children with absent fathers show higher aggressive and noncompliant behavior, especially in boys, and early onset of sexual activity for both adolescent boys and girls, as well as lowered educational achievement in adulthood (cf. Ellis *et al.*, 2003; Geary, 2005: 490) and poor social attachment patterns (Bakermans-Kranenburg *et al.*, 2004) – another collection of links between fathering and adjustment in the non-kin social milieu. Furthermore, fathers who play with their children have positive effects on child popularity (Carson *et al.*, 1993). Paternal deprivation before age four has a more disruptive effect on a child's development than at a later age (Biller, 1974). Fathering also benefits children through *improved mothering* (cf. Flinn, 1992), which could therefore apply to stepchildren as well.

Father absence, as much as familial discord or lack of closeness, appears to independently predict menarche (Ellis and Garber, 2000), and earlier menarche is associated with absence of positive father relationships (Moffitt *et al.*, 1992), divorce, or father absence. Girls with a warm relationship with their fathers experience menarche later than girls living with emotionally distant or absent fathers (Ellis *et al.*, 1999). The earlier a new, non-father male figure enters a girl's life, the earlier she reaches puberty (Ellis and Garber 2000). This leads Kaplan and Gangestad (2005) to argue for a facultative *adaptation* present in girls that detects a conflict of interest between mothers and others over degree of investment in her. If she can expect (consciously or unconsciously) to receive less investment, a short-ened pre-reproductive period may optimize net reproductive benefits and motivate daughters to seek support from romantic partners, a process that is accelerated when mother–boyfriend conflict is increased (85–86; Ellis and Garber, 2000).

Neurobiological substrates of father symbols

What the above studies show, in broad strokes, is that the perceptual/conceptual system appears to have mechanisms in place that detect or represent a specific type of male figure that has "fathering" connotations – no doubt through very complex mechanisms. Nevertheless, children can apparently detect the presence of the genetic father in the family environ-ment to some degree, and they use this information to coordinate behavior and physical development, a fact that is particularly evident in girls according to research, but likely it is equally if not more important to boys – further research is needed here to confirm this suspicion. The link between children and fathers appears to have effects on *social adjustment* in children of both genders that are independent of maternal factors – this independence is another argument for a "polytheistic" approach to arche-typal symbols, as fathers are not merely male mothers to the developing organism, but are separate differentiations of the parental attachment system. The father image consists of male aspects of the perceptual/conceptual system that contains the above *feelings* (much like the mother symbol) along with it and provides the target domain for father *symbols*.

Mythic explorations of father symbols

The legacy of the father to his son can be found in the universally prevalent myth of the resurrecting son. Examples of the resurrecting sons are provided by Stevens (1998):

> Osirus, Zagreus, Dionysus, Tammuz, Attis, the Dictean Zeus, Orpheus, Mithras, Ba'al, Baldur, Adonis, Wotan/Odin, and Christ . . . their birth is often announced by a star, they are born of a virgin in a cave, they are sometimes visited by wise men, as children they teach their instruc-tors, they commonly predict their own death and second coming, they die on trees, descend into the earth for three days . . . and they are

resurrected. They never attain full maturity, and are always identified with their divine father. The initiatory symbolism of dying gods is very apparent, therefore, and it is usual for initiates to identify with them as they pass through the ritual.

(257)

Note the complex relationship between the dying god and his father, his death and resurrection (which recalls the death–rebirth links given previously). Throughout mythology the father is seen as "manifested in" the imagery of "dominion, solar and sky power, spiritual, moral and civil authority, reason and consciousness, law, the elements of air and fire, warlike spirit and the thunderbolt . . ." (Tresidder, 2005: 178). Note that many of these are visuospatial ways to depict the tremendous emotional impact the father archetypal process has on the developing mind.

Jung felt that "A father's legacy for the daughter is always a *spiritual one*; that is why fathers have such an enormous responsibility for the spiritual life of their daughters" (2008: 395, emphasis added); recall that the father's relationship with his daughter can actually affect her physical development – the presence of a nurturing father can switch the adolescent to a more long-term mating strategy, which involves a later onset of her period and more secure attachments. Perhaps the subjective correlate of this behavior variation is part of what Jung was intuiting when he made his statement about fathers and daughters.

Other connections exist cross-culturally with father gods associated with the sky, heaven, light, lightening bolts, weapons, dominion, and traditions that oppose base instincts (Cirlot, 1971). The sky, for example, is nearly everywhere associated with supreme father gods cross-culturally (Eliade, 1958). The sky has a long history of very close symbolism across cultures; virtually all cultures throughout history have generated similar symbols of sky fathers who possess great wisdom, represent supreme authority and dominance (and also freedom from submission), are responsible for fertilizing the earth through rain and severe weather, and through culture are usually differentiated into many lesser deities more concerned with day-to-day emotional concerns (Eliade, 1958). Throughout mythology, rain often symbolizes a sexual union between the heaven and earth (Jacoby, 1964), and in fact the "creative storm," like the belief among the ancient Norsemen that Thor's lightening fertilized the fields, is a universal symbol (Cirlot, 1971). In any case, the common thread running through these symbols is the overriding sense of order and social harmony, cutting across all aspects of life, involving law, consciousness, day, and divine authority. Given the above studies show the importance of the father in fostering social navigation, regulation of affect, social competitiveness, proper physical development, social dominance and even improved mothering, it becomes apparent what this imagery is intuitively about.

The father spirit

Presently, much like the mother goddess, then, all of us have two fathers – the physical father, whose behavior will be variable, and the Great Father, who is timeless and godlike, and has a separate set of agendas, expectations, demands, and blessings to the mother goddess. Whereas the mother goddess seems to embody strong but vague notions of more intimate kinship and self-relatedness – both to others and to the physical world in general – it seems the father god embodies our relationship to the less kin-related social order and all its complexities. How this symbolic being will behave probably depends a lot on the subject's experience of her own father, but not necessarily *only* upon this experience, since much of it appears to be innate, geared toward specific psychobiological needs and impulses. A person with an angry, abusive father may find a similar father symbol punishing him in a dream or fantasy – but on the other hand he may find refuge in a more benevolent father symbol. Often in therapy one encounters a rigid dichotomy in these cases, with "good father" and "bad father" symbols vying for attention. But the ways father gods manifest are not *infinitely* variable; rather, they correlate with the ancient father-attachment system. If the physical father acts "in accordance" with this *expected* or archetypal father, all will be relatively well, but of course no father is a god, so sooner or later they will separate in a person's mind (especially when a young man becomes a father himself), and this can be a positive maturing progression or a violent schism. In terms of religion, it seems that many have the subjective impression that the "essences" (another innate idea) of the sky, storms, dominion, wisdom, and so on are related to this father god.

The point is that, like with the mother, the human brain understands father imagery, and it comes with a lot of emotional significance; so much, in fact, that it can apparently affect our developmental physiology. The ideas, intuitions, and nameless abstract feelings that get symbolized as the father god are therefore not inconsequential; he is correlated with powerful emotional significance that stretches to the activities of deeper brain layers, and also has a mentality and intent, much like dream characters. To say "this situation/experience *is like* a father" is therefore a serious symbolic statement. Furthermore, he is an animate symbol that is not merely a reflection of the actual father – if this were the case, how could we explain why we even care about the actual father in the first place? The reason we care is because we are programmed to – the brain has a system in place that rapidly acquires a "father figure" or "father image" and invests it with deeply emotional meaning, and it can use this same program to generate father images, symbols, and characters independently of the physical father. These images will be meaningful symbols of otherwise mysterious phenomena in the environment and the unconscious systems that have "father-*like*" attributes.

Two cases are illustrative here. The first is an adoptee, Mr. Grey, who suffered from depression, chronic irritability, and very impulsive, self-destructive behavior for several years, particularly when he discovered a small amount of information about his biological father. Though he knew very little about his biological father, except that he lived in another country and was somehow involved in sports, Mr. Grey fantasized about his father as being a consummate athlete. He mentioned several times that he would often seek out older men to be his "mentor," and share his experiences with them in attempt to deal with his depression and irritability, but he would later flee from these relationships in dissatisfaction. Meanwhile, the image he had of his biological father had acquired a godlike status no mortal father could live up to. Unfortunately, he also fled therapy for similar reasons, and continued to dream of saving up enough money to meet his biological father, who lived in another country. In him there seemed to be a desperate longing to connect with this father image, who had great things in mind for him; and when he spoke and thought about his biological father, he seemed to be experiencing this Great Father, and had a very difficult time managing his emotions toward this mighty figure. This "father god" had manifested to Mr. Grey, and his ambivalent relationship with him – awe and fear – played itself out in other relationships in life. Furthermore, as Mr. Grey did not communicate with either this image or the physical person he had "imbued" with this godlike aura, he was unable to navigate the internal conflict he had with respect to such a father character.

Another case, Mr. Black, was a war veteran suffering from severe Post Traumatic Stress Disorder (PTSD), who had multiple difficulties in his work and social relationships, though interestingly not with his family. During the course of his treatment, a dream character emerged of his grandfather. Mr. Black recalled good memories of his grandfather, who had died many years before Mr. Black began dreaming of him. In his dreams, however, his grandfather appeared to be coaching him through the very challenging symptoms he was experiencing. We were able to identify the importance of this figure and I predicted that he would show up in later dreams to offer his advice and encouragement. Sure enough, he did, as if remembering the previous interactions (or perhaps remembering my positive interaction with him in Mr. Black's waking life), much like McNamara's (2009) studies on dream characters. This interaction, between Mr. Black and the image of his grandfather, became more conscious as a result. The subsequent recognition that his grandfather continued to play an important role in his subjective world, and the rejection of the literalist complaint that he was "just in my head," allowed him a freer and more profound relationship with this figure, which led to continued improvements therapeutically, and, tellingly, in his work and social relationships. In our final session he spontaneously mentioned his grandfather lovingly.

In these two cases we seem to be dealing not so much with the supreme father *god* per se, but rather ancestral "father spirits," in the case of Mr. Black, of a *grand*-father, and in the case of Mr. Grey, of a strongly constellated image of a father who dwells "far away" and has ideal qualities of dominance and physical prowess. These two cases have cultural parallels in typical widespread beliefs that ancestors continue after death to interact with us and assist us in our lives, as well as the recognition that ritual interaction or communication with these subjective "beings" leads to better integration and less internal conflict. Here we can see how images can spontaneously shift in time from the personal/specific toward the archetypal.

Chapter 9

The child

Out of all the intense activity between the males and females, fathers and mothers of the last few chapters emerges the child. As we will see, infant recognition mechanisms of the perceptual/conceptual system arouse strong feelings of attachment, which include approach and protection from harm as well as many other nuances.

For example, mothers can identify their offspring in a set of matched photographs after five hours postnatally, in a crowded nursery by odor following a single exposure six hours postnatally, and by voice two days after birth (Bjorklund and Pellegrini, 2002); this appears to be an inadequate level of stimulation to be possible without innate "nudging." How this is accomplished is still a mystery, and may be related to subtle facial features or other as-yet-unspecified cues, but the fact that it works is not a mystery at all.

Just as in the anima and animus, there appear to be innate recognition aspects of the brain that orient to child-specific stimuli. In fact, parents of attractive infants are more attentive and affectionate toward them (Langlois *et al.*, 1995), two emotion-laden qualities of behavior, whereas physical deformity, lethargy, poor tone, or lack of so-called pedomorphic characteristics may increase risk of abuse (McCabe, 1988). Pedomorphic characteristics, which include relatively large eyes, small noses, and rounded heads are attractive to parents and others in general (Zebrowitz, 1997); furthermore, active infants with higher APGAR (appearance, pulse, grimace, activity, respiration) scores – a measurement of birth health – are less likely to be victims of infanticide (reviewed in Duntley, 2005: 239).

Parenting behavior is inextricably bound to the CARE circuitry of all mammals; these circuits are highly conserved throughout the animal kingdom, which obviously includes humans, and is therefore deeply innate. Mothers do not need to "learn" to want to care for their infants; they do so naturally as long as they have an intact CARE system,[1] which works via brain oxytocin and opiod systems. Fathering behavior is also dependent upon CARE circuitry, which includes a properly functioning arginine-vasopressin (AVP) system (Panksepp, 1998). These systems are universal and innate, though they are not invulnerable to environmental influence. They can be interrupted by severe stress – on the positive side they are affected by nursing, which would have been universal in the ancestral environment: newborns who nurse in the first hour after birth stimulate a surge in maternal oxytocin levels, which have been observed to shift the mother's priority to self-groom for the purposes of attracting new mates to grooming their infants (Insel, 1992). By contrast, non-nursing mothers are more likely to suffer from post-partum depression, commit infanticide, and have thoughts of harming their babies – one wonders what subtle long-term effect mass bottle feeding may have had on civilization.

High stress can interrupt this system; mothers who have experienced early trauma have consistently higher brain concentrations of the stress hormone cortisol and display fewer nurturing behaviors, social attachment, and breastfeeding (Nemeroff, 2008). Conversely, subsequent activation of the mother–infant bond strengthens this system, in that women who have been mothers previously show increased nurturant feelings in subsequent encounters with infants over women without children (Corter and Fleming, 1990).

This is evidence for a system that is somewhat flexible to environmental influence along certain trajectories. According to neuroscience, "All mammals have neuronal operating systems that evolved to help prepare them to take care of infants. . . . We now know a great deal about the nurturance systems of the mammalian brain" (Panksepp, 1998: 248–249). The intrinsic CARE brain circuitries, which utilize oxytocin among other things, "appear to be the key participants in [the] subtle feelings that we humans call acceptance, nurturance, and love – the feelings of social solidarity and warmth" (Panksepp et al., 1997; Panksepp, 1998). This system is more pronounced in mothers than fathers but is present and active in both parents in humans. Note that the CARE system evolved from earlier reptilian circuitry controlling sexuality and egg-laying.

A variety of studies show that sensitive and attentive fathering behavior is correlated with increased cortisol levels, higher prolactin levels and lower testosterone levels in these fathers compared to other men (reviewed in Geary, 2005: 493), reflecting the hormonal differences in mating strategies explored in the previous chapters between the "investing" and "dominant" males. Furthermore, in mammals showing paternal care, such as prairie voles, elevations in the hormone AVP prepares males to be receptive to and care for infants (Bales et al., 2004) – recall that AVP appears to be associated with reduced aggressiveness and increased activity of CARE circuits in human males, and that the neural circuitry of the CARE system that generates male sexuality is present in deep brain regions – it is important to note that there are more estrogen-responsive oxytocin cells in this area in females than males, and this is likely a result of estrogen induction (Jirikowski et al., 1988). Damaging this area eliminates all parenting behavior in laboratory animals (Numan, 1994; Numan and Insel, 2003). All these areas are highly conserved and present in all mammals.

To summarize, then, there appears to be a variety of innate predispositions to recognize children via cues of pedomorphic characteristics, kin relatedness, infant viability (correlated with attractiveness), and nursing behavior, related to intact CARE systems in the paleomammal brain. Like all the other symbols, this means the child is well understood by the brain, and so it will be used to symbolize things less easily grasped, including parts of our own personality or mysteries of life; the child image itself appears linked to many deeply felt but very difficult to quantify emotions.

Mythical aspects of child symbols

In symbolism, Jung argued, the Child represents the "preconscious, childhood aspect of the psyche" (Jung, 1959b: para 273). Here we see the SELF IS A CHILD mapping in action. Jung continues to theorize that the child symbolizes an exposure to adversity, as in the perilous birth accounts of heroes appearing cross-culturally (Campbell, 1949). The mythic child, however, despite being continually exposed to danger and destruction, contains a tremendous divine latent power within. Jung (1959b) observes that the child

> is a personification of vital forces quite outside the limited range of our conscious mind. . . . The urge and compulsion to self-realization is a law of nature and thus of invincible power.
>
> (para 289)

> This essential "divine child" quality is frequently symbolized as a flower, an egg, or the center of a mandala, a dream image of a son or daughter, a king's son or witch's child, a chalice, golden ball or jewel. It represents the seeds of future possibilities and wholeness.
>
> (para 270)

Here we can see Jung struggling with this image so much that he is using other symbols to explain this one – not unusual when dealing with emotionally powerful symbols, and a frequent occurrence in Jung's writings. The child is also repeatedly used to depict purity, innocence, potential, and also "mystic knowledge" (Tresidder, 2005). Cirlot (1971) observes that the child frequently appears to embody the future in general. Jung (1954) postulated that the brain symbolized the child as a positive figure representing the synthesis of conscious and unconscious aspects of the mind – what he called the "transcendant function." This is the kind of thing that can be verified only by detailed case study – and shows the art of understanding symbol meaning.

Child symbols

The child image is another animate symbol. It can be a baby or child; the important aspects are the so-called "pedomorphic" characteristics, which have strongly instinctual "cuteness" connotations that inspire caretaking and/or vulnerability, which are likely in place due to their obvious adaptive value in *Homo sapiens*. In considering these symbols, one should note that kin-relatedness and infant viability, both innate aspects of the system, may be included as part of the nuances of this imagery.

One fascinating clinical example was reported to me by a woman who had been pregnant, but then lost her baby, which caused her tremendous bitterness. Following the baby's death she was plagued with nightmares of being pregnant with "nothing," hearing babies screaming, and seeing severed limbs. At other times she dreamt of baby animals she was supposed to be taking care of drowning in fish tanks. After discussing the possibility of trying to connect symbolically with this child somehow, and treating it like a personality with a mentality and a "spiritual" existence, she decided to get a tattoo of a small bird with a flower and an egg in an inconspicuous place, and reported this as being highly symbolic of her lost baby. We explored the Celtic and Germanic symbolism of the raven as messenger from the Otherworld, such as the two ravens of the liminal god Odin,[2] the egg as a typically encountered symbol representing renewal and rebirth (such as found in Easter games, and reflecting much older pagan renewal rituals), and the flower as a symbol of conscious reflection and solar imagery (discussed in later chapters) to bring this symbolism into greater conscious awareness. Interestingly, she stopped having nightmares about the lost baby, and more peaceful dreams about the child came afterward.

Unlike the mother and father symbols, which represent our origins and the expectations placed upon us from the beginning, the child symbol is a future symbol; one which calls part or all of ourselves to make a generative act (the anima/animus and other unknown spirit beings are perhaps intermediate symbols). The child is full of promise and potential – godlike – and yet is more *us* than the father, mother, anima, or animus. In other words, the mother and father expect us to *be* something, whereas the child is perhaps our urge to *do* something. Maybe this is (as Jung suggested) like nest building in birds. Birds probably don't know why they're doing it, but something in them tells them to nonetheless; if the child symbol emerges in our minds, it is possible that the urge toward a creative act is being symbolized as well, though since our brains are much more complex than those of birds, it could be a great variety of things being symbolized. Regardless of what the components of this symbol are neurobiologically, the subjective sense that it is an agent, with purpose and intention, appears to correlate with major shifts in unconscious system functioning.

Another example comes from my own dreams – long before this book was finished, I had recurrent dreams of taking care of a small child. This child was often in danger and I was charged with protecting it. Interestingly, the child was not my own, but rather I had been tasked to take care of her (it was usually a little girl). She was usually the daughter of someone very important like the president or a foreign power of some kind. Thus she had an air of divinity and power to her, but there were times when she had been abused or was in peril. This dream continued for over a year, until I finished the first draft. Thereafter this "elf-child," for lack of a better word, disappeared. Thus, perhaps, one might see the childlike spirit behind the great deal of work that went into this book; like most symbols she defies an easy explanation or reduction, and is best left on her own terms.

Mr. Literal: "But I don't see a baby anywhere and I don't understand what you mean. Therefore it doesn't exist."

Me: "I thought I shot you."

Chapter 10

The shadow

Nothing great happens without anger.

Thomas Aquinas

Often the first thing encountered in therapy is a person's anger; this is because it so often has no way of being expressed overtly due to social pressures. Instead it comes out in many other ways, including symptoms; in dreams one finds violent beings, and in mythic expression one finds demons, giants, ogres, trolls, and horrendous beasts. But aggression is simply what it is – RAGE behavior is a part of all vertebrate species and is a part of the environmentally "closed" reptile brain functioning. So rather than repress it, dismiss it, explain it away, or otherwise pretend we can make it disappear, we should face our inner demons which are often one of the first beings encountered in therapy. But what triggers RAGE behavior in humans and other animals? Why did it evolve and what purpose does it serve?

Reputation and social status account for the way in which we navigate the social environment; evolution made this a powerful motivator for behavior because in the ancestral environment, loss of social status would have had devastating effects on survival and reproduction (Buss, 2004). In fact, the most frequent triggers for homicidal fantasies are threats to a person's social status (Buss and Duntley, 2003) – likely a reaction to the survival implications for social loss; this particular result is highly relevant for understanding such subjective imagery. When the "resource" threatened is a mate rather than commodities, men and women engage in tactics ranging from vigilance to violence. Men (and other male animals), in particular, are more likely to conceal their partners, display resources or threaten violence against rivals. When the threat comes from the female herself, males are more likely to display submission and self-abasement, including groveling and promising to partners to convince them to stay, whereas women will enhance their appearance and induce jealousy in their partners to demonstrate their other mating prospects (Buss and Shackelford, 1997). Such, apparently, is the power of the woman.

Survival tendencies therefore have required that humans have an innate capacity for violence and aggression in order to protect or garner resources; the immediate cause of this behavior is likely the RAGE circuitry shared by all vertebrates and is correlated subjectively with feelings of intense anger. The tendency for competition in humans due to the harsh necessities of natural selection has a number of neurobiological consequences. Neuroscience has shown that frustration of goal-directed behavior triggers the RAGE system, which leads to higher levels of aggression as well as darker prejudices toward minorities in children (Dodge, 1986). Males are highly sensitive to slights in reputation because of the ancient equation of social dominance and reproductive success – natural selection has therefore constructed males that are generally more aggressive than females and more concerned about social status due to its direct relation to reproductive success and the necessity to compete for females due to females' increased investment in offspring, though humans display a wide variation in these subtle differences. For example, boys are more assertive than girls by 13 months of age (Goldberg and Lewis, 1969) and spend 65 percent of their time in competitive games versus 35 percent in girls (Lever, 1978). Boys engage in more rough-and-tumble play (DiPietro, 1981), a fact reproduced cross-culturally (Whiting and Edwards, 1988). Rough play appears to establish social dominance, which boys rate as more important than girls do (Jarvinen and Nicholls, 1996). Dominance appears by age six and actually predicts later dominance nine years later (Weisfeld, 1999). Culture of course influences these basic behaviors to a high degree, but culture does not appear to *define* them.

Females compete as well. As stated by evolutionary psychologists:

> Ecologically or socially imposed monogamy tends to equalize the fitness distribution of the sexes and creates two-way selection. We, therefore, expect that women would compete with one another in the currency of attributes that are valued by men.
>
> (Campbell, 2005: 635)

Overall, while men compete by exaggerating their superiority, promiscuity, and popularity, women compete by altering appearance artificially to exaggerate youthfulness and fertility (cf. Buss 1988). Furthermore, since paternal uncertainty is a fact of mating due to our biological heritage, men are more cross-culturally concerned about fidelity in long-term sexual partners, which probably leads to the infamous sexual double standard (cf. Brown, 1998), which women are actually more likely to enforce than men (Baumeister and Twenge, 2002). Cross-cultural studies show that women primarily compete by disparaging rivals' appearance and sexual reputation (Campbell, 1986; Joe-Laidler and Hunt, 2001), all by way of rumor spreading, gossiping, ostracism, and stigmatization, beginning by age six, and typically increasing more in girls than boys, who compete more overtly (Campbell, 2005).

The aggressive instincts that have their roots in resource competitiveness can obviously extend to full-blown violence. In fact, humans appear to have evolved *facultative adaptations* to murder and vengeance (Buss and Duntley, 2003) in order to preserve resources and ensure reproductive success and inclusive fitness (in the form of lost or gained resources, mates, or social status/reputation) in certain high-stakes situations, which are continuous with those found in other animal species (Ghiglieri, 1999). In other words, destruction lurks in everyone because it can result in improved inclusive fitness when properly triggered; no amount of enculturation will be able to eliminate this because it is a part of our neurobiology. In response, defenses against homicide (i.e. counter-adaptations) also exist. Specifically, selection has favored homicide defense adaptations that lead to the avoidance of unfamiliar surroundings – especially territory controlled by rivals, locations where ambush is likely, traveling by night, or avoiding enraging others of the same species (Duntley, 2005: 236).

Part of this counter-adaptation is aimed toward detection of threats. The perceptual system, for example, appears to be hardwired to detect threatening facial features; threatening faces are more quickly found than happy faces among neutral distractors (Öhman *et al.*, 2001b). Evidence suggests that humans need very little experience to identify kin and appear to have evolutionary adaptations for kin or self-recognition (reviewed in Burnstein, 2005); facial resemblance in the form of morphed photographs, for example, has been shown to increase trust in others (DeBruine, 2002).

Furthermore, people tend to automatically categorize others as within their "group" or "outside" the group; for example, when people are placed randomly into groups they immediately tend to feel more negatively about the other group, even when religious affiliation, sexual identity, and cultural variables are factored out (Tajfel *et al.*, 1971). The male is seen as the prototypical outgroup member (Zárate and Smith, 1990), perhaps reflecting the male predominance in social group dynamics and the ancestral likelihood of encountering a male before a female, who is more likely to have a more limited range and be sequestered further in the group's territory in ancestral environments. This propensity to view outgroup members as male is also directly observed in dream research (Van de Castle, 1994), and should not be surprising considering the fact that males are more likely to be physically aggressive.

Thus there is evidence that humans have a multitude of adaptations designed to classify some humans as suspicious enemies while classifying others as "kin" or members of the "inside" group, and to mobilize powerfully aggressive urges toward those that threaten one's resources or mates. There are mechanisms within the perceptual/conceptual system designed to detect aggressive enemies and avoid danger and physical harm. Aggressive self-defense involves more than physical attack; it also involves denigration of reputation and social subterfuge (particularly for females), all of which help to preserve the organism's resources, which include not only commodities but social rank and mating prospects.

Neurobiological substrates for shadow symbols

The RAGE and FEAR systems evolved in vertebrates to protect organisms from the threat of danger, in part from other members of the same species. One mapping we have already considered is the angry, defensive predator symbols from Chapter 4, such as Ms. Green's "bear spirit." Many other variations of this are possible. Some symbols appear as shadowy people, that is, human-shaped figures enshrouded in darkness. This "shadowy" aspect derives from a different mapping involving light and darkness (this imagery will be discussed in later chapters). For the moment, note that since humans are diurnal creatures adapted to daylight activities, we are more vulnerable at night. This was particularly true of the ancestral environment, and as such we have a variety of adaptations that orient FEAR and other emotional systems toward the avoidance of darkness. Animal or human symbols that have this aspect or "coloring," then, will therefore include this ancient spontaneous link in meaning between darkness and safety; in other words, the two aspects will combine into a polysemic metaphor. Thus angry faces, and shadowy, animistic, or threatening features are all quickly and easily recognized by the brain and labeled with high degrees of RAGE and FEAR significance.

The human recognition mechanism in the perceptual/conceptual system has a heightened sensitivity to faces in general, and to *angry faces* in particular (discussed previously). Like snakes, these are recognized quickly and will be readily used to express things symbolically. Such RAGE activity *in the context of* threatened resources or bodily threat in the environment will be "translated" into either physical or verbal attack in symbolic terms. Another important aspect to remember is that these undifferentiated urges are directed toward the preservation of the subject – they are not simply "infantile urges" or "narcissistic fantasies." They are primitive drives that mobilize the organism toward the preservation of self and future reproductive success. These urges can vie for conscious attention and direction, which can be observed in violent conflicts occurring in dreams or reverie material. Also consider that humans have instincts directed at resource *acquisition* as well as resource defending. Resource acquisition, however, involves the SEEKING or LUST systems. If the subject colors this image with darkness, thus making it a "shadow" character, it likely reflects the archetypal connotations of darkness with fear, the unknown (un*seen*), and harm avoidance. The composite image is therefore a "positive and negative" figure, in that it aims at resource acquisition and other SEEKING affects such as satisfaction and fulfillment, colored with fearful nuance. Animals can be used for these urges just as much as humans, and, in my experience, when people dream of aggressive animals, it is because their aggressiveness is less conscious. As they become in touch with it, or such forces become more dominant in consciousness, they tend to dream of aggressive humans. My colleagues and I observed this pattern in a study of the dreams reported by combat veterans while still in theater overseas (Wyatt et al., 2011).

Mythic explorations of shadow symbols

Indigenous myths, as well as folklore and legend, often equate the shadow with the "alter ego" of an individual (Cirlot, 1971). Jung described the shadow as the "dark side" of the personality, which means anything that has been repressed. It can include basic instincts, and so shares similarity with the Freudian "id," but it can also contain positive, creative impulses that for whatever reason the ego has repressed. Furthermore, it has an "archetypal core" of pure destructiveness, recalling the evolutionary adaptations for murder (Buss and Duntley, 2003). For Jung, the shadow represented

> a moral problem that challenges the whole ego-personality, for no one can become conscious of the shadow without considerable moral effort. To become conscious of it involves recognizing the dark aspects of the personality as present and real. . . . Closer examination of the dark characteristics . . . reveals that they have an *emotional* nature. . . . With a little self-criticism one can see through the shadow – so far as its nature is personal. . . . In other words, it is quite within the bounds of possibility for a man to recognize the relative evil of his nature, but it is a rare and shattering experience for him to gaze into the face of absolute evil.
>
> (Jung, 1959a: 8–10)

Also relevant are frequently appearing "wild man" symbols – savages that appear in folk tales throughout the world, which include ogres, giants, and so on (Cirlot, 1971).

A ubiquitous "shadow" character, in the Jungian sense, that exists in all mythology is the "trickster," who manifests as various instinctive gods or animals that delight in creating havoc and acting impulsively; he is often also a cultural hero. Characters such as Loki (Norse myth), Coyote or Raven (American Indian myth), Satan (Biblical myth), Eshu (West African myth), Prometheus (Greek myth), Lucifer (Medieval Christian myth; literally, "light bringer"), Huehuecoyotl (Aztec myth), Puck (Celtic myth), the Monkey King (Chinese myth), Seth (Egyptian myth), Kitsune (Japanese myth), Maui (Polynesian myth), and many others (Henderson, 1964) are all "trickster" characters that solve (and create) various problems through guile, dumb luck, or impulsive and unorthodox actions; interestingly, most are male (Tresidder, 2005: 486). Jung equated these trickster characters with repetitive manifestations of shadow symbols in their various negative and positive aspects (Jung, 1959b). In other words, they represent cultural variations on the basic theme that repressed or unwanted feelings find a way to manifest themselves despite such defenses. The trickster is the shadow person who eschews cultural norms and concerns about social niceties and acts on pure whimsy, vindictiveness, or impulsiveness, sometimes with disastrous results as shown in Norse mythology, for example, where Loki's machinations are prophesied to bring about Ragnarök. Another, less malicious, character identified by von Franz (1964a) is the "old friend," which she equates with a symbol of a forgotten self. In this case the character and behavior of the "old friend" should provide further detail as to the symbolic meaning of this image – the "forgotten" nature of these images is symbolized by their "dark" or "unknown" qualities.

Understanding the shadow symbol is often the first aspect of any therapy – this is because it is a mostly personal symbol, consisting primarily of any aspects of the personality that are rejected or repressed by the conscious self during development – thus these figures are more related to personal history than god figures are. The reason these aspects do not simply disappear during development when we are taught to "just say no" to them is that the more distasteful urges, such as competitiveness, aggression, unfettered sexuality, and hatred are innately hardwired in our RAGE and SEEKING circuitry. In certain brain states, then, in the context of increased activity of these systems, we encounter symbols of people or animals that express these aspects of experience – the following dream provides an example. Here Mr. Brown, who was a very anxious and depressed middle-aged man who overextended himself to please others, dreamed:

> I was clinging to a pole in the ocean. Another man was clinging to another pole next to me, he was a movie star, strong and confident. Below the two of them circled a shark. He told me I was going to have to deal with the shark, but I refused and clung tightly to the pole.

This dream came before treatment began. Here we can surmise that the shark, being a dangerous, unpredictable and aggressive animal, may be correlated with RAGE systems – but this would oversimplify the nuance of the symbol as it appears. When considering this image consciously, the patient said he did not feel it wanted to harm him, but was simply swimming. Furthermore he felt that sharks were "often misunderstood." His conscious (repressive) attitude toward anger or aggression, embodied quite well by a shark, can be seen in his refusal to "deal with" the shark, and in so doing he is left "high and dry" (dreams often play on words like this).

The dreamer associated the movie star with someone who was "cool and collected" and a "man of action" – perhaps this symbol reflects SEEKING brain activity, which was also repressed, judging by his refusal of the man's suggestion. Movie stars, in modern settings, take the place previously occupied by culture heroes such as Beowulf or King Arthur – and in fact the *characters* movie stars portray are usually much more relevant to the dream in this case. This is because movies occupy the same position previously occupied by the storyteller or cultural gathering in which legends and folk tales were told and/or performed, and it is the "spirit" of these characters that is influencing the dreamer in these cases. At other times, movie stars embody cultural/societal values. In any event, the intuitions regarding this dream were verified by further clinical material.

The evolutionary adaptations we have inherited, including those that can potentially incite homicidal behavior, emerge from ancient reptile-brain structures that are universal in all vertebrates – humans are naturally no exception. They exist not to create strife and mayhem, but rather to preserve the organism's inclusive fitness. Nature is morally neutral here; the only thing that preserves a behavior is its reproductive success. Humans, however, have adaptations in place that aim toward maintenance of reputation, trustworthiness, and harmonious social rank placement. But these adaptations evolved much later than the more ancient methods of violent agonistic competition for resources (Stevens and Price, 2000). The guilt that these later adaptations produce is therefore sometimes at odds with the vengeful destruction of the RAGE circuits. So it seems the human mind is born into conflict. This observation is further supported by McNamara (2009), who reviews the way our very genes can compete with each other to produce intrapsychic conflict.

Refusal to accept the darker aspects of the personality, then, is doomed to failure; the best one can hope for is to accept and be conscious of them, not to let them dominate behavior but to try to use them in a more controlled and socially appropriate manner; Freud called this "sublimation." When it comes to religious and mythic thinking, it is immediately obvious that such primordial affects and images are only partly dependent upon personal history and identity; such wrathful quasi-autonomous "spirits," pictured variously as demons, giants, monsters, animals, and whatnot can invade our consciousness in a variety of settings, either as humans and animals in dreams and reverie, or as moods and personality shifts during waking states, because these symbols do not depend on unconscious systems walled off from the world; rather they act *in concert* with the environment, and sometimes produce extremely powerful psychological effects on the conscious self, which are very hard to distinguish from ancient, widespread descriptions of malicious spirit possession (McNamara, 2009).

Chapter 11

The dreamscape

In the last few chapters we have discussed the way the mind perceives animate symbols – images with mentality, purpose, and even memory. Evolutionary psychology and various neurosciences explain why our brains are well suited to formulate experience in terms of animals and beings moving about. But these are not the only "spirit" perceptions. Humans did not evolve in a vacuum; we evolved in a specific environment – most likely the African savannah. Furthermore, our evolutionary history built upon highly visual arboreal primates that predate *Homo sapiens*. Just as there are innate attentional biases and cues in our perceptual/conceptual system regarding animals and humans, there appear to be similar mechanisms that are used when processing environmental data. Aside from the division between animate and inanimate objects, which is an innate classification, we further differentiate environmental information to a degree that seems to be quite detailed. This system aids survival by biasing certain environments as more "attractive" – note again how imagery is innately tied with meaning – in the same way it orients certain physical features (like symmetry) as more attractive than others.

For example, humans innately find savannahs and savannah-like landscapes beautiful, starting in childhood, but we also reliably acquire a desire for a landscape that is familiar, easy to explore and easy to remember (Pinker, 1997: 376). In fact, evolutionary psychologists have determined that there are likely domain-specific algorithms for landscape preference based on our hunter-gatherer ancestry as well as strong attentional biases toward weather changes for similar reasons – they were both intimately related to survival and inclusive fitness for the organism *Homo sapiens* (reviewed in Stevens, 1998: 100–102).

Studies on landscape preference in humans has shown consistent results that humans not only prefer natural environments to man-made ones (Kaplan, 1992) but also that savannah-like landscapes are preferred among natural environments, particularly in children under age nine (Balling and Falk, 1982). Other qualities of landscapes that attract our innate systems for attention and desire have been worked out by evolutionary esthetics research (Orians and Heerwagen, 1992). These qualities include semi-open space that is neither completely exposed nor overgrown, even ground cover, views of the horizon, large trees, water, changes in elevation and multiple paths leading out (all of which mimic the savannah). Kaplan (1992) defines "mystery" as another key to landscapes that has this effect on the human perceptual/conceptual system: paths bending around hills, wandering streams, gaps in vegetation, all pointing to hints that the environment needs further exploration. Houses are primarily valued for their refuge qualities, such as small cozy spaces, and "mystery" such as multiple levels, bends, windows, and so on (Orians and Heerwagen, 1992; Kaplan, 1992; Cosmides *et al.*, 1992). These biases likely evolved to orient the system toward finding refuges that were well defended and secret so as to protect against predators and rival tribes in the Pleistocene epoch, since they represent the environment *Homo sapiens* evolved in.

Mealy and Theis (1995) found that the relative attractiveness of a landscape varies with mood – when mood is positive, landscapes that showed greater "prospect," meaning prospects for exploration, were preferred, whereas negative moods were associated with landscapes that offered comfort or "refuge." Subjects reporting positive moods preferred vast expanses and overviews, whereas subjects reporting dysphoria preferred enclosed, protected spaces.

Finally, natural events such as sunsets, storms, clouds, darkness, and fire, all long recognized universal symbols that shape dream imagery and mythic storytelling, have been shown to evoke emotions that arrest the senses in preparation for what is to come (Cosmides *et al.*, 1992), and have obvious survival advantages for hominids navigating the ancestral environment. Whether or not there are "storm recognition" acquisition systems remains an open question,[1] since the size of storms, accompanied by the loudness of thunder and the impressive visual effects of rain and lightning may account for their evocative character. In other words, more basic algorithms that orient to size, noise, and changes in light may combine to create the subjective orienting effect of a storm (another case of complexity within complexity). Storms orient most animals to find refuge, and, without good reason to suspect humans to be different in this urge (though recognizing that humans have the ability to ignore it), would recurrently find a further connection linking storms with ominous portents and the need to gain shelter, as well as being "outward manifestations" of the many thunder gods of the world.

Environmental symbols

Here again we have evidence of image evoking mood, and the reverse of this process probably occurs in spontaneous imagery, where mood evokes image, such as was found in mental imagery studies. Symbols that emerge using environmental imagery are likely to be mapping "prospect," "refuge," or "exploration" as a part of their metaphorical meaning. It appears from the above landscape preference data that humans have an innate set of cueing mechanisms that can generate "savannah-like" imagery, which would provide the target domain for a variety of MENTAL STATE IS A LOCATION mappings, which are found cross-culturally (Lakoff and Johnson, 1999; see also Chapter 2). Since the savannah is viewed as esthetically pleasing, is the ancestral environment, and appears to be related to mood changes, possibilities include links between instincts, sadness, or seeking with savannahs, refuge, or prospect imagery. Jung equated dream environments that were more natural as representing a more "primitive" state (2008), a hypothesis that finds interesting parallels in the above research.

SELF IS A HOUSE: human shelter-making is an absolute universal, as is the designation of a "homeland," even when individuals hardly ever visit such a place (Brown, 1991); consequently, there may be psychological cues or attentional biases that orient toward both "home" and shelter imagery; these studies have not been done to date. Alternately, the already present tool-use aspects of the brain, which detect "artificialness" (Boyer and Barrett, 2005), combined with the above "refuge" seeking system that orients with mood, may cue to any enclosed area and the use of tools to construct them. In any case, houses and other areas of refuge can provide the target domain for various MENTAL STATE IS A LOCATION symbols, wherein moods/ mental states will be closely linked to the type of imagery mentioned (explored in more detail in Goodwyn, 2010b).

All of these are further examples of the brain using basic metaphorical thinking methods, which describes mental states (difficult to conceptualize) in terms of locations (easy to conceptualize). Since humans are territorial mammals, territory that is designated as "home" will be subject to a number of perceptual/conceptual biases. For example, evolutionary psychologists believe humans are adapted to elevated FEAR activity when in hostile or "external" territory, possibly as an adaptation to avoid murder (Duntley, 2005). Thus dream and fantasy symbols using houses are likely to include associations with more introverted "homeland" mental states, and represent the relationship between the subject and their designated "homeland" – though this is likely to be a symbolic homeland, or perhaps the subject himself. The differentiation is also found in esthetics research into refuge and prospect, which correspond to the PANIC or FEAR systems (refuge) or SEEKING (prospect). Imagery involving the subject searching and exploring reflects SEEKING activity, wherein the subject is "finding new things" in the location or "discovering secrets" – therapy patients often report dreams in which they are in a house exploring secret doors they never knew were there; often this corresponds with the intense self-exploration that goes on in therapy. Contrast this with the many strikingly similar reports of "shamans" or folk healers worldwide (Eliade, 1964;

Haule, 2010) who travel to distant worlds and encounter gods and ancestral spirits in their trance reports. In the latter case, the journey is noticeably *away* from home; this I would argue is because these trance-journeys are not concerned with self-exploration the way psychotherapy is, but with journeying into subjective realms (i.e. mental states) that are more archetypal and independent of personal history. Psychotherapy typically involves understanding your own "house" before you start wandering into realms "beyond."

Another frequently encountered dream report involves fleeing or attempting to find a safe haven from enemies (or whatever), or trying to protect the location from "outsiders" or other visuospatial threats – these threats are themselves likely to be still more symbolic characters, animals, or situations. Thus the environment appears to be mentally subdivided into basic "homeland" versus "outside" divisions. This is reflected in the worldwide symbolism that divides the local "home" environment from the "outside" environment that consists of demons, "chaos," death, giants, foreigners, the dead, and so on (Eliade, 1952).

Recall from Chapter 2 the fact that even humans born blind are able to understand three-dimensional landscapes with point of view, obstruction, and objects moving throughout; thus the ability to generate never visualized environments is an innate ability, as is dreaming about such environments.

Tree symbols

Humans evolved from arboreal primates with binocular color vision; navigating arboreal environments meant the difference between life and death, so one would expect aspects of the brain to orient at least somewhat to trees as a result of this heritage. Evidence for this recognition system is limited but significant. In indigenous cultures, trees often provide shelter or gathering places, as well as survival uses. Subjects in the United States, Argentina, and Australia rated the attractiveness of acacia trees that varied in trunk height, branching pattern, density, and shape. Trees rated as most attractive were, not surprisingly, from savannas and considered high quality in adaptive value for humans, such as having moderately dense canopies and trunks that bifurcated near the ground – contributing to ease of climbing and concealment (Orians and Heerwagen, 1992). This provides evidence for a tree-recognition mechanism within the perceptual/conceptual system that tends to organize experience using tree symbols and possibly tags them with some kind of difficult to describe affective significance. Concealment is one of the aspects of "refuge" described above, in that dysphoric moods unconsciously produce a bias toward concealing, containing environments.

The so-called "cosmic tree" has multiple manifestations throughout the world, such as the cosmic trees of Vedic India, ancient China, and Norse myth, with its magnificent Yggdrasil, as well as central and north Asiatic shamanism, which speaks of the cosmic tree traversed by shamans; this symbolism is paralleled in the shamanism of Indonesia, the Arctic, and South and North America (Eliade, 1964: 49). The symbolism of the cosmic tree is actually "almost universal" (Tresidder, 2005: 485), and usually comes complete with a spiraling snake at its base, fertilizing waters gushing from its roots, and spiritual birds nesting in its branches, which stretch into heaven. Thus it appears that such symbolism recurs so easily due to some kind of innate tree-orienting system in the brain. I have explored this symbolism extensively elsewhere in light of Norse mythology (Goodwyn, 2010b).

The tree is often used to represent life, death, eternal life, and "absolute reality" throughout many cultures (Cirlot, 1971). Christ, for example, was depicted in medieval art and poetry, such as in the Old English poem *The Dream of the Rood*, as being crucified on a tree rather than a cross (Tresidder, 2005), which combined the "tree of knowledge" with the "tree of life" symbolism. The mysterious Germanic God Odin also hung upon the world tree in order to obtain deep mysteries and magical knowledge, and this tree stretches throughout all worlds and binds humanity-cosmos-time-gods and many other subjects (Goodwyn, 2010b). This "tree imagery," then, is therefore an essentially "mystical" (which to me means highly symbolic or ineffable) way of formulating life experience that has a potent subjective "truth" that complements the neuroscientific truth.

Even modern evolutionary biology has a "tree of life"; note that many ancient presages of this idea exist in the numerous symbolic works that depict the "cosmic tree" with animals in accordance to the ubiquitous GREAT CHAIN OF BEING metaphor (Lakoff and Johnson, 1980), with dragons and snakes at the roots, lions, stags, or unicorns at the surface, and birds in the foliage. This is essentially a GREAT CHAIN OF BEING IS A TREE mapping. Finally, trees are known to grow according to the laws of chaos theory; treelike patterns can be found in nature in such varied instances as crystal growth and blood vessel patterns (Prigogine and Stengers, 1988; van Eenwyk, 1997), thus many patterns in life are likely to be symbolized as trees by hominids with arboreal ancestors, simply because of their structural similarity. This is a good example of a mathematical principle governing an archetypal image, as noticed before by Jungians such as Saunders and Skar (2001).

Other plants

Given that plants beside acacia trees would have been present in the ancestral environment, it is possible that cues that orient toward other plants, such as flowers – which signify fertile land with abundant nutrients and possible prey locations – might have found their way into the perceptual/conceptual system as well. Unfortunately, there is no empirical data at present to support or refute this notion, though there is extensive evidence that humans of all cultures have used plants medicinally and in highly symbolic ways (Moerman, 2002; Pollington, 2008; Storms, 1948). Symbologists have also noted that plants often find their way into many symbols.

The lotus, for example, which is a symmetrical flower, is usually symbolic of the sun, and frequently represents a "mystic union" of various opposites such as sun and moon, male and female, spirit and matter, day and night, death and rebirth, eternal regeneration and immortality, and order emerging from primal chaos (Stevens, 1998: 249); it thus shares many of the tree symbolisms explored previously, and since it is symmetrical it acquires this meaning as well (symmetrical symbolism is explored later). Thus the lotus is actually a highly complex symbol containing many parts that all flow together into a meaningful whole; the plant, symmetry, fundamental divisions, and vertical levels all go together into this (beautiful) symbol – the perception of which, when taken seriously as a subjective "truth," can lead to a certain level of ineffable wisdom and meaning, though this level of conscious reflection is probably rare, particularly in noisy modern environments.

Fruits would have been very important in the ancestral environment since we are omnivores. Interestingly, fruit symbolism is frequently associated with enticement and fertility, and is often equated with the body: "apple cheeks, cherry lips, breasts like peaches, buttocks like melons, teeth like pomegranate seeds, etc." (Stevens, 1998: 383); fruit symbols appear to be used to visualize or embody the strong feelings of temptation and lust.

When Jung (2008: 218) outlined his understanding of landscape symbolism, he observed that plant symbols often meant healing, and recounted numerous parallel myths of magic healing herbs in Babylonian myth, astrological symbolism, Greek mythology, alchemy, and indigenous myth, linking them to various alchemical and biblical symbolism of water and finally of "enlightenment." Others note that plants are frequently found as symbols of death and rebirth (Cirlot, 1971).

Indigenous cultures everywhere use plants as medicines and in religious ceremonies – what might be the neurobiological origin of this behavior? At this point it is difficult to say, but the usual explanation invokes "trial and error" with cultural transmission; that is, somebody somewhere "discovered" that eating such-and-such a plant made someone feel better, and this passed down from generation to generation. I would hope at this point that one might be skeptical that this is the *only* mechanism for explaining this behavior – in any case "cultural transmission" is increasingly viewed as less likely the sole method of learning among cognitive anthropologists (Whitehouse and Laidlaw, 2007; cf. also Goodwyn, 2010b). After all, why would humans play around with plants like this in the first place without some kind of instinctive motivation? It seems likely that in addition to the mechanisms of transmission and trial and error, there exist cues and biases in the perceptual/conceptual system that looks for and uses particular plants (or classes of plants), motivated most likely by vague impulses. These impulses would drive the curious behavior aimed specifically at plant experimentation, possibly with some idea that plants can be useful for healing, "rejuvenation," "purification," or some other hazily defined innate concept.

In fact this seems to be the case; for example, historians (Pollington, 2008; Storms, 1948) note that plants used in magical healing rituals among ninth-century Anglo-Saxons were usually chosen for their appearance or behavior, that is, their symbolic qualities. Moreover, the fact that humans everywhere use plants for decoration is interesting in itself – indeed why are flowers beautiful? Without some kind of innate preference in place for some biological reason, it is very difficult to fully explain this behavior.

Vertical symbols

The infant research on gravity is evidence of an innate understanding of vertical orientation and gravity; infants understand gravity by six months (which, by the way, is about the time they acquire greater freedom of movement – good timing that is probably not a "coincidence"). It is likely that primates like *Homo sapiens* with arboreal ancestors have innate orienting predispositions for dealing with vertical dimensions and learning about verticality. Verticality, then, is prime material for symbol making.

Furthermore, an innate predisposition to explore landscapes, such as scaling peaks for the sheer pleasure of the view, is likely to have been adaptive (Appleton, 1990), and one that may be driven by the SEEKING affective system. The predisposition to find high vantage points "beneficial" or "desirable" – which again links image with affect – would provide a clear survival advantage to a species with excellent binocular day vision, particularly one capable of advanced complex planning. This would provide an innately guided MORE KNOWLEDGE IS UP mapping, and is reflected in numerous religious symbols of verticality. Note also that higher ground provides an advantage in tribal warfare, which was prevalent throughout all of our ancestral history (and plagues us to this day), which may have provided a further basis for equating "higher" positions with positive motivations.

The symbol of the tree, ladder, or staircase, which represents "ascension" is also found worldwide:

> *It gives plastic expression to the break through the planes necessitated by the passage from one mode of being to another* . . . [and is placed] in a "center" . . . it makes communication possible between the different levels of being, and, finally, because it is a concrete formula for the

mythical ladder, for the creeper or the spider-web, the Cosmic Tree or the Pillar of the Universe, that connects the three cosmic zones.

(Eliade, 1952: 50–51, emphasis in original)

The symbol of the "Three Levels" (the spiritual world of the gods, the material world, and the underworld of the dead) spans all world cultures throughout history (Eliade, 1952: 40–50). These three levels are nearly always transected vertically by a "center" axis; the myth of the "center" is ubiquitous throughout world religion and myth, for example the giant rock of Batu-Ribne of the Samng pygmies, the Dur-an-ki or "link between Heaven and Earth" of Nippur, Larsa, and Sippara, the Rock of Jerusalem (Hebrew myth), the gate of Apsu (Babylonian myth), the *mundus* of the Romans, Mount Neru (Indian myth), Heraberazaiti (Iranian myth), the mountain Himingbjörg or great tree Yggdrasil (Norse myth), Mount Tabor (Palestinian myth), Golgotha (Christian myth). These symbols, which transect the heavens, earth, and the underworlds (and all their parallels), often consisting of a great mountain, rock, or tree, also comprise the "center of the world" and are linked to the anthropomorphic symbolism of the world as a person, wherein this symbol is the person's "navel." Thus mythic understanding of vertical symbols appears to show a ubiquitous tendency to regard "spiritual" matters, which I equate with an emotionally charged symbolic subjective experience. The three levels (which also borrow number symbolism, which I explore in the next chapter) are also "transected" by a method of ascension symbolized by an ancestrally valid and strongly personal mode of travel (climbing either a rock, a tree, or a mountain) that is designated as the "center" (which borrows symbolism of the "homeland" or the "us versus them" categorization). These religious symbols therefore combine a large variety of archetypal connotations together into a coordinated unit; it is no wonder they survive so well in the human mind – they are combinations of many universal components. The parts of these symbols exist in every intact human brain, and so can emerge spontaneously in everyone; they are therefore not likely to be solely dependent upon cultural transmission except in the details – which are nonetheless important for a full understanding and context.

Recall from earlier chapters the way animal symbols are used, and the way our theory of mind (TOM) capacity helps to build them. Since (flighted) birds live in the air, they would naturally acquire all of the vertical symbolism described previously; this explains why birds are so often symbols of "spirit" and other vague but innate notions.

Finally, human brains and bodies have an innate biological system that orients along a vertical axis: the vestibular system. This system, which includes the inner ear, automatically tracks balance along the vertical dimension, and detects movement via the inertia of fluids in the labyrinthine canals. This provides a concrete reference point for target domains of a variety of mappings, all of which are innate, and are probably the specific systems accessed by the ubiquitous vertical mappings that have already been identified by Lakoff and Johnson (1980, 1999, 2003) and Lakoff and Turner (1989), and include the MORE IS UP ("stocks *soared* to new heights today"), HAPPY IS UP ("my spirits are *lifted*"), GOOD IS UP ("things are finally *looking up*"), ALIVE IS UP ("he *rose* from the dead"), CONTROL IS UP ("I'm trying to get *on top of* this situation"), STATUS IS UP ("she dresses very *high* class"), RATIONAL IS UP ("humans can exercise *higher* reasoning functions," "take the moral *high ground*"), and so on. In other words, humans understand verticality well and apparently "up" is preferable, providing another meaning-image connection. Haule (2010) reviews evidence that the "three-tiered cosmos" pattern is indeed "hardwired," a system I review extensively using the example of Norse mythology elsewhere (Goodwyn, 2010b).

Left/right symbolism

LEFT/RIGHT SYMBOLISM: The mind does not appear to organize concepts as identical along the left-right axis either. The evidence of this comes from a variety of sources. First, many languages attribute value distinctions to "right" and "left" directions in the same way. "Right," in English, means "correct" or "conventional," for example. *Droit* (French) means right, but also just, law, and uncorrupted, whereas *gauche* (left) means ungainly, unseemly, awkward, or warped. *Aristeros* (Greek for left) means insane and "wrong," whereas *sinister* (Latin for left) means corrupt and evil. *Na levo* (Russian for "on the left") means underhanded or "on the sly." The Jungian analyst Anthony Stevens (1998) has related this terminology to neurobiology – our evolved specialization of the hemispheres, with the left hemisphere controlling the right half of the body, and the right hemisphere the left half:

> since in the great majority of people the left hemisphere is dominant, most of us are right-handed. The right side is our competent, effective side; our left is clumsy, awkward, *gauche*, and this has probably been the case since protohominid times.
>
> (122)

One might protest that Russian, English, French, and Greek are all Indo-European and so may have similar meanings because of robust cultural transmission. But Stevens also points out that cross-culturally the "right" has been associated with the sun, the masculine, day, summer, the sacred, the known, life, health, good, and Heaven, whereas the "left" is often associated with the moon, the feminine (in male-dominated cultures, naturally), night, winter, the profane, death, illness, evil, and Hell, essentially equating all these things in an IS RIGHT/LEFT metaphorical mapping (such as GOOD IS RIGHT, BAD IS LEFT, etc.). These connections with our handedness that are consistently found throughout the world suggest a frequent association of dexterity with a variety of concepts using the innate handedness as a target domain. I feel this reasoning is on the right track, but there may be more to our neurobiology than handedness at work.

For example, neuroscientists have worked out that the left and right hemispheres operate in several fundamentally different ways. Experiments in split-brain subjects have shown that the left hemisphere is more conscious, more analytical and rational, and more verbal than the right hemisphere. In contrast, the right hemisphere is less conscious but more aware of our surroundings and our internal milieu, is more holistic in judgment rather than reductionistic, and more emotional (Gazzaniga, 1995; Gazzaniga et al., 2002). Solms and Turnbull (2002) have observed that the right hemisphere is necessary for deeper emotional processing in maintaining psychological health, whereas the left hemisphere is more precise and rational, but frequently oblivious to these matters and prone to repression, denial, and other defenses. Furthermore, the right hemisphere is more neuronally connected with the deeper emotional circuits, whereas the left hemisphere sees these things more "at a distance" (Damasio, 1999b; Panksepp, 1998). Ramachandran et al. (1998), operating on years of studies of patients with various left/right lesions, as well as summarizing the clinical research, observe:

> The basic idea here is that the coping strategies of the two hemispheres are fundamentally different. The left hemisphere's job is to create a model and maintain it at all costs. If confronted with some new information that does not fit the model, it relies on Freudian defense mechanisms to deny, repress, or confabulate; anything to preserve the status quo.[2] The right hemisphere's strategy is fundamentally different. I like to call it the "devil's advocate," for when the anomalous information reaches a certain threshold, the right hemisphere decides that it is time to force the organism to revise the entire model and start from scratch. The right hemisphere thus forces a Kuhnian paradigm shift in response to anomalies, whereas the left hemisphere always tries to cling to the original model.
>
> (42–43)

Thus we have much more than an "association" with physical dexterity – we have a basic underlying difference between hemispheric processing styles. The equation of knowledge and the sun with the "right" is a reflection of the more conscious processing of the left hemisphere, and utilizes the ubiquitous KNOWING IS SEEING associations. Given Ramachandran et al.'s observation that the left hemisphere tenaciously hangs on to theories and "what is known" (or thought to be known), the equation with a questioning right hemisphere that is more unconscious but more deeply aware of the internal and external environments certainly would lend itself to innate UNKNOWN, EVIL, DARK, or ILL IS LEFT connotations – in fact, the characterization as the "devil's advocate" is quite apt, since the right hemisphere appears to be a "Mephistopheles" to the left hemisphere.[3] More emotional, more unknown and mysterious, but having deeper knowledge of the inner and outer world, it is also less verbal, less precise, and more prone to irrationality and chaos. And everyone has both types of processing in their brains. Animals that have no differentiation of the hemispheres would probably not have this dichotomy; humans do, and it is likely that this is the neurobiological source behind this symbolism and why the same metaphors appear cross-culturally. If this were a matter of convention or culture, these metaphors (if they appeared at all) should distribute randomly, or at least follow patterns of diffusion. Since they don't, the neurobiological origin seems more credible.

Anything on the "left" symbolically, then, may represent left as darkness, unconsciousness, "evil" or "sickness" (meaning anything that disturbs the status quo of the left hemisphere), "the profane" (meaning bodily functions and emotionality) and "Hell" (meaning anything opposing the idealized "Heaven" of the left hemisphere).

Color symbolism

A common assumption in linguistic analyses of color terms and concepts has been that they are completely arbitrary; this hypothesis has not withstood more recent analyses, however (Brown, 1991). In analyzing over 100 languages worldwide across many cultures, Berlin and Kay (1969) found basic universal principles apply to the way humans organize color information. First, they found that while languages vary in the number of color terms used from two on up, there are some basic commonalities. Some languages, for example, divide all colors into only two broad terms like "light" or "dark"; this does not mean that subjects *cannot differentiate* the colors, which would suggest that language dictates thought – a hypothesis not supported by psycholinguistic evidence (Pinker, 2007); rather, subjects using these "two-color" languages merely lump dark colors together and light colors together and give them a single name. The way in which these categories are devised, though, is not arbitrary. Two-color languages, for instance, *always* use "black" and "white" equivalent terms. If a language has three terms, the third color singled out for labeling is *always* red. Four- and five-color languages *always* include green and yellow. The sixth is blue, the seventh is brown, and the eighth through eleventh colors are always purple, pink, orange, and gray. These basic eleven colors are found in all other languages, and this "hierarchy," since it was never violated, suggests a universally acquired organizing principle in the mind that assigns particular importance first to black and white, then to the color red, followed by green and yellow, then blue and the rest. Note also that colors that attract the most attention are red, yellow, green, and blue, and these colors are preferred by children (Tresidder, 2005: 116).

What might be the neurobiological principles behind this organization? First, note that the initial actual colors (red, green/yellow and blue) are primary colors in optics, as well as the set-wavelengths of the color-detecting "cones" of the retina. Before that, the more numerous "rods" differentiate light and dark, which may explain their order in the hierarchy. The fact that red is classified first may suggest an innate attentional bias in the perceptual/conceptual system, for the simple reason that redness in the environment may mean someone or something is bleeding – which would be important for survival purposes; this hypothesis calls for more specific study. The other colors may correspond biologically with the fact that humans evolved in a diurnal environment where yellow (the sun) and green (vegetation) were particularly important, followed by blue (the sky), brown (the earth), and the other finer differentiations. Symbologists have recognized this link between color symbolism and nature, pointing out that green is usually used to represent potency and vegetation, yellow the sun, blue the sky, spirit and truth, white purity and light (which includes the Chinese symbolism of funerals), and black with death, secrecy, mourning, or evil (Tresidder, 2005).

Evolutionarily the white/black primacy of color conceptualization makes sense considering that light and dark differentiation occurred first before color differentiation did. The linguistic evidence is unfortunately all we have to evaluate the color-processing aspects of the brain; however, these alone suggest quite a bit. Diurnal creatures such as humans can use color as a way to navigate the environment, so we might be able to make an educated guess that there are subtle emotional biases in the brain that "tag" certain colors with certain (likely quite vague or thematic) meanings. These meanings would automatically find their way into our symbols unconsciously, as spontaneous mental images often reverse the image → affective label processes given above to generate an affective state → image process.

In understanding symbolism of the color red, Jungians postulate that "red is the color of fire, of blood, of wine, the color of embers and of inebriation . . . red stands for life and death, for fertility and danger" (Brunner, quoted in Jung, 2008: 346), to which Jung adds that red "stands for *blood, passion*, and *fire*" (Jung, 2008: 366, emphasis in original). Red is generally seen as "strong," "heavy," and emotive" in world symbolism (Tresidder, 2005). The fact that redness cues the brain to the exclusion of all other colors, which I postulate is due to the potential importance of noticing blood for survival reasons, would equate "danger," "emotion," or "life and death" connotations certainly. Note also that activation of the RAGE and LUST circuits elevates blood pressure and blood flow (Panksepp, 1998), providing another link between these "passionate" affects and blood, which flood the skin capillaries during these moments, and consequently *redden* the skin. The link with fire may have an attentional bias in that fire use is an absolute universal (Brown, 1991), and there are even cases of individuals who have pathological fascination with fire (in the impulse control disorder pyromania) – both suggesting that the perceptual/conceptual system has attentional biases that recognize fire as emotionally important (more research needs to be done in this area, however, to directly test this possible bias). Since both RAGE and LUST circuitry elevate body temperature (Panksepp, 1998), a universal RAGE OR LUST IS HOT becomes obvious. The link between heat and fire is a tight one, perhaps made by early learning mechanisms in combination with innate predispositions, but otherwise usually resulting in fairly universal RAGE OR LUST IS FIRE mapping. The most important point here is that the use of the color red to symbolize affects is not arbitrary or a contrived cultural custom, but perpetuates due to our shared neurobiology.

In general, colors have come to be understood to represent a number of meanings when compared cross-culturally. In a variety of systems, red represents the color of the gods, including fire and the sun (Hermetic philosophy), grey represents a mixture of light/dark, as well as ghosts – perhaps a visualization of the "light" world of the living and the "dark" world of the dead. Blue contrasts red and indicates a calming state, and is usually considered "good" (Tresidder, 2005). Blue has been depicted as the mantle of the virgin Mary, is linked with water and unconsciousness, and the sky and spirit realm, and is linked with green in depictions of the Egyptian underworld and land of disembodied spirits (Jung, 2008). The Jungian analyst Jacoby equates blue with thinking (1964: 338), whereas red is associated with the sun, passion, masculinity (testosterone elevates blood pressure and body temperature, which may encourage a universal HEAT, BLOOD, RED → MASCULINE link) and war, and is frequently linked with black and white, for example in medieval Christian art where black represented evil, red the resurrection, and white the transfiguration. Interestingly, this exact color hierarchy is also found in Ndembu and Andamanese symbolism (Stevens, 1998: 148). Note also the alchemical symbolism of black-white-red-gold (yellow), which represents the process of "spiritual transformation" from base matter (black), to illumination and revelation (white), through suffering and love (red), and finally to transcendence (gold). Interestingly, the white–red–gold progression is also present in Taoist symbolism (Cirlot, 1971). All of these colors are early in the hierarchy; black and white come first, then red, then green or yellow.

Green is often a symbol of life and hope, but also of death and lividness (Jacoby, 1964), and green is frequently the color of vegetation and putrefaction. Green and yellow come after red in the color hierarchy, which may represent a bias in the brain that has adapted to vegetation, wherein refuge but also predators, including rival tribes, lie. The link between green and life makes sense if the brain motivates us toward "green" stimuli in combination with the "animacy" categorization (described previously); thus the link between green and life. Others note that brown is linked to earth symbolism. The above link of green/yellow with animate objects would find its opposite in brown colors, or "inanimacy" (i.e. rocks, dirt, etc.). Of course, there are many brown animals, so this differentiation is not perfect – it may only cue to environmental surroundings (green forests, grasslands as opposed to dirt and rocks). Here again red is associated with surging emotionality; there are many more associations to color symbols in a variety of systems, many of which are taken to extremes and are contradictory (Cirlot, 1971). The question here is how much these associations lean toward the archetypal, as opposed to the personal. In my estimation, only the colors that are "early" on the hierarchy are likely to have more archetypal meanings; further differentiations are likely attached later and vary more across cultures.

Light and dark

The fundamental division of day and night is likely a part of the makeup of all animals, since feeding, resting, and exploring all vary on the basis of available light in the environment. Humans are diurnal creatures that hunted and foraged during the day, and returned home at night. This pattern is evident in our neurobiological adaptations. For example, natural selection has favored homicide defense adaptations that lead to the avoidance of unfamiliar surroundings – especially those controlled by rivals, or in locations where ambush is likely, and especially traveling by night (Duntley, 2005: 236). Darkness cues the FEAR system to be more vigilant against danger when far from "home" territory as an adaptation against physical harm. When the FEAR brain circuits are directly stimulated in humans, subjects frequently give highly metaphorical reports of "entering a dark tunnel" or being "lost at sea" (Panksepp, 1985) – note how here the stimulation of these circuits generates visual symbols directly – a rigorous demonstration of affect → image. Humans readily acquire fears of dark places, heights, approaching strangers with angry faces, sudden sounds, snakes, and spiders (Gray, 1987), and children under two years of age typically have innate fears of sudden noises, strange objects, pain, and loss of physical support (Panksepp et al., 1998), and later easily acquire fears of animals, strangers, the dark, and drowning (Panksepp, 1998: 220–221), providing evidence that certain imagery has direct access to FEAR circuitry in humans and may provide universal DESPAIR IS DARKNESS, FEAR IS DARKNESS, ISOLATION IS DARKNESS images. By contrast, note that mice (which are nocturnal foragers) appear comfortable in darkness and actually fear light (Panksepp, 1998). Perhaps this means that if mice could visualize heaven, it would be a dark hole instead of a "bright light." In humans, black is normally representative of death, solemnity, darkness, secrecy, or the unknown, sickness, and evil, and has also been utilized to symbolically depict humiliation, death, sorrow, and mourning (Stevens, 2002: 147) – all of these mappings probably emerge from the above differentiations of the more general DANGER IS DARKNESS symbol.

Light is everywhere equated with knowledge (via the KNOWING IS SEEING metaphor; Lakoff and Johnson, 1999), and this meaning is expanded to include "mystical awareness," moral virtue, "higher consciousness" and "spiritual" thought. Light is everywhere used to represent Divinity, such as the descriptions of the Buddha as always emitting light, Christ's saying "I am the light," the Hindu conception of Brahman as "the light," the blue light of Krishna, numerous Old Testament metaphors of God and light, and various gods of light throughout history, such as Balder or Freyr of Norse myth. Conversely, darkness is equated with the physical world, the unknown, with primordial undifferentiated chaos and the "seeds of creation," but also with gloom and evil, but only *after* differentiation of the "primordial" darkness into light and dark (Cirlot, 1971). The color white is commonly "Associated with light, sun, air, holiness, perfection and innocence" (Stevens, 1998: 148), and yet it is linked to death in Asian, ancient Greek, and Roman funeral rites, which may therefore symbolize the upcoming "enlightenment" of the afterworld or "purity of the spirit," rather than the grief of the survivors.

Consider, for example, the numerous systematic metaphors that equate understanding (which is favorable) as "seeing," such as UNDERSTANDING IS SEEING ("I *see* what you are talking about," "I *view* things differently from you"), or CLEAR IDEAS ARE LIGHT ("your ideas are *insightful and brilliant*," which also contains the INTELLIGENCE IS LIGHT mapping). Thus, since apparent seeing is "favorable" (image → meaning/affect), we would expect spontaneous brightly lit images to reflect "favorable" → light images.

The colors of black and white appear as pairs throughout symbolism of the world. Numerous indigenous cultures have face or body painting rituals that use black and white in combination, and there are a number of myths that involve twin animals of each color, such as horses (Indo-European myth), the watermaidens of Hispanic folklore, black and white knights of medieval folklore, the two birds released by Noah after the flood (Old Testament), the white and black gods Bielbog and Chernobog (Slavic myth), and the Yin–Yang (Taoism). Here black appears to symbolize the primal, undifferentiated, unconscious source of new creation, whereas white represents illumination (mystic or literal), learning, or conscious differentiation that is nevertheless dependent upon the black (Cirlot, 1971).

Furthermore, the division of things into pairs of opposites, which occurs in the inferior parietal lobe, can provide the source domain for the PAIRS OF OPPOSITES ARE BLACK AND WHITE mapping.

Finally, growth hormone is secreted mostly during sleep, and consequently most wound healing is done during sleep. This, along with our diurnal habits, means there may be a connection between healing or rejuvenation and night, sleep, or hibernation.

Temperature symbols

As we saw in Chapter 3, the neural systems for separation-distress evolved from brain circuitry involved in pain and *thermal regulation*, both of which have been shown to be affected by manipulations in opioid systems (Panksepp, 1998). These systems, which are present in all mammals, therefore provide the neurological source and target domains for several mappings. EMOTIONAL PAIN IS PHYSICAL PAIN is one, based on the close link between both neurological systems. The link between social attachment and temperature regulation provides the source and target domains of the ISOLATION IS COLD and the AFFECTION IS WARM mappings. As I mentioned before, Jungian dream analysts often see winter dreamscapes as symbols for the lack of feeling a person is experiencing, whereas: "Fire and flame symbolize warmth and love, feeling and passion; they are qualities of the heart, found wherever human beings exist" (Jacoby, 1964).

Several other common mappings that can be sourced to this basic neurobiological link include the EMOTIONAL SEPARATION IS COLD, and the PASSION, RAGE, OR LUST IS HOT mappings. Recall that activation of the RAGE system results in elevations of blood flow, body temperature, heart rate, blood pressure and muscle tension and may represent the neurobiological links between ANGER IS HEAT or PASSION IS BLOOD.

Natural versus artificial

Specific brain regions exist that are dedicated to artifacts (Gazzaniga *et al.*, 2002); living things and artifacts – and more specifically *hand-held tools* – activate different cortical brain regions when measured by neuroimaging techniques (reviewed in Boyer and Barrett, 2005) and provide evidence that evolutionary inference systems exist that process information in terms of its possible use as a tool or weapon (104). This provides the target domain necessary for a variety of IDEA IS A TOOL mappings, which will be universal. It also provides the necessary differentiation for the division of environments into "natural," like a forest, or "artificial," like a building – this distinction colors symbolism a great deal. Recall also that humans prefer natural environments esthetically.

Alive and dead

By age four, children appear to be able to reliably distinguish living from dead animals as well as dead from sleeping animals; this skill develops robustly and with the same time frame in both modern and indigenous cultures (reviewed in Barrett, 2005). Thus "there are reasons to suspect that the agency system might contain a very specialized device whose function is to distinguish living agents from dead ones" (reviewed in Barrett, 2005: 213). Furthermore, chimpanzees "exhibit innate fear of deathlike appearances in other chimpanzees" (Hayden, 2003: 184), which suggests a strongly archetypal character to images of death linked to strong affects in our primate family. This system further aids in the categorization of animals as "meat," which makes sense since humans are omnivorous and in the ancestral environment obtained a significant portion of calories from predation. Like other innate systems, then, this ability can be used by the symbol-making mechanisms as a source or target domain, such as the previously discussed DEATH IS REBIRTH association. Innately acquired and emotionally tagged images of skulls and death, therefore, may be using this innate, well-understood domain to represent many things symbolically such as transformation or metaphorical "lifelessness." I have found that patients who feel alienated, numb, or distant from SEEKING often dream of death-spirits, skulls, skeletons, or "zombies"; the walking dead are a common folkloric element, such as the *draugr*, "roaming dead," which often make their mischief in the dreams of the characters in such stories (Turville-Petre, 1975; Davidson, 1988, 1993). Haule (2010) also reviews other various widespread folklore beliefs of the mischief and destruction the dead can bring about.

Pure and impure

A branch of evolutionary psychology known as "error management theory" has shown that humans have aversion reactions to diseased people or food, and are biased toward requiring very little evidence to warrant the crude categorization of "contaminated" and a lot of evidence to warrant categorization of "uncontaminated" (Haselton et al., 2005). In other words, disgust comes easily, as do ideas of "purity" and contamination. This is argued to be evolutionarily protective, due to the fact that a false negative is potentially much more costly than a false positive; thus "disease-avoidance mechanisms will be biased and tend to evince disgust and avoidance at many stimuli that are safe" (734). A bias, of course, presupposes an innately guided mechanism that organizes things into the two categories, much of which finds its way into religious and mythic symbolism of that which is "pure" (or white, light, desirable, etc.) and "impure" (or "dark," "undesirable," "evil," and so on) and hence into dream symbolism as well.

Water and air symbols

Water symbols can be found throughout world religion (Eliade, 1958), and are usually associated with things "emerging" from the "unknown," using a variation of the already recognized IDEAS ARE OBJECTS mapping (Lakoff and Johnson, 1980). This symbolic emergence when merged with water symbolism "repeats the cosmogonic act of formal manifestation; while immersion is equivalent to a dissolution of forms. That is why the symbolism of the Waters includes Death as well as Re-Birth" (Eliade, 1952: 151). What Eliade is talking about here are basic conceptualizing propensities. Just as we formulate objects moving about, so we understand fluidity and easily conceptualize things as fluid (Pinker, 2007).

Another example of this metaphor is evidenced by the multiple parallel myths of the heroic "descent" into the primal waters to battle the sea monster, such as Christ entering the Jordan (New Testament), Job and the Behemoth or Jonah and the Fish (Old Testament), and the "waters of death" mythologies of ancient Asia and Oceania, or Thor battling the Midgard Serpent. Water is also very commonly portrayed as "purifying" or "regenerating," as reflected in the numerous "deluge" myths that have recurred throughout the world as well, as seen in the tales of Orpheus (Greek myth), and similar stories found in Polynesia, Asia and North America, and the story of Christ descending into Hell (New Testament), and the visions of Ragnarök. Here the water symbols are borrowing the aforementioned "contamination" recognition and aversion mechanisms of the brain and combining them; it is also possible that washing may be a separate instinct (as observed in other animals, such as raccoons) that was selected to avoid contamination, providing a closer link between water symbolism and crude unconscious "purification" concepts. These would generate SPIRITUAL CLEANSING IS WASHING connotations, found all over the world as baptismal rites.

Water appears to be understood by the unconscious mind as a "source of life." For example, very many creation myths begin with a god forming the world out of a "primordial sea" (Bierlein, 1994; Sproul, 1979), and everywhere water appears to symbolize life, the source of life, immortality, and liquid in general, and the border between life and death (Cirlot, 1971; Tresidder, 2005). Current evolutionary theories continue this idea of life emerging from the sea – this might be seen as an odd coincidence, though perhaps not: the so-called laws of nature that we see in the world also constructed the brains that perceive them. So we're probably not as clever as we think we are.

In any case, note that many myths depict the land of the dead as separating the land of the living by a body of water (Bierlein, 1994). Jung equated water with unconsciousness or saw it as a symbol of the unknown that could either be suffocating or rejuvenating (1964, 1974, 2008), which finds a parallel in the Great Mother images, the latter meaning creating another impetus behind "baptismal" rituals worldwide as symbolic "rebirths." Similarly, Freud equated water symbolism with birth (1969).

These connotations put water in opposition to air symbolism, which is usually equated with lightness and freedom. Note also that "the creative breath" of life is a ubiquitous metaphor for animation worldwide (Cirlot, 1971; Tresidder, 2005). Air is also linked with thoughts and ideas, which brings us back to bird symbolism; for example, the Norse god Odin's twin ravens are named "thought" and "memory." If water depicts physical life, then air seems to depict its animation, that is, through the ANIMATION IS AIR or WIND connections. Neurobiologically, air is understood well for the simple reason that breathing is essential for mammalian life to continue. The rhythmic contractions of the diaphragm and the biochemical monitoring systems are part of the "reptile brain" and are therefore universal. They are necessary for sustained life and the system has very powerful motivational systems intact to ensure continued breathing and air supply. Consequently, breathing and air have tight links to affective meaning! Air and water then become excellent material for symbol making by the brain, such as found in ANIMATION IS AIR links. The innate system involving breathing, which has controls ranging from unconscious to fully conscious, is used here. Vague holistic ideas of "life energy," which find neurobiolgical correlates in the SEEKING system, also provide differentiations such as SEEKING IS BREATH, WIND, OR AIR, and are frequently observed in images of being "filled with the breath of life" found in poetry, myth, ritual, and dream images. An intact SEEKING system is required for the sustaining of life, which further links it to these images of air.

Pain and grief

The evolutionary proximity of pain and PANIC systems and the fact that electrical stimulation of pain regions in the brain provokes separation cries in animals and intense feelings of sadness in humans, which can be regulated by opioids, lead Panksepp (2005) to argue for a neurological basis for cross-culturally appearing metaphors connecting social loss and physical pain (53). I could not agree more. When viewed metaphorically, both systems provide the source and target domains for EMOTIONAL GRIEF IS PAIN and the converse PAIN IS EMOTIONAL GRIEF symbolism.

Chapter 12

Deep archetypes – time, number, causation

The archetypal processes I explore in this chapter I am calling "deep" archetypes. This is because they deal with dimensions present in many images and symbols and likely correspond to very fundamental ways we formulate and organize experience, like the image schemata identified by Knox (2003).[1] Number, for example, plays a part in every symbol – after all, for any given particular image, there is either one or more of them. As it turns out these concepts have a strongly innate basis, and this should not be a surprise. These "deep archetypes" do not generate individual mappings, however, because they are so abstract; rather, they color aspects of other images.

Number

According to Jung, number or the attribute of numerosity

> may well be the most primitive element of order in the human mind, seeing that the numbers 1 to 4 occur with the greatest frequency and have the widest incidence. In other words, primitive patterns of order are mostly triads or tetrads . . . [number is] an *archetype of order* which has become conscious.
>
> (Jung, 1919: 456, emphasis in original)

As it turns out there are some interesting parallels between this and other Jungian statements about number and what is known empirically about the way we process number information.

For instance, it is known that there exists an abstract system of number representation that is present and functional in infants (Wood and Spelke, 2005; Butterworth, 1999, 2005). Developmental psychologists recognize that "a predisposition to numerically relevant data is built into the architecture of the human mind" (Karmiloff-Smith, 1992: 99). Number sense, or the ability to understand exact quantities of up to four, is present in infants and toddlers, as well as monkeys (Butterworth, 1999; Dehaene, 1997;

Devlin, 2000; Weise, 2003); animals can discriminate between two and three objects (Garnham, 1991), and toddlers as young as four discriminate between writing, drawing, and number notation (Karmiloff-Smith, 1992: 144–145), even though they cannot read or write themselves.

Note that we are not talking about *numbers*, but the concept of numerosity; that is, the propensity to organize stimuli into "things" or clusters. Many indigenous languages, for example, do not have number words that go beyond "two," but conceptually humans can recognize numerosity up to four and sometimes more (Pinker, 2007: 138–141). The concept of number, like most innate concepts, is not easily defined, and yet children understand them. Children, in fact, can recognize numerosity even in disparately shaped objects and even entities that are not discrete objects such as events, holes, puddles, or collections (Bloom, 1996) – to illustrate, when going through the grocery store "express" lane, do you count a six-pack of carbonated drinks as one "item" or six "items"? Why? One could argue either way; this hints at the brain origin of these ideas as *organizational principles*, which will of course be used in symbols.

Children understand complex numerical principles of item indifference, order indifference, and cardinality without needing to be taught any of this (Gelman and Gallistel, 1978) and use different rules for number notation than other types of drawing (Sinclair *et al.*, 1983). Though external number notation systems are not universal, however, counting, arithmetic, and number conservation appear to be (Karmiloff-Smith, 1992: 107). The concept of number appears to apply to conscious processes as well; memory researchers have found that we can consciously hold about seven "chunks" of information in working (that is, conscious) memory at a time (Miller, 1956).

So in what way do these innate concepts apply to symbols? Since the above evidence suggests that innate concepts of number do not extend beyond four (after which we use either estimation or recurrent iteration to extend the numbers if our culture teaches us to), I will consider their symbolic meanings with emphasis. It should be no surprise, then, that the natural numbers one through four (and to a certain extent one or two multiples of these) are the ones that have been attributed the most meaning mythically.

The Pythagoreans (Greek number mystics) and the Chinese both equated the number four symbolically with one, and felt that numbers "cycled" from the wholeness and unity of one, to the binary "evenness" and duality of two, to the "active" ternary principle, and finally to the "fundamental" quaternary structure of four that both divides and unifies. This *progression* through the *non-quantitative* characteristics of the numbers also has commonly attributed meanings, in that unity tends to be divided into binary "pairs of opposites," which in turn engenders the combination of these two opposites to create a new aggregate entity, which is symbolized by the number three, which finally is linked to the original unity as four elements – the original, the divided opposites, their union, and their entirety (Cirlot, 1971; Tresidder, 2005; Jung, 1959a).

The number one is associated cross-culturally with unity and wholeness, the creative essence or supreme divinity, whereas the number two represents either duplication or binary division of one thing into a pair of opposites – the basis of which is correlated with activity in the inferior parietal lobe. Cirlot (1971) compares the number two with "echo, reflection, conflict and counterpoise or contraposition . . . it is expressed geometrically by two points, two lines or an angle" (232). The number three seems to represent the active synthesis of dualism, is geometrically represented by triangles and the "spiritual" (i.e. psychological or conscious) combination of opposing principles; it also divides the vertical world into upper, middle, and lower. Three is often associated with synthesis, reunion, resolution, versatility, omniscience, and growth (Edinger, 1972; Tresidder, 2005). Note also the constant reference to the number three in fairy tales worldwide, such as three witches, three days (which "coincidentally" is the length of the new moon), three wishes, three trials, three wise men, three kings, three-headed gods such as Cerebrus, Hecate (Greek myth), or Brigit (Celtic myth), the three deities of sun, moon, and storm (Inca myth), three treasures, and so on – these seem to point to a theme of change and transformation, thematically. This may be related to the rhythmicity of three, as it takes a minimum of three pulses to establish a rhythm in time, and the fact that it takes a minimum of three members to form a "tribe" – that is, a family. Jung felt that the number three was a "relative totality" such as the spiritual totality of the Trinity (1959a: paras 351–352).

The number four is often equated with totality, is visualized by squares or crosses, and seems to represent a union of physical and psychological balance and totality – a characteristic it shares with the number one. Symbologists note that the number four often symbolizes comprehensiveness, ubiquity, solidity, power, organization, stability, and the earth (Tresidder, 2005). The cosmos is frequently divided into four rivers springing from the "tree of life," as seen in Babylonian, Iranian, Christian, Teutonic, Nordic, Hindu, and Buddhist mythology. Other references are the four columns supporting the earth (Egypt), the four giants supporting the earth (Central American myth), the four dwarfs supporting the earth (Norse myth), the four letters YHWH of God, the four evangelists, the four animal guardians, the four horsemen of the Apocalypse (New Testament) and many others.

Concerning the number four, Jung felt that the

> quaternity is an organizing schema par excellence, something like the crossed threads in a telescope. It is a system of co-ordinates that is used almost instinctively for dividing up and arranging a chaotic

multiplicity, as when we divide up the visible surface of the earth, the course of the year, or a collection of individuals into groups, the phases of the moon, the temperaments, elements, alchemical colours, and so on.

(Jung, 1959a: para 381)

Four is found everywhere in the way humans divide complicated subjects, such as the four elements, the four seasons, four directions, the four beats of musical "common time," the four bodily "humors" of Hippocrates, the four fundamental forces of particle physics, the four equations of Maxwell, the four laws of thermodynamics, the four dimensions of space-time, the four quadrants of the Cartesian coordinate plane, the four phases of matter (gas, liquid, solid, and plasma), and even the four basic emotion systems of SEEKING, PANIC, RAGE, and FEAR. All of these divisions, note, have the implicit understanding that while the considered entity is being divided into four, they are all aspects of an overarching unity. Stevens (1998: 119–120) points out that even our biological makeup appears to have this structure, observing the four elements of life (hydrogen, oxygen, nitrogen, and carbon), the "quaternary alphabet" of four bases of DNA (a binary alphabet would have sufficed), and the four primal molecules of primordial life (water, carbon dioxide, methane, and ammonia). The point of this discussion, however, is *not* to try to convince anyone that the number four has any "supernatural" attribute "in itself" (a statement I would find difficult to *define* much less prove), but rather that it appears to be linked to the way in which *Homo sapiens* organizes information at a very basic level, and that this is linked to our neurobiology and carries with it deep symbolic meaning that is nonetheless difficult to verbalize. The fact that our brains organize things in the way that nature organizes things should be surprising only if one ascribes to the dualist fantasy that there is no connection between the two; this is not the case, however – mind and matter are two aspects of the same substance.

Number symbolism extends beyond four essentially by combining the above elements in novel ways, such as the number five as representative of "four symbolism plus the center," or the "perfect" number seven, which combines the symbolism of three (heaven, earth, and the underworld) and four (north, south, east, west, etc.), for example, or the extensive use of the number nine, a tripled triple, in Indo-European myths (West, 2007). These appear to be natural extensions on the above system, rather than new, completely different connotations associated with numbers beyond four. The zodiac, for example, shows this propensity to divide into quaternities, double quaternities (eight divisions), or triple quaternitites (twelve divisions). Zodiacs that divide the cosmos existed in Inca, Neolithic Chinese, Indian, Mesopotamian, Egyptian, Grecian, and European cultures (Stevens, 1998: 255–256) and usually implied cycles of involution and evolution, masculine and feminine, death and rebirth.

Numeric multiplicity, or groups of objects of indeterminate number, is frequently associated with negativity or chaos, as in swarms of insects or other animals in symbology (Cirlot, 1971), suggesting an UNCON-SCIOUSNESS OR DISINTIGRATION IS MULTIPLICITY symbolism, and its opposite, the COHERENT CONSCIOUSNESS IS UNITY mapping.

With regard to the way in which numbers shape symbols, the Jungian analyst von Franz postulates:

> In most cases when any archetype constellates, it first manifests as *one* archetypal image in a dream. When it moves toward the threshold of consciousness it generally appears doubled, as two identical or nearly identical images. . . . Three groups of beings symbolize that that very archetype is actively possessing the ego, forcing upon it actions or thoughts. That is why fate gods are so often triadic. When the same content appears in its four-phase it has reached its best possibility for being realized in our consciousness . . .
>
> (von Franz, 1988: 283–284, emphasis in original)

There may be a parallel in this description and the way in which ideas are differentiated from raw impulses through the various levels of consciousness. If one takes the analogy of DNA replication and mutation, new genes frequently come about through the process of a single gene first being replicated (duality), then of one of them becoming mutated (binary division into opposites – in this case in terms of function). A third replication and mutation will naturally be compared in function to the other two, and a fourth will represent a "balanced" comparison of two binary gene pairs. Ideas may go through a similar process as they become conscious; that is, any concept as it goes through the cycles of reevaluation will become divided on the basis of whatever "characteristics" one is measuring or differentiating by, twice, to form a quaternity (which we innately understand). Further divisions don't have the innate grounding, symmetry, or balance that the quaternity does. Finally, number symbolism is a big part of images of what Jung called the Self (capitalized) archetype, which I will discuss in a later chapter.

Causation

The propensity to organize events in terms of "causation" is an innate impulse we share with other primates (Hauser and Spaulding, 2006). Causation-related intuitions such as helping, hindering, allowing, preventing, and, of course, *causing*, are concepts that develop in infants as young as six months old (Premack and Premack, 2003). These innate intuitions are mapped onto a variety of metaphors spanning all kinds of concepts, and are not simply acquired by "association," as once postulated by Hume. Like mentality and "intent," it is a subjective label; causation is in fact a difficult concept to pin down exactly, and it does not easily map to what we know about physics, which sees the universe as a huge collection of wave/particles inexorably progressing according to deterministic and probabilistic equations – at this level of analysis, "causation" simply does not appear to make much sense. Nevertheless, it is a part of our primate birthright to think in terms of causation, and it permeates our thought and language (summarized in Pinker, 2007: 208–225).[2]

The concepts, then, of helping, hindering, allowing, preventing, and causing should be observed in symbolic narratives in a general way rather than a strictly analytical way. In other words, if in a dream or fantasy a subject is walking along a path and finds herself blocked by an animal, the symbolic interpretation of this event may have a causal basis – that is, whatever it is that the animal symbolizes is "hindering" the subject. Thus causation is an innate concept that structures symbolic narratives, and represents an important dimension to understanding the context of the symbols. As mentioned previously, it colors symbols of "origin," such as the ORIGIN IS THE MOTHER mapping, wherein the mother is seen as the "cause" of the child.

Time

Jung argued that the archetypes have a timeless nature about them, and compared the archetype to instinctual behavior, such as nest building in birds. In such an instinct, he argued, "the end is anticipated . . . it is a timeless condition . . . the beginning, middle and end are just the same" (Jung, 1990). The nest building behavior, then, has an independent and timeless quality about it from the point of view of the bird.

What does empirical research say? It appears that our brains contain a variety of rhythm generators to organize our subjective world, which possibly include calendar mechanisms that respond to lunar cycles and seasons (reviewed in Zimecki, 2006), which may be linked to melatonin activity in the brain (Panksepp, 1998: 125–130); these biorhythms have been shown to influence dream production (Nielsen, 2004), and hence autonomous mental imagery.

The importance of innate time conceptualization in our brain is also affirmed in emotional neuroscience:

> there is little doubt that the 24-hour biological clock of the [brain region known as the] suprachiasmatic nucleus guides the distribution of behaviors in all vertebrate species, or that the neuronal regulators of sleep are conserved in essentially all mammals . . .
>
> (Panksepp, 1998: 304)

Also, sleep is not the only state in which there are 90-minute cycles; there is evidence that the waking state is subject to a cycling analogous to the 90-minute rapid eye movement / nonrapid eye movement (REM/NREM) cycle; only because there is so much input of sensory data during waking life it is much more subtle than the sleep state (Nielsen, 2004; Solms and Turnbull, 2002: 189).

Apparently our conceptions of time and space are related to "religious" feelings. Brain scans on Franciscan nuns engaged in "centering prayer" (a Catholic method of silent prayer with the intention to create communion with God) and Buddhist monks engaged in transcendental meditation have found that brain regions in the parietal lobes have reduced activity (Newberg et al., 2003; Newberg and Waldman, 2006), and this is associated with reports of feelings of timelessness and a loss of spatial dimension, that is, a sense of "oneness" with the universe or God (depending on the religious beliefs of the subject). They also showed an increase in activity in the frontal lobes, which among other things has been shown to be active during the conscious processing of religious beliefs. The reduced parietal lobe activity is significant because this area has been implicated in the processing of time sense and self-awareness and is reduced in other activities in which we become "absorbed" in an experience. Contrast this with the frequent introduction in fairy tales "a long time ago in a far away land," both invitations to lose oneself in time and space, and the near-universal religious concept of "sacred time" wherein practitioners perform rituals with the aim of recreating the legendary age of gods and heroes of myth – this "sacred time" is separate from and outside the "secular" or "profane" time of our mundane everyday experience. Rituals are enacted that relive the sacred time, which is cyclical and primordial, and contrasts with the linear, progressing type of profane time in which we carry out our day-to-day activities (Eliade, 1949). In these rituals, the return to sacred time is often symbolized as a "mystical" (i.e. *metaphorical*) union with Paradise, found in images of Christ, Buddha, and Mohammed "ascending" into Heaven, among other things. Note also that many indigenous societies have a conception of time that is cyclic, wherein the world is successively created and destroyed, that parallels lunar symbolism of birth–death–resurrection (Eliade, 1952: 72).

Thus the understanding of time appears to have two basic "types" neurobiologically: first is the "linear" time of the conscious self (Damasio, 1999b), where the latter brain areas,[3] when down regulated, appear to mediate a "timeless" feeling that is a simple rhythm which exists "before" the conscious linear expression of time, and so shares many similarities with Eliade's "sacred time." Perhaps what is happening is that the subjects in Newberg and Waldman's (2006) studies are willfully bringing themselves into a state that is closer to our lower levels of consciousness,[4] only in a controlled manner that still allows for some conscious processing to occur.

This research is still very young, however, and more definitive statements will likely be made in the future.

Interestingly, symbologists have noted that the snake is also frequently associated with time; examples include the snake as keeper of time (Greek) or the Wheel of Life (Buddhist myth), the keeper of the universe (Norse and Indian myth, alchemy), the keeper of the ecclesiastical year (Christian myth). Snakes are also commonly symbols of immortality through shedding of skin (numerous indigenous folk and fairy tales, Gnostic, Manichean, and Persian myth), and the spinal cord and vital force (Kundalini yoga) as well as eternity (Mithraic mysteries). These are all examples of universal TIME IS A SNAKE, or possibly SACRED TIME IS A SNAKE or SACRED TIME IS A PERSON (i.e. GOD/SAVIOR) symbols, as both time, snakes, and human imagery have innate mechanisms and can serve as source and target domains. As Lakoff and Johnson (1980, 1999) have already observed, time gets mapped onto visuospatial imagery all the time, as seen in the TIME IS A RIVER and TIME IS A LINE OR CIRCLE mappings found everywhere in human thought. The bottom line here is that time is one of those things the brain struggles with; hence all the symbolizing with circles, snakes, arrows, lines, and all that. Time, then, is not a single phenomenon, but can structure our subjective world in different ways depending on how "deep" we go into the brain/mind.

Opposites

The inferior parietal lobe of the brain appears to be responsible for the classification of objects into rudimentary categories of "opposites" (Bagley et al., 2006). This process is responsible for a number of religious symbols, particularly in creation myths, in which God or the gods divide the universe into pairs of opposites such as land and sky, light and dark, male and female, human and animal, and so on (Bierlein, 1994; Newberg and Waldman, 2006). Add to this further ubiquitous categorizations such as the "us and them" grouping. Also, recall the color symbolism of "black and white" that gets mapped from this innate idea of opposites, and the hypothesis that numerosity arises from a succession of binary divisions and syntheses, at least innately up to the number four, whereupon individuals tend to think more in terms of rough estimates (Pinker, 2007).

The concept of "opposites" therefore has an innate basis that correlates with activity in the inferior parietal lobe, which incidentally is the same region that is downmodulated in the "transcendant" experiences described in the experiments of Newberg and Waldman (2006); this naturally leads to a hypothesis that these deeply "religious" experiences are associated with not only a diminished emphasis on time and space, but also the differentiation of opposites. This phenomenon, if correct, would be able to describe the subjective experience of "one-ness" or "at-one-ment" described by its practitioners in neurobiological terms. Either way, it appears that Jung's intuition that in the unconscious mind things are "undifferentiated" and "timeless" may have merit. The experiences of the subjects in Newberg and Waldman's experiments present an interesting twist here: the "opposites" are well understood by the brain, and hence are used in symbolism all over the place. But the subjects in these studies appear to be deliberately ignoring the very thing that makes time, gods, or whatever more easily understandable, thinking instead more in purely symbolic terms, all while fully conscious. This gives us some more direct evidence that purely religious thinking is specifically *non* concrete.

Chapter 13

Complex recurrent symbols and self symbols

In the previous chapters, I have been building up a method through which we may be able to conceptualize the symbols that appear in dreams, fantasies, and also myths in terms of their neurobiologically based archetypal meanings. But symbols do not normally emerge in isolation; rather, they are usually presented in a narrative fashion and interact with each other in very complex ways. Jungians have long maintained that dreams in particular seem to have repetitive themes even to higher levels of complexity than single animal or person symbols experienced in isolation. It is beyond the scope of this book to explore these in any depth; rather, I will briefly consider a few of these to give an idea of how neurobiology can help us understand symbolic meaning in these more complex cases.

PSYCHOLOGICAL DEVELOPMENT IS A JOURNEY. This is actually a differentiation of the more general CHANGE IS MOTION IN SPACE mapping (Lakoff and Johnson, 1980, 1999, 2003), and can provide the narrative basis for the insertion of numerous other symbols. An example of this might be a dream or fantasy narrative of a person grappling with a difficult problem, symbolized by that person traveling a road that is tough, easy, bumpy, or whatever. I will provide an example of a dream reported in my own practice:

> I am riding a bicycle along a road through the woods, and you [the therapist] are riding ahead of me. While riding I see a large eagle soaring above me, flying alongside a large bat of the same size. Finally, you and I come to a crossroads. To the right is a steep decline with rocks at the bottom. To the left is an easier path through the woods. You go down the steep decline, and disappears into the woods, whereas I choose to go the easier way, in order to "meet up with you later." In so doing, however, I get lost in a "town," and try to get directions from the people in "the buildings," but they keep telling me the wrong directions.

At the time of this dream, the patient, Ms. Grey, was worrying about the upcoming termination of therapy (due to circumstances beyond either of our control), and asserting her own independence from her experience of an at times overcritical and overbearing family. As one can see, one way to interpret this dream is a symbolic narrative of the PSYCHOLOGICAL CHANGE IS A JOURNEY mapping. This mapping uses the visuospatial system to symbolize the struggles going on in the patient's life in compact symbolic and nonverbal form. As one can see, there are many themes going on in this dream. I am not only myself, but her idea of "the therapist" in herself, my "spirit" as it appears to her. I have of course never actually ridden a bicycle with the patient nor traveled through the woods with her, however, this easily overlooked aspect of the dream symbol was obviously constructed by her for some reason that goes beyond simple memory retrieval, since she could not have remembered it!

The termination was apparently depicted as a literal separation along the "crossroads," with me going downward and to the right (recall the rich archetypal symbolism of verticality and left–right orientation) into a more dangerous path that was frightening to the dreamer. Note her choice to take the "easier path" to the left, which often means less conscious. Note also my own willingness (in the dream) to go places she found scary – a commentary on my own possibly at times overly enthusiastic technique; I found this "dreamed critique" useful in future sessions by backing off somewhat to make her more comfortable and improve the therapeutic alliance, which is so crucial to therapeutic efficacy (Ahn and Wampold, 2001). The easier path, however, resulted in her entering an environment that was a more "modern," and hence "artificial" (recall the archetypal symbolism of environment and artificiality), place with buildings and "people."

The people here are unknown male "maintenance workers." These denizens of the generic "buildings" she visits in trying to find me are full of opinions and directions but get her nowhere; meanwhile, I'm gone and not helpful to her – reflecting the upcoming separation. One could argue that the workers are undifferentiated aspects of the dreamer in this context – that there are a multiplicity of them rather than a more archetypal number such as one through four suggests a somewhat chaotic organization. If so, they only give her a "blah blah" type of advice but are at least not danger-ous; rather, they are somewhat passive and "dormant" in her own mind, perhaps cueing that the patient's own positive tendencies of assertiveness, exploration, independence, and analytic dispassion are dormant and unattended (a statement supported by a large body of clinical material). They also reflect the *relational pattern* of passively following me and "men in general" (thinking in terms of generic symbols) that mirrored her waking patterns that were prevalent prior to and partially during treatment, and caused by underlying insecurity.

The eagle and bat are an interesting pair of images – it is unlikely that these are "randomly" placed in the dream. I will return to these characters in the next chapter when I describe symbol dimension analysis. The point here is to show the overall structure of a psychological change or struggle being depicted as a journey.

Self symbols

Perhaps Jung's most profound and frankly difficult hypothesis is his proposal that the unconscious mind contains an entity he entitled the Self. The Self archetype, Jung argued, was a kind of homeostatic function that integrates the various conflicting parts of the psyche and guides them toward balance (Jung, 1919, 1953a, 1959a). Jung postulated that there was a class of images that were representative of this dimly grasped process and that they were usually symbols of *wholeness and integration*. These symbols, usually found to have circular and quaternary structure, he called "mandala" symbols, named after Buddhist symbols used in meditation (1959a: para 59).

Symbols that Jung felt referred to the Self included a variety of images including circles, spheres, or quadratic figures such as crosses, geometrically formed crystals, cities, castles, churches, houses, and vessels, or wheels, each with subtle nuances (Jung, 1959a: paras 351–354). The content of these spaces, furthermore, has significance, such as water within the house or vessel, fire or animals, and the inhabitants of these spaces might be same-gendered gods or godlike humans, princes, priests, historical figures, beloved, admired, or successful family members – anything that "transcends" (metaphorically speaking) the subject. In other words, he proposed a class of metaphors that include THE SELF IS A HIGH-RANKING PERSON, THE SELF IS A HOUSE, and THE SELF IS A MANDALA. It "transcends" the subject because it includes more than just the conscious self; it consists of the entire mind, all the instincts, unconscious circuits – in this respect it also includes all of existence, since for Jung our subjective universe as we know it is constructed in no small part by the mind, a stance confirmed by neuroscience (Solms and Turnbull, 2002).

Jung went on:

> Like all archetypes, the self has a paradoxical, antinomial character. It is male and female, old man and child, powerful and helpless, large and small . . . though this does not mean that it is anything like as contradictory in itself. It is quite possible that the seeming paradox is nothing but a reflection of the enantiodromian [fluctuating back and forth] changes of the conscious attitude which can have a favourable or an unfavourable effect on the whole.
>
> (Jung, 1959a: para 355)

I would add that since the Self is a symbol, it is ultimately ineffable – this often leads to contradictions because if it had no contradictions, it would easily be described concretely, and hence one would not need to represent it with a symbol.

Thus the Self "contains" pairs of opposites, and exists "before" and "after" things are differentiated into pairs of opposites – remember the subjects of Newberg and Waldman's experiments, where they suspended thoughts of opposites to consider a religious symbol. For Jung, the Self archetype was "projected" outside the mind onto supreme godhead images cross-culturally. Obviously this language strains comprehension – it is no wonder Jung was often accused of mysticism. But Jung's intuition some-times surpassed his ability to describe and communicate his ideas; before we dismiss the concept of the Self as incomprehensible, we should explore what neuroscience has to say on the questions Jung raised.

The neuroscientist Joseph LeDoux (2002) attempts to define what he calls "the self" in terms of neurobiology; note that this is a different "self" – more concerned with what is identified by the organism as belonging to itself than Jung's more comprehensive Self, but it's a start. LeDoux (2002) maintains that "the self" must include unconscious aspects as well as conscious aspects, which leads him to define it as

> a notion that can be conceived of along an evolutionary continuum. While only humans can have the unique aspects of the self made possible by the kind of brains that humans have, other animals have the kinds of selves made possible by their own brains. To the extent that many of the systems that function nonconsciously in the human brain function similarly in the brains of other animals, there is considerable overlap in the nonconscious aspects of the self between species. . . . If we are to understand how the mind, through the brain, makes us who we are, we need to consider the *whole* mind, not just the parts that subserve thinking.
>
> (23–24, emphasis in original)

In this case LeDoux argues for a more complete definition of the self that transcends conscious thought to include unconscious thought; this is closer to Jung's conception when he describes the Self in non-symbolic terms. LeDoux continues, describing what he is calling the self to be a unit in charge of maintaining *homeostasis*, including both explicit and implicit aspects, both learned and innate, finally settling on a definition of the self as

> the totality of what an organism is psychically, biologically, psycho-logically, socially, and culturally. *Though it is a unit, it is not unitary.* It includes things that we know and things that we do not know, things that others know about us that we do not realize. It includes features that we express and hide, and some that we simply don't call upon. *It includes what we would like to be as well as what we hope we never*

become . . . different components of the self reflect the operation of different brain systems, which can be but are not always in sync. While explicit memory is mediated by a single system, there are a variety of different brain systems that store information implicitly, *allowing for many aspects of the self to coexist.*

(31, emphasis added)

In particular, he emphasizes that memory, which is a function of neuronal synaptic connections, can arise not only from experience, but can also come "about as a result of ancestral rather than personal history" (66). Note the numerous similarities in LeDoux's definition of "the self" and Jung's defi- nition, made decades earlier and without the advantage of mountains of neurobiological data. One might even imagine that Jung was grappling with the same entity LeDoux describes; only Jung's description was somewhat more confusing, *and* Jung was emphasizing the way in which the above entity is *symbolized* in the mind. This added an additional layer of difficulty to the analysis.

Mythic explorations of self symbols

Just to give an idea of how complex this gets, Jung felt that the Self was symbolized in many ways. Not only was it represented by geometric images such as the sphere, circle, cross, or mandala, but also the stone, the quaternity, the *prima materia*, the egg, and the God-Man such as Christ, Attis, Dionysus, Mithras, Buddha, or Krishna. Note that the typical "difficult thing described in terms of easy thing" metaphorical mode of thinking strongly applies here. The Self could also be symbolized by animals such as the elephant, horse, bull, bear, bird, fish, or snake. The mountain and lake, as well as flower and tree, symbols can also represent the Self archetype (Jung, 1959a: paras 356–357).

Jung usually described the Self as an entity that was frequently rep- resented as a "mandala" (which means "magic circle"), which is any geometrical shape that has a circular structure with a quaternary division of some kind. As evidence of this, he showed how these "mandala" symbols have been observed all over the world from the furthest antiquity. These symbols (to Jung) meant psychological balance and wholeness, as well as the ineffable core essence of one's being (Jung, 1959a; von Franz, 1964a). Examples are Buddhist mandalas, the pagan cross of Celts that was later Christianized into a cross with the circle in it, the Germanic sun-wheel or medieval symbols of Christ surrounded by the four Evangelists (which mimic symbols of Horus and his four sons of Egyptian myth), the garden of Eden (with its four rivers that flowed from the tree of knowledge), the clock (divided into four groups of three divisions), the *quadrata circuli* of alchemy, and ubiquitous architectural designs throughout the world, particularly of temples and places of worship. Part of the mandala is the circle, which appears to be one of man's oldest symbols, appearing everywhere throughout history (Jaffé, 1964). Furthermore, the mandala is another instance of the widespread symbolism of the "center," wherein it is depicted as representing a protecting circle around the religious initiate, the sacred space of contemplation or ritual communion (Eliade, 1952).

Other Jungians, like von Franz (1964a), understand the Self to be often symbolized as a "royal" or "superior" character such as a king, queen, president, or mythic figure, such as a magician, priestess, god, or goddess (208–209), citing Hermes (Greek myth) or Merlin (Arthurian legend) as examples. The Self can also be symbolized by a "Cosmic Man," or world-encompassing human. Examples of the Cosmic Man are also abundant in mythology, as it appears many mythological systems have a world-man symbol; examples are Purusha (Hindu myth), Gayomart (Persian myth), Adam (Talmudic lore), P'an Ku (Chinese myth), and Ymir (Germanic myth), and also include god-men such as Christ, Krishna, Buddha, the "Son of Man" (Old Testament), Adam Kadmon (Jewish mysticism), the Great Man (Native American myth) or Anthropos (Greek myth). Finally, the Self can be depicted as an animal (von Franz, 1964a: 220–221), when representing the instinctive "just-so-ness" that animals have in comparison to humans, or as a stone, due to its seeming permanence and raw, concrete materiality far removed from conscious thoughts and fantasies – much like the philosopher's stone of European alchemy, or the numerous stones used in worldwide indigenous religions; note the equation of the Christ with the "foundation stone" or "spiritual rock."

Paleolithic man apparently found stones fascinating and polished them (von Franz, 1964b: 225); the human "essence" apparently becomes symbolized as an ESSENCE OF SELF IS A STONE mapping, where the human "essence" of the subject is mapped to the target domain of an immutable stone. Ancient indigenous societies held beliefs that stones were resting places of gods and spirits (Jaffé, 1964), and we still practice placing "headstones" on the graves of the dead in modern society. Modern "new age" spirituality often attributes various magical properties to stones. The stone is frequently depicted as a symbol of "being, of cohesion and harmonious reconciliation with self" (Cirlot, 1971: 313) due to its durability and non-biological character. Meteorites, in particular, have easily captured the imaginations of ancient peoples as objects of awe. Stones are used worldwide to adorn grave sites, and "magic" stones figure into mythology everywhere.

Neurobiological substrates of self symbols

How are we to understand all of this symbolism in neurobiological terms? At first glance it seems unresolvable due to the sheer variety of ways in which the Self is supposedly symbolized. In fact, it appears that the Self can be so variously represented because the symbols are actually representing several distinct but interrelated ideas. LeDoux's "self," which is similar to the nonsymbolic descriptions Jung gave of the Self, may be a neuro-biological correlate of this experience. It includes not only what we feel ourselves to be – meaning the conscious ego – but also the other 95 percent of what goes on in our minds, especially our emotional selves, meaning the singular conscious explicit system and all the implicit systems. Hard, inanimate objects in the ancestral environment, particularly those that are brown or grey, which utilize quickly recognized colors (black and white in the case of grey) and have clear boundaries, would fit the bill for use by the conceptual system to create this symbolism due to the common meanings attributed to boundedness, solidity, permanence, and so forth. Beyond this symbolization is the concept of "essence," or the innate propensity to ascribe objects as having an immutable quality that endures changes in shape or even consistency; even children classify ice, liquid water, and steam as "the same" despite radical changes in appearance, and the same "logic" applies to animate and inanimate objects.

Jungians make the distinction that a person who represents the Self will appear more "noble," numinous, famous, or otherwise "transcendant," in relation to the symbolizer. Social status is ingrained into our psychology just as it is in other cohabitating mammals, which allows for an archetypal image of the Self as a very high-ranking person. When considering animal Self symbols, one may expect the animal to have some kind of "superior" quality to it as well. Animals and people are always prime material for symbol making due to our innate propensity to formulate subjective experience in terms of animals moving about. Note that even LeDoux's "self" is a system inextricably bound with the surrounding environment, and hence it would be a mistake to consider all of this to be an entirely "internal" phenomenon – the "organizing center" includes both internal and external aspects of a person (blurry at the deepest levels, recall) as they interface with the environment. Thus the organizing center applies to subjective experience as a whole.

The depiction of the Self as a geometrical shape such as a sphere, mandala, or square has some basic innate foundations. The brain has already been shown to be capable of spontaneously constructing innately specified basic shapes (or "geons"; cf. Biederman, 1995; also the congenital blind studies reviewed earlier). But a mandala is a more complex matter. Recall from the previous chapter the "deep" archetype of number, wherein "four" has various qualities associated with dividing up complex subjects into manageable chunks; in fact, two pairs of opposites that work in combination. This quaternary structure suggests the union of the concepts of wholeness and division, such as the four quadrants of the Cartesian coordinate plane – they are four, but also one, and the quadrants are opposites that "work together" to form a coherent whole. Mandalas therefore incorporate not only the innate concept of the circle, but also of "fourness." But even more important is the concept of symmetry. Recall that humans (and most other mammals) use a recognition system that places high value on symmetry – another image/meaning link – in mate selection because it results in higher-quality mates due to the correlation between harmful genetic mutation load and asymmetry – symmetry is always "preferred" in mate choice because it reflects genetic quality. Since humans, and in fact *all vertebrates*, have a bilaterally symmetrical body plan, as opposed to say the radial plan of a sea star, this preference for symmetry in mate choice runs very deep. Is symmetry therefore esthetically pleasing *in general* or is it specific to mate choice only? Given the high value placed on symmetry in human art, architecture, and even mathematical physics (such as modern theories which tout "super-symmetry"), I am inclined to believe the latter. Thus it seems that the propensity to seek out symmetrical mates and invest them with high esthetic value has "bled over" into other concepts that lie outside mate choice – in other words, symmetry is innately understood and will be used to symbolize things.

Jung felt that the Self was a symbol of balance and wholeness; the concept of "balance" is a symmetrical one, in that two "entities" are "equally" present, neither dominating the other. Balance is also hardwired into our vestibular systems, and is favored particularly in bipedal animals whose survival depends upon maintaining upright posture – this links symmetry and "balance" with "favorable" connotations, even if only vaguely intuited. Given these facts, note that the circle is mathematically the most symmetrical of all two-dimensional shapes (as is the sphere in three dimensions) – thus the link between the concepts of "wholeness," "symmetry," and "balance" are easily mapped into the innate concept of the circle. When placed symmetrically, quaternary symbolism obtains this additional esthetic significance – combining the two geometric figures doubles the symmetry. Note also that children around age two and older all over the world spontaneously draw mandala symbols consisting of circles, squares, and crosses (Kellog, 1969; Edinger, 1972), perhaps in response to a natural tendency to formulate experience according to this organizing principle.

But there is another way in which this mapping becomes readily made that has to do with neuroanatomy: the *visual system itself* is actually a *circular field divided into four quadrants*. The retina is itself a circle, and due to the organization of the brain's visual tracts, incoming sensory data are divided into four equal quadrants that distribute evenly to the visual centers of the brain – in other words, our entire visual field is literally one big mandala! Everywhere one looks, then, complex visual data is being divided into four, with an emphasis on the center. Contemplating mandala symbols, then, sends symmetrical data to all four quadrants of the visual cortex simultaneously – perhaps it is this feature that correlates with subjective feelings of "balance" in those meditating on them, and spontaneously generates symbols during moments when such "balance" is felt to be needed or symbolized. The important point is that these features of mandalas are not inherent in the drawings or symbols in themselves, but rather that the emotional or symbolic meanings that become entangled with them are due to our particular neurobiological makeup.

Finally, the link between symmetry and mate selection may even provide a further nuance that links fecundity with visual symmetry, which might explain why Jungians often equate Self symbols with "fertility," "new life," "renewal," and so on. Apparently, then, what Jung described as the Self is actually a family of many spontaneous symbols. These various products of the brain work with a variety of innate "building blocks," in this case, LeDoux's "self," essences, balance, animacy/inanimacy, possibly color, social dominance, human and animal recognition mechanisms, shape, symmetry, fecundity, numerosity, and the hard facts of our visual system's anatomy. Jung argued that mandala figures in particular emerged during states of "crisis" or conflict – such as that described by LeDoux wherein various unconscious circuits are not working coherently with the conscious self or with each other. The emergence of mandala images, to Jung, represented attempts at healing or restoration of balance and resolution of this conflict, and they were often given the name of a god by the subject. This intriguing prospect has to my knowledge only been tested once, and this was by Jung himself. Here, Jung recorded the dreams of one of his analysands, the Nobel laureate physicist Wolfgang Pauli. To minimize interference and the possibility of suggestion, Jung had an associate record Pauli's dreams over an extended period – Jung had no contact with Pauli whatsoever during this time and Pauli was unfamiliar with Jung's ideas. At the time, Pauli reported that he was going through an emotional breakdown related to a recent divorce. In all, Jung recorded 400 dreams, and found a significant change in imagery: the first 50 dreams included a 2–9 percent incorporation of circle-quaternary symbols, whereas the last 50 included 11–17 percent mandala symbols (Jung, 1974) – an overall change from roughly 1 in 25 dreams to roughly 1 in 7 dreams. The increase in mandala shapes increased as the patient improved.

Contemplating the cosmos

Much like the war god and the anima and animus, the biological data I review above shows how the innate *imagery* of the Self is conjured up by the mind using a kind of universal symbolic and preverbal "language." Stones, oceans, mandalas, and so on are used to make spontaneous symbols for specific reasons when the Self wants to create a metaphor for something. Due to the implications of wholeness, essence, balance, symmetry, animacy, fertility, and completeness, these symbols are excellent images to represent the totality of all the innate aspects of the mind – including its dynamic attempts to self-regulate – but because it is a symbol, the image is really the best way to describe it. Thus the subjective experience of this massive, world-creating, unconscious and ineffable subjective process at the brain–mind–environment border is likely to be frought with awe, wonder, and meaning, and hence visualized with big symbols like God, Allah, Christ, Buddha, Wyrd, Tao, Bramha, mandalas, or the philosopher's stone; novel creations such as animal gods or cosmic/galactic images are possible as well and could potentially arise in anyone with an intact central nervous system. Interestingly the key difference in these many types of Self symbols is the sense of personality within them. Some are personified, but others are not – which may explain some of the key differences in these religious systems at a very fundamental level.

Part 3

Conclusions

Chapter 14

Meaning

The dissatisfaction of large segments of the modern world with the scientific/technological assumptions of the official version of Reality may well point to an "exhaustion of an intellectual impulse," very much like what happened when the medieval myth broke down at the time of the Renaissance. It is unlikely that science will be abandoned, but it seems no longer to be *enough*.

John Haule, *Jung in the 21st Century*, 2010

Like all metaphorical perceptions, archetypal symbols are "true and not true" – they represent relational patterns between things in the lived experience of the person. They are inherently ambiguous and ultimately ineffable, and sometimes have strong personalities. The ineffability is the main reason for resorting to metaphor in the first place, but the ability to maintain this ambiguity is also neurobiologically based, probably in the brain regions known as the orbitofrontal cortex and the dorsolateral pre-frontal cortex, places that, if damaged, make patients have a hard time maintaining a symbolic level of thinking. Such is the case to a lesser, nonpathological extent in dreams, wherein these and other regions of the brain are downmodulated – symbols that emerge during this time feel literal and concrete. Another example is psychosis, which many have observed shares similarities with dreams and mythological themes. But there is another side of this, and that is when one takes a symbol and decides that if it is not literally true it must be "false." I suspect this is the source for the dismissal of dream imagery and especially religious concepts, arguably the most symbolic and profound of all human creations, as "mere nonsense." Taken literally, they certainly are nonsense. But given the prevalence of symbolic thinking, perhaps another look at how we treat symbols is in order.

Symbol and "belief"

Much of this boils down to just how seriously we are going to take an autonomous symbol. I once had a patient who dreamt that he was bringing home a fish to put into an aquarium, but when he opened the bag, a giant snake came out and slithered away into a creek bed. Of course, we can always whisk such things away, confident that they are meaningless or "random," but there appear to be several reasons why dream and fantasy images are probably not random or meaningless.

First, evolutionary psychologists have shown that the brain appears to have evolved a number of highly sophisticated mechanisms to maximize inclusive fitness. The specific goals of *Homo sapiens*, being a highly social, omnivorous primate with a predatory niche in savannahs, produced adaptations for technology, mating, parenting, kin selection, social striving, and creative cognition aimed at acquiring and communicating literal and metaphorical knowledge in lieu of other endeavors (Carroll, 2005). New symbols, then, might reasonably be assumed to be related to these issues more often than they would be random and meaningless, since brains that waste valuable resources (such as conscious processing) generating meaningless imagery would likely be selected out over evolutionary time.

Second, non-random physiological influences on the brain can influence imagery, much of which is unconscious. For example:

1   An environmental change or stress can cause variations in concentrations of hormones like corticotropin releasing factor (CRF) (Nemeroff, 2008) and inflammatory molecules (Pace *et al.*, 2007).

2   These changes in hormones have been shown in numerous studies to have direct correlations with mood through a variety of well-defined brain regions (reviewed by Miller, 2008; see also Raison *et al.*, 2006; Musselman *et al.*, 2001). Note that here is where we cross the brain/mind boundary, by correlation as always, and link brain states with subjective mood reports.

3   Daytime mood reports are furthermore known to correlate with symbolic dream imagery (Kramer, 1993, 2007; Koulack, 1993; Koukkou and Lehmann, 1993), for example by increasing imagery of death and mutilation in subjects about to experience bipolar episodes (Beauchemin and Hays, 1995).

Generalizing, this link of effects would look like this:

Environmental stimuli
↓
Direct correlations with mood via various brain regions and cytokines
↓
Effect of mood on dream imagery
↓
Dream symbol as meaningful holistic metaphor of unconscious brain/mind-environment state

The above chain of events traces a hypothetical pathway from molecule to symbol with several well-documented links, none of which are "random" but all of which are meaningful to the organism.[1]

Third, since studies in mental imagery have shown that focusing on emotionally charged images can affect the emotional response of subjects (Kalin, 2008), and there is powerful reciprocal innervation between these areas of the brain (LeDoux, 2002), it is probable that the reverse process occurs – that is, that emotional states give rise to specific images related to those emotional states, rather than random, meaningless images. One study reviewed earlier showed exactly this phenomenon; that is, when FEAR circuits, which along with other emotion centers are heightened during dreaming, were directly stimulated in humans, subjects frequently gave highly metaphorical reports of "entering a dark tunnel" or being "lost at sea" (Panksepp, 1985) – note how here the mere stimulation of these circuits generated visual metaphors directly.

Fourth, recurrent dreams provide more evidence against meaningless random imagery. As Van de Castle points out, the well-documented occurrence of recurrent dreams, reported in over 50 percent of adults in surveys (Cartwright and Romanek, 1978; Browman and Kapell, 1982; see also Hartmann, 1998), poses a serious problem for "random image" theories of dreaming:

> Physiological theorists who claim that dreaming represents purely random neuronal firing . . . have a difficult time explaining how the same well-formed and constructed dream can keep reappearing for weeks, months, or years. The odds against such a pattern being random would be astronomical.
>
> (Van de Castle, 1994: 341)

Finally, Kramer's (2007) data, which I mentioned early on, suggests dream content is non-random and, furthermore, not just mindless churning through memories.

Thus new undirected symbols are unlikely to be random and meaningless, but related to species survival, emotional expression, and the activities of unconscious circuits in the deep layers of the brain/mind; furthermore they are likely to be metaphorical (Lakoff, 1997) and hence expressions of ineffable intuitions based as much on innate brain-environment patterns as personal history (Goodwyn, 2010a; Hobson and Kahn, 2007).

The living, breathing symbol

The previous section outlined how meaningful symbols may originate; once present in consciousness, there is good evidence that imagery and meaning – both key components of a symbol – can affect brain and body physiology.[2] Jung felt that understanding and "amplifying" symbols was essential for achieving mental balance and alleviating suffering (1919: para 316), but was unable to explain how something mental could affect something physical, except through an appeal to plausibility:

> Psyche cannot be totally different from matter, for how otherwise could it move matter? And matter cannot be alien to psyche, for how else could matter produce psyche? Psyche and matter exist in one and the same world, and each partakes of the other, otherwise any reciprocal action would be impossible. If research could only advance far enough, therefore, we should arrive at an ultimate agreement between physical and psychological concepts.
>
> (Jung, 1959a: para 413)

Ways mind affects brain/body have been rigorously demonstrated in studies of the so-called "placebo" effect. Long maligned as a nuisance phenomenon and confounder of research trials, the placebo effect has finally emerged in some literature as a legitimate subject of study in itself (Benedetti, 2009; Kradin, 2007). As will be seen, placebo effect studies provide us with examples of ways in which symbolic experiences can affect brain and body physiology.

For example, significant and persistent placebo responses have been observed in a variety of mental and physical disorders, including irritable bowel syndrome (Vase et al., 2004), depression (Khan et al., 2007; Leuchter et al., 2002; Vallance, 2007), pain (Colloca and Benedetti, 2005), and Parkinson's disease (Colloca et al., 2004; McRae et al., 2004). Other disorders known to respond to placebo include arthritis, ulcers, hypertension, warts, cancer, and epilepsy (Benedetti, 2009; Kradin, 2007). One famous study showed that for chronic knee pain a "sham" procedure was effective and showed persistent alleviation of symptoms – equal in effectiveness to a common knee surgery (Moseley et al., 2002). In a large meta-analysis of depression therapies, Sapirstein and Kirsch (1998) concluded that 73 percent of therapeutic responses were due to psychological factors surrounding the administration of antidepressant medication and other nonspecific factors, as opposed to 27 percent due to the drug itself. Other studies have shown placebo effects to be highly significant and inducible via *symbolically meaningful* visual, auditory, and olfactory stimuli as well as *ritual*; all had conscious as well as unconscious effects (Koshi and Short, 2007). Interestingly, the placebo effect is not unique to humans – it has been observed in other animals (Ader and Cohen, 1982).

Most ailments can improve with placebo – or "nonspecific" – interventions, and these appear to depend greatly on the subject's state of mind. Shapiro and Shapiro (1997) suggest that modern treatments do not maximize the potential placebo enhancement of treatment, and furthermore placebo response appears to be state-related rather than trait-related.[3]

Other factors include the subject's state of suggestibility and expectation of cure (Bandura, 1997; De Pascalis *et al.*, 2002; Price *et al.*, 1999), number of visits during a treatment course (Thomas, 1987), and the perceived *meaning* of the symptoms (Brody and Brody, 2000). Also, more frequent administration of a medication, larger pills, newer pills, and even the *color* of a pill can enhance or diminish placebo responses, as does the physician's optimism/pessimism, reputation and personality, and what the patient is told about the treatment and by whom (Moerman, 2002). One dramatic case observed a euglycemic patient with multiple personalities in which one of the alter egos was an insulin-dependent diabetic (Rossi, 1992) – further evidence that mind can profoundly affect brain and body. The medical anthropologist Moerman (2002) argues that the placebo response should be reconceptualized as a "meaning response," citing a large array of studies. Others argue that the placebo response may actually be an evolutionary adaptation (Thompson *et al.*, 2009).

The mind/body researcher Richard Kradin observes that many aspects of the doctor–patient relationship can promote well-being, including "touch, gaze attunement, imagery and meaning" (2007: 147; see also Colloca *et al.*, 2008; Oken, 2008). Kradin argues that placebo and nocebo response are types of Jungian complexes (Kradin, 2004), recalling that Jung (1919) suggested that complexes were *mediated by internal images*: "Might mental images mediate placebo responses? The idea at first sounds odd, but the fact is that images are linked to most responses by the nervous system" (Kradin, 2007: 186).

Elsewhere he observes that the data on the placebo response argues for a comprehensive self-regulation system, which of course was presaged by Jung in a "crude but characteristically prescient manner" (190) in his theoretical construct of the Self, discussed previously. Finally, Kradin's research points to a system that has both innate and early developmentally idiosyncratic factors, is nonlinear in response, is strongly correlated with unconscious mind-body physiology, and can be invoked in therapy:

> Rather than as a mechanistically ineffective treatment or as a confounder of clinical trials, it may soon be accepted as a scientifically objective endogenous mode of healing rooted in nonlinear mind-body physiology.
>
> (197)

The mechanism of the placebo effect is currently under investigation, but so far has been shown to be related to highly conserved brain systems (Kradin, 2007; Benedetti *et al.*, 2005; Lidstone and Stoessl, 2007; McNamara, 2009; Mayberg *et al.*, 2002; Oken, 2008). Kradin recommends that to maximize placebo improvement, physicians should construct a narrative for the illness, including its "cause," its meaning, and implications for recovery. Humphrey (2002) argues that the placebo response is *amplified* by conviction in the religious (and hence symbolic) descriptions of symptoms, whereas McNamara (2009) points out many similarities between placebo and ritual responses. Others argue similarly that

> although the placebo itself may be inert, the process of administering and receiving the placebo treatment may not be, embedded as it is with learned expectancies and symbolic meaning.
>
> (Koshi and Short, 2007: 10)

Koshi and Short continue by arguing that placebo is highly significant, and does not equal "quackery": "Studies mentioned here showed that meaning can have considerable physiologic action. . . . Therefore, placebo is not the equivalent of 'no therapy'" (13).

What these studies seem to show is that the ways we symbolize our present state are no mere mental ephemera but real, living and breathing effects that can alter our neurobiology to a significant extent. This should not be a surprise – after all, the brain is not separate from the body, nor the environment, which is something ancient peoples have always felt, but for some reason modern humankind tends to forget.

I think it possible that someday the *knowledge* of how the placebo effect works will be sufficient to invoke placebo effects. The subset of subjective symbolic expressions of a patient's state of being that fall under the category of emotionally moving, ubiquitous, deeply ineffable, and originating in the deep layers of the brain/mind I define as *archetypal* symbols – including interactions (via rituals) with the subset of these that have intent and personality. These interactions are likely to bring about significant changes in brain/mind functioning.

Interacting with symbols

Jung advised his students to "learn as much as you can about symbolism and forget it all when you are analyzing a dream" (Jung, 1950: para 483). The reason he said this was probably to avoid the pitfall of reducing symbols to *signs*. Each symbol, he argued, must be taken as an individual expression whose meaning must be gleaned carefully. If we are to understand symbols as sensory metaphors, then, what Jung was apparently afraid of was reducing patient's symbols to "dead metaphors."

Dead metaphors (Jackendoff, 2002; Lakoff and Johnson, 1999; Pinker, 2007) are metaphors that have been used for so long they are no longer considered metaphorical; clichés (like "seeing red"), aphorisms ("power corrupts"), and banal phrases such as "spilled his guts" (meaning told all his feelings) are examples of "dead" metaphors. Dead metaphors are therefore symbols that have been reduced to signs. Carefully analyzing a symbol can "resurrect" it and make it a "living" one – such that a symbol that was previously just a "figure of speech" becomes a meaningful experience. There is an interesting parallel in this concept and religious symbols; dead metaphors are frequently found in religious symbolism and reflect the slow generational transition of a symbol into a mere place holder. This process was often decried by Jung:

> once metaphysical ideas have lost their capacity to recall and evoke the original experience they have not only become useless but prove to be actual impediments on the road to wider development.
>
> (1959a: para 65)

The cross is a good example: it is a mandala, and so carries the meanings of balance, unity, and division and apparently represents many other "deep" ideas – that of the nexus between heaven and hell, life and death, father and son, gods and man, matter and spirit, immortality, sacrifice, the Great Tree, and the promise of a brotherhood of mankind. But mostly people just think "cross = Christianity" and that's it, and never mind the fact that the cross has been used throughout the world outside of Christian influence, such as in the case of the sun-wheel. Thus a potent "religious" symbol can become a dead metaphor to most people except the devout, who must work to keep the symbolism alive subjectively; this applies to religious as well as non-religious symbols, including dream and fantasy images. Perhaps the most damaging effect when the symbol "dies" is the loss of its ineffable nature and the tendency to forget that (to use a Christian example) a cross is not *literally* anything but a hunk of wood. Its "as if" nature is lost, and hence its mystery and sacredness, which are crucial aspects of every symbol – more on this below.

Symbolic thinking in modern culture

It seems that the difference in modern and ancient thinking on this subject is that ancient thinking was largely in symbolic terms. It was undifferentiated in terms of the objective, physical contribution and the unconscious psychological contribution, as is the case now – all of it was considered equally. As we will see, when it comes to symbols, this is an advantage. Furthermore, science has provided so many of the details to many of our experiences, such as the moon, animals, or the wind, that the symbolic way of understanding these things has been drowned out by reams of minutiae, crammed into children's heads during their formal education. The moon is no longer the outward manifestation of a goddess, time, or inner healing – it is a large mass of inanimate rock filled with craters more or less randomly distributed, orbiting the earth mindlessly in accordance with mechanistic laws. Satisfied, we state "That's all it is" (which we never proved, by the way). When observed "objectively," which means stripped of human meaning, then, the symbolic meanings humans have attributed to the moon become "illusions" or "merely psychological" – whatever that is supposed to mean. But the two are not mutually incompatible. Speaking of the moon more poetically as inducer of madness or goddess of the night, however, sometimes invites chuckles, since everyone knows that "it's just a hunk of rock." This negative attitude, contrary to some opinion, is not due to being excessively reductive; actually, it's the result of not being precise enough about our definitions – and their limitations.

Why? Because it is based on an unfounded assumption: that objects all have inherent properties "in themselves" that exist "out there." But the concept of "an object" doesn't even exist in itself! It's created by the visual system to organize sensory data, as are most of our beloved concepts that we use to understand the world. So, searching for gods or meaning in the "objective" universe is wrong-headed – like searching for the objective existence of "good" scientifically. If we are going to bias ontological truth solely on physical parameters, we must logically be prepared to do so with *all* our concepts – not just a select few. Declaring that evil does not exist except "merely" in our minds implies that it is less "real" than mass, velocity, or molecular structure. But our everyday lived experience is only partially contingent on the so-called physical world, unless we are prepared to declare that nothing has meaning, since science has shown that the universe is a collection of molecules bouncing around in accordance with probabilistic and deterministic laws. But this is not true; patterns of this molecular soup emerge from the chaos, but *patterns* require an observer to discern the meaning inherent in such a pattern – even quantum mechanics cannot escape the necessity of an observer.

Empirical science has sought to observe the physical world with as little interference from psychological influence as possible. That is the reason for all the carefully controlled experiments, the ubiquitous concern over "observer bias," the importance of "blinding" and reliance on instrumentation that strip away all pretense of meaning from the "raw data" that is acquired. Thus empirical science seeks to understand the "objective world" as it impinges upon our senses *before* we "mess it up" with all of our biases and preconceived notions. This methodology is crucial to our understanding of the physical world, which includes the body and the physical side of our anatomy and physiology, especially the brain. The method itself, by design, strips away psychological meaning – to say that science has proven that the universe is "merely" atoms and impersonal forces, implying that the universe is meaningless, is therefore circular: strip away the meaning we attribute to the world, and the world becomes meaningless! But how could it be otherwise? Meaning does not exist "in itself," without reference to an embodied human observer to find it meaningful.

The opposite of the above fallacy is also frequently made: that since all meanings we attribute to the world come from "inside" our head, all meanings are created equal. But this denies the fact that meaning must have raw material to work with, which must by necessity come from the physical world (which includes the myriad processing systems in our brains that cannot be influenced by conscious thought). Not only that, but it denies the specific mechanisms through which meaning is generated, much of which is also outside our direct conscious control and originating in our neuro-biology. This link between symbolic meaning and biology has already been noticed by the Jungian analyst Anthony Stevens:

> The results of cross-cultural studies indicate that analogous symbol-isms, whether of religion, myth or folk tale, are so consistently and universally apparent that it is hard to escape the conclusion that the propensity to create them is implicit in the mind-brain of humanity . . . what the dictionaries and encyclopaedias of symbols have hitherto failed to recognize is that symbolism has its roots in neurology and the evolutionary history of our species as much as in the ancient religious and artistic traditions of human culture.
>
> (1998: 20–28)

Another difficulty encountered in dealing with religious symbols is our propensity to argue that they are "incoherent," meaning frequently contra-dictory. While it is true that the folk psychology intuitions used to create symbols certainly tend to be contradictory at times, if at least some of them are appreciated as *symbols*, much of this difficulty is relieved. This is because myths, gods, and religious ideas are often contradictory or "paradoxical" by nature simply because of their necessity as symbolic expressions – in other words, anger is like fire, but you can't cook a hot dog with it (the symbol of fire for anger is therefore "contradictory" in some ways, but this is nothing new). Metaphors are often capable of several interpretations that are mutually contradictory (Lakoff and Johnson, 1980, 1999, 2003), but this is because they are metaphors that cannot be expressed any other way concretely without resorting to using *other* metaphors/symbols. We should not be surprised, then, nor dismissive, of archetypal symbols for this reason. If whatever a symbol expressed could be stated in a completely coherent and clear fashion, which has more to do with our limited neurobiology than anything else, we wouldn't need to use symbols to describe it in the first place.

Symbols help to create life experience – much like the mind creates the life experience of the emotional importance of one's own child. Stripped of all psychological meaning, physically the infant is "nothing but" a collec-tion of molecules in a particular configuration. When psychological mean-ing is restored, the experience of the infant is restored to its proper place in the parent's subjective world.

The symbols emerging into consciousness still need to be understood on this subjective, meaning-oriented level. The above sciences, through a renewed understanding of the symbols' origin, may shed some light onto this process, since it provides mechanisms and origins, but that will still be incomplete information. To point to the neurobiological origin of such symbolism and say "That's all it is" would be a mistake, much as understanding the origins and mechanisms of the color of blood do not completely characterize the particular way redness is experienced by the subject or in understanding the ineffable core of meaning behind the metaphor "seeing *red*." The fact that this metaphor is so common that it is cliché only speaks to the fact that these ineffable cores of meaning are not impossible to understand – but the fact remains that anger is not and cannot ever be literally "red," and trying to force the metaphor this way makes it appear ridiculous (beware Mr. Literal!). Complex metaphors such as gods (or any other religious or scientific metaphor such as the "bread of life" or the "electromagnetic *field*"), when taken literally, are affected the same way. The linguists Lakoff and Johnson observe that we

> don't have a choice as to whether to think metaphorically. Because metaphorical maps are part of our brains, we will think and speak metaphorically whether we want to or not. . . . Further, since our brains are embodied, our metaphors will reflect our commonplace experiences in the world.
>
> (2003: 257)

They go on to explain just how prevalent and necessary metaphors are to human understanding:

> Metaphors are not merely things to be seen beyond. In fact, one can see beyond them only by using other metaphors. It is as though the ability to comprehend experience through metaphor were a sense, like seeing or touching or hearing, with metaphors providing the only ways to perceive and experience much of the world. Metaphor is as much a part of our functioning as our sense of touch, and as precious.
>
> (Lakoff and Johnson, 1980: 239)

Metaphors are conceptual in nature; language is secondary. Abstract concepts have a literal core but are extended by metaphors that are often mutually inconsistent; however, the abstract concepts are not complete without the metaphors:

> For example, love is not love without metaphors of magic, attraction, madness, union, nurturance, and so on . . . we live our lives on the basis of inferences we derive via metaphor.
>
> (Lakoff and Johnson, 2003: 272–273)

The origin of symbol "mystery"

This is because all symbols exist to help us understand things we could not otherwise comprehend in concrete terms. In the above sections I have argued that archetypal symbols are non-random, emotionally laden metaphorical constructs originating in the deep layers of the brain/mind as it interacts inextricably with the environment, which at the deepest level is highly conserved and universal. Furthermore I have argued that these symbols (among others) can affect brain/body health, and that techniques such as symbol analysis may maximize a symbol's therapeutic efficacy.

The quality of *mystery*, I argue, is an important component of maintaining a symbol's life. According to Lakoff and Johnson (1999, 2003), we use metaphors as tools to understand things. That is, metaphors are used to link things we understand with great clarity, like objects moving in visuospatial fields, with things we understand poorly, like nebulous feelings, vague intuitions/patterns, ephemeral concepts like society, life, gods, the universe, and so on (examples in Lakoff and Johnson, 1999). Furthermore, what determines whether or not we understand something well or poorly (i.e. its mystery) is a function of our neurobiology; because we are descended from arboreal primates, we have a highly developed visuospatial capacity and hence we process this sort of information with great clarity.

For example, the cognitive anthropologists Laidlaw and Whitehouse point out that

> cognitive scientists have developed quite a rich picture of the strengths and weaknesses of human cognitive capabilities. Some things we appear to do brilliantly: for instance, we recognize faces and remember patterns of behavior we have seen or heard on only a single occasion, perhaps days or weeks ago, perhaps under very different circumstances from those in which the remembrance occurs. Or we make astonishingly accurate and convergent interpretations of other people's emotional states based on cues so subtle that giving formal description of them and/or subjecting them to experimental measurement is extremely difficult. Even the world's most powerful supercomputers have difficulties performing tasks of this kind. . . . at the same time even an average home computer can carry out tasks that are utterly beyond our mental faculties . . .
>
> (2007: 15)

Among some of these well-understood capacities are detecting agency, intent, animacy, and "purpose" (Atran, 2002b; Boyer, 2001; Pyysiäinen, 2009), which makes symbolic beings (gods, spirits, etc.) all too natural, particularly when they are "animated" with the help of unconscious systems that appear to have all these qualities when active. Thus, interacting with the world in terms of spirits and gods is extremely natural and uses just those particular capacities we excel at. Why then should we not use them?

At some point in evolution we acquired the ability not only to *imagine* objects moving (using the same neural machinery), but to further represent less easily understood things *as if* they were objects moving. Thus we have two abilities that build on the extant sensorineural machinery, one that uses it to imagine objects less dependent on external input, and another more sophisticated one that uses the imagery system to imagine objects and link them to other concepts "as if" they were the same by using deeply innate ideas (Pinker, 2007). Hence we can see an object rising, and using the same system we can *imagine* or *dream about* an object rising even when away from that object, and finally we can say "My mood is elevated today," which is using the nebulous concept of "mood," and treating it *as if* it were a rising object.

The advantage of this ability is that it allows us to contemplate things outside of a narrow range of domains, such as the nature of life and death, the "essence" of being, time, society, vague but powerful emotions, and many other concepts. The trade-off, however, is that while it allows us to *contemplate* these things, we cannot understand them with the clarity that we understand concrete experiences like visuospatial data. Anger is "like" fire – this metaphor is so common that it is cliché, but strictly speaking anger is not fire and fire is not anger. It is *like* fire; as it is, this word "like" is actually a bit mysterious. No matter how we think about it, anger is not literally the same as fire; the only way we can explain what this "means," then, is to list off the qualities of their similarity. Anger makes us hot, can burn out of control, is destructive, and so on – this is an "amplification" of this symbol, which magnifies the appropriateness of it and (if convincing, which is a subjective judgment) results in an interesting feeling of the mysterious way anger is "like" fire. But this mystery derives from the ineffable core of meaning that all metaphors share, and cannot be expressed in concrete terms, but only in other metaphorical terms. Furthermore, once it is literalized, the symbol "dies" and becomes useless for understanding and emotional impact.

Lakoff and Johnson (1999) provide examples of literal sensorimotor experience used as metaphors (objects, movement, concrete images, etc.), and I extend this idea to include animate symbols, arguing that since evolutionary psychologists have uncovered innate animal recognition/ motivation and meaning-attribution mechanisms in the mind (for example), this is an innately prespecified concept that can also be utilized to represent things symbolically because it is a concept we have a clearer understanding of due to our species history. But there are many more of these problem-specific algorithms than animal recognition mechanisms. Evolutionary psychologists have observed a large array of problem-specific mechanisms that could potentially be used to create metaphors.[4]

A prime example of this kind of learning is the "cheater detection algorithm" (mentioned in earlier chapters), which Cosmides and Tooby (2005) convincingly argue is innate and universal and cannot be accounted for by any known generic learning mechanisms. Notably, they show how subjects given problems that are logically identical to "cheater detection" problems but do not involve social exchange fare consistently poorly, and practice does not improve this difference. This capacity, then, appears to be something the hominid brain simply understands *better* than other ideas; hence I argue it will be reliably utilized to create metaphors. In fact, throughout history humans appear to have done this: giving gifts and initiating social reciprocation – via sacrifice, for example – has been and is a significant part of every major religion (Smith, 2004: 222–227), even if it is primarily a cerebral exchange and not concretized into any particular ritual. Hence the ritual interaction of a god *symbol* (representing something deeply ineffable but nonetheless perceived) and the conscious hominid becomes a dialogue between the human and those concepts far beyond the hardwired capacities of the brain.

Throughout this book I have outlined many other problem-specific cognitive abilities and adaptations that I argue would be well-suited to metaphor construction. This finite collection of preferred environmental data sets explains why humans easily acquire languages, attachment styles, mate selection tactics, snake phobias, and predator inferences (Buss, 2009) but must spend years of study acquiring the ability to read, write, understand quantum mechanics, or play the piano, even though there is nothing inherent in any of these domains *in themselves* that would make them more or less difficult to comprehend – it is our brains that make them more or less comprehensible. Thus I have argued that these species-specific domains will be readily available for use in metaphor construction; furthermore, this is one reason why similar symbols appear cross-culturally.

The Great Mysteries

Understanding why these universal symbols are mysterious is important to preserving and using a symbol in therapy. I speculate that the mystery derives from the dichotomy of well-understood versus poorly understood domains. The basic idea is that since the brain/mind was selected over deep time to organize subjective experience using a specific set of processes related to our survival as complex animals living in a certain Earth-based environment, other domains were left out. Beyond the boundary of the species-specific domains lie realms of experience our brains are poorly equipped to process with great clarity – these domains I am *neurobiologically* defining as the Great Mysteries (GMs). The only reason we even contemplate these domains is because of our capacity for metaphor: the ability to comprehend a non-species-specific domain, like "life," "time,"

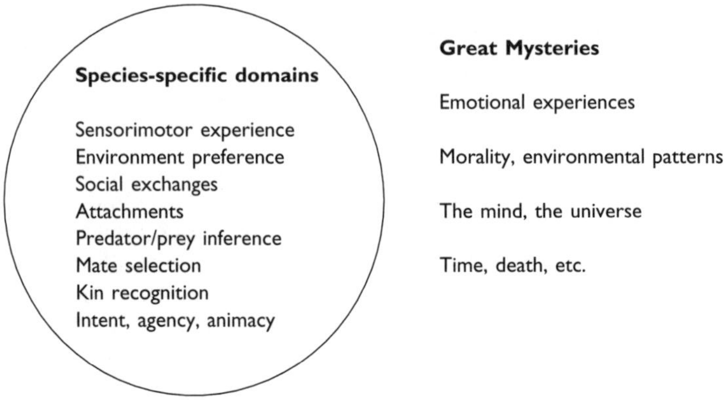

Figure 3 Species-specific domains and the Great Mysteries (GMs).

Note: Other species-specific domains include innate ideas such as cause/effect, object, numerosity, and many others; (for examples see Buss, 2005; Lakoff and Johnson, 1999, Pinker, 1997). Some readers may wish to compare this analysis to the cognitive anthropologist's (cf. Atran, 2002b; Barrett, 2004; Pyysiäinen, 2009) division of cognition into "intuitive" and "reflective" thinking; both are used (usually in concert) to devise symbols to understand the GMs.

"death," or "the cosmos," and contemplate it *as if* it were a species-specific domain, such as objects or animals moving (gods), a great tree, or whatever. By tacking the mysterious word "like" between them, humans have the ability to ponder the domains of the GM and extend our comprehension beyond the species-specific domains; however, we pay the price of concreteness for a certain ineffability of meaning (see Figure 3). This is not to say we cannot understand them – clearly we can on a certain level, just not as well as we can process data that lies within the species-specific domains.

Thus the further away we get from the species-specific, the more symbolic our attempts to understand these domains must become, for the simple fact that we have biologically limited brains.

Haule (2010) argues that gods "arise as our cognitive imperative struggles with a zone of uncertainty surrounding questions of who we are and why we do the things we do" (205). This "zone" varies across times and cultures, but the GMs above will always be in this zone of uncertainty; hence some dimensions of experience will always be the domain of the gods.[5]

All the things that the brain/mind has innate prespecification to comprehend cognitively and linguistically due to their pragmatism in species survival will be better represented and better comprehended in the brain than what lies beyond these domains. Therefore, outside this "boundary" lies the GMs – mysterious for the reason that we have few innate organizing principles to attend to them, and so natural selection has not seen fit to mold the brain in such a way that would make these domains more concretely understandable; thus the necessity to ponder them using ineffable metaphoric images or animate symbols like gods. Importantly, we should note that emotional experiences are *outside the boundary* because we appear to be ill equipped to concretely define them without using metaphor to a large extent. This may be because consciousness appears to have evolved to service our emotions (Damasio, 1999b; Panksepp, 1998, 2005, 2006) rather than the other way around; in other words, Nature hardwired us to *want to* behave in ways that maximize inclusive fitness, but not necessarily to cognitively understand those wants. Regarding emotions, Nature seems to say, "Just do it, and don't ask questions." This creates an "externalizing bias" in the brain, in which we tend to conceive of things going on in our head as external agents acting upon us from "outside."

Furthermore, some symbols are more mysterious than others. Certain metaphors, such as the primary metaphors outlined by Lakoff and Johnson (1999), like SEEING IS KNOWING, HAPPY IS UP, STATES ARE LOCATIONS, and so on, are apparently fairly easy to grasp from an early age, and so are not very far beyond the species-specific border. As we brave "farther" beyond the border, however, building more complex metaphors from these, we must resort to more symbolic expressions more distant from the species-specific realm. Thus one can imagine that we live on a species-specific "island" surrounded by the GMs, and the farther we go into the water and away from the island, the deeper we tread into the mystery.

Symbol systems, science, philosophy, and religion

Throughout history, humankind has developed ways of understanding the farthest reaches of the non-species-specific domains I call the GMs by way of systems of complex symbols so metaphorical and ineffable they can only be appreciated in terms of *other* metaphors and symbols.

Viewed symbolically, many domains of the GMs seem to have been cross-culturally represented in similar terms, normally of humanlike figures (gods, ghosts), animal "spirits" (like Mrs. Green's bear *fylgja*), and almalgam figures (theriomorphic gods, elves, trolls, fairies, etc.), as well as deceased loved ones. Dreaming of loved ones after their death happens frequently (Van de Castle, 1994), which may again be metaphor shaping dream imagery (Lakoff, 1997). In this case, a "ghost" image is used as a compact symbolic expression of all the feelings, subtle environmental cues, affects, introjected qualities, unconscious perceptions, and self-biased memories of the person *in the subject*; considering the degree of brain physiology we all share, the distinction between "self" and "other" becomes blurry and mysterious at best, and calls into question just how one could differentiate the *image* of a person in a subject from the *actual* person; it is certainly not "merely" a memory. Like "phantom limb pain," a subject can continue to vividly experience a person even after they are gone – they "live on" in the symbolic subjective world constructed by the brain/mind. Either way, the deceased loved one continues to behave with a coherent personality and may even remember previous interactions, and as such their "spirit" lives on in this manner in the subjective world of the dreamer.

Other systems of symbols besides religious ones include the relatively newer disciplines of science and philosophy. Science uses symbols to represent aspects of the GMs also – the probability *waves* of quantum mechanics (which are hard enough to comprehend symbolically much less literally), chemical *bonds*, where elements connect *as if* by strings, biological *selection*, wherein species change *as if* acted upon by a selecting agent. Philosophy has numerous other examples (Lakoff and Johnson, 1999). But a key difference between these systems and religions is the aspect of *participation*. In a ritual, not only is the practitioner a "believer," but he or she also participates in the mysteries.[6] Through an interaction with the god, the practitioner "merges" with the god-symbol, which is usually an *archetypal* symbol, and becomes a part of the GMs *as if* she and it/they are "one." Thus "mystic union" or at-one-ment means *metaphorical/symbolic* union, with the caveat that the mystery underlying this activity derives from the ineffable core of meaning embedded in the system's metaphors, and the fact that the boundary between self and environment becomes very blurry outside conscious awareness. In these cases we are often so far from the species-specific, in representing huge universal ideas like the world, life and death, cycles of being, essence of being, "purpose," the meaning of existence, deep affects, barely conscious inklings, and the difference between self and other, that the symbols *by necessity* become impossible to explain in concrete terms. Comparative analyses can perhaps give greater understanding of their "meaning" but never exhaust the possibilities, because of the ineffable nature of the symbol. In fact, "meaning" is a sneaky term here, because it assumes we can explain a symbol fully in concrete terms when we simply can't. The symbol can be described and redescribed in many ways, but the "true meaning" (if there even *is* such a thing) cannot be concretized without committing a literalistic error.

Participation separates religious/mystic systems from others; though the philosopher deals with symbols of great mystery, he is never "one" with them, and neither is the scientist, who for her part seeks to validate a (usually less ambitious) symbol system by repeated experiments. But scientific symbol systems only erase deeper symbolic mystery on the surface; strictly speaking, electrons are not waves or particles, molecules are not "bonded," species are not "selected," any more than the course of the universe is literally directed by human-like creatures floating in the sky. But thinking about these things "as if" they were (symbolically) true brings an ineffable sense of understanding and perhaps meaning to our subjective inner world, so long as literalism is avoided.

This "participation" seems to consist of a (perhaps unconscious) recognition that the human brain/mind emerges spontaneously from the primordium of matter/energy, through the union of the parents and the body of the mother. Mind and brain are one, and hence brain/mind and GMs are also "one," though the particulars of natural selection have made it difficult for the small conscious perception of the mind to comprehend the "bigger picture" it rests upon. Participation in a symbol system becomes the only way to "connect" this conscious self with the GMs. I suspect this requires effort because the conscious self has such a high "filter" (Watt and Pincus, 2004) and allows only so much unconsciously processed data into it. Subjectively this frees consciousness but also isolates it from its unconscious grounding. The unconscious layers of the brain/mind require no such effort because they do not have such filters. Hence the symbolic expressions of the more unconsciously derived dream and fantasy symbols reflect this "union."

In the "neurotheology" experiments of Newberg and Waldman (2006), reduced parietal lobe activity was correlated with feelings of timelessness and loss of spatial dimension; that is, a sense of "oneness" with the universe or God (depending on the religious beliefs of the subject) – it is apparently (among other things) a "lowering" of the filter that separates us from the GMs. This filter gives us great cognitive powers but appears to make us fundamentally rather lonely beings – perhaps it is for this one reason that attachments are so important to us, as attachment is one very important way in which we "reconnect" with the world, through others in a social context. In any case, participation, with mystery, may very well be another factor that maximizes a symbol's "potency," or ability to affect mind/body. Haule (2010) presents fascinating evidence that such symbolic thinking is facilitated by various altered states of consciousness such as dreaming and ritual. Furthermore, he argues that the capacity for these states evolved for this purpose due to their ability to aid in various species goals.

Differentiations of Jung's concepts

Archetypal symbols use archetypal *imagery*. This imagery has multiple aspects; in fact, symbols seem not to be constructed as self-contained entities ready to spring up fully formed, but rather emerge as part of a constructive process that incorporates many innate, unconscious, and vague intuitive *themes* such as "light and dark," "agency," "purpose," "mate seeking," "dominance," "vertical dimension," image schemata, and so on into a coherent whole. In other words, there does not appear to be a one-to-one relationship of archetypes-as-such to archetypal images, as Jung postulated; rather, they overlap considerably, as observed by later Jungian theorists such as Brooke (1991), Edinger (1972), and von Franz (1999), and more recently Haule (2010), who observes that they are "complexities within complexities." The "collective unconscious," then, is not so much a group of archetypes-as-such waiting to be "activated," but rather a massive array of innate concepts, schemas, evolutionary adaptations, and abstract images ready to be combined in novel ways to generate a bewildering array of emotionally charged symbols spontaneously – but their source is still innate, and in nested hierarchies.

Meaning and "religious" considerations

Psychology, since its inception, has frequently had an uneasy relationship with religion. Curlin *et al.* (2007) have argued that a traditional antagonism between psychiatry and religious concepts began when

> Freud equated religion with neurosis . . . [however] Some recent developments suggest that this historical antagonism is waning . . . the historic division between psychiatry and religion may be narrowing.
>
> (1825–1830)

Jung obviously disagreed with Freud on this point (Jung, 1961), and Jungian analysis frequently enters the realm of a patient's spiritual or religious beliefs – another reason Jungian psychology has been dismissed as "mysticism" – but considering a patient's religious beliefs appears to be a natural part of symbol interpretation, and I think this is because religious symbols are derived from the same mechanism all other symbols emerge from, with the added components of *participation* and *mystery*. But despite the separation of psychology and religious thought, there appears to be a call for a more integrated approach that includes the consideration of a patient's spiritual "health" – without, obviously, espousing any particular religion (Bienenfeld and Yager, 2007). The reasons for this are based on the literature; religious patients, for example, have been shown to benefit from treatments that include their religious beliefs (Meador and Koenig, 2000). Religious belief is apparently positively related to mental health, including longevity (Helm *et al.*, 2000), lower stress (Koenig *et al.*, 1998), lower blood pressure (Larson and Koenig, 2000), and lower risk of suicide and drug abuse (Kuritzky, 1998), and it appears to be protective against adolescent depression (Miller *et al.*, 1997). McNamara (2009) suggests that religious belief as well as ritual are probably evolutionary adaptations, a conclusion drawn by many others (Haule, 2010; Hayden, 2003). All of this data further supports the idea that subjective symbols have profound mental and physical effects on health, particularly when they are "participated" in.

The dimensional analysis of symbols

In any case, archetypal symbols appear to be unconsciously constructed entities that are created via numerous innate ideas. Each of these contributors can be thought of as a "dimension," which I define as *aspect of meaning*. These correspond to what are essentially "themes" that "urge" behavior, feeling, and thought in one direction or another. They are not precise; rather, they are innate abstract idea-themes that are used combinatorially by the brain to generate a huge array of nonverbal images designed to grasp the present state of the organism/environment. When used, these various themes combine in a unique way to generate a particular symbol that comprises all of these themes to varying degrees. That is why I am calling them the "dimensions" of the symbol; it is an attempt at understanding this process in reverse – given a particular symbol, I ask, which themes did the brain use to generate it?

The themes are manifold, due to the large array of adaptations in the brain, and include all the innate concepts such as intentionality, objectness, image-schema, affect, essence, self, other, animal, gender, number, mother, father, enemy, tree, time, causation, morality, theory of mind, and visuo-spatial representation: all concepts generated via natural selection during the long evolution of our species. These ideas are rapidly acquired early in development and provide a substrate that we use to formulate our subjective world.

Dimensions

Let me state plainly that reducing any symbol into its components will unfortunately nullify some of the meaning that is inherent in the particular way the components are put together. A living human, for example, is composed of carbohydrates, fats, proteins, and DNA. But then, so is a dead human. They are of course *not* the same. Thus the "truest" way to appreciate a symbol is at face value as a whole. As Eliade warned, "To translate an image into a concrete terminology by restricting it to any one of its frames of reference is to do worse than mutilate it – it is to annihilate, to annul it as an instrument of cognition" (1952: 15). That is not my intent; rather, I wish to pick out thematic material in a symbol that might otherwise go unnoticed. Once all of the dimensions are considered, the reconstruction of the symbol will help gain *conscious* access to its meaning as completely as possible. Going through this exercise helps to bring the symbol into conscious appraisal in order to facilitate whatever you intend to do with it, whether that be to participate or not.

Internal/external axis: This axis includes all the boundary making related to "in-group" versus "outgroup" delineations. All cultures differentiate "home" versus "out there," and relate the home to the "center," and so many symbols may have this aspect as well.[7]

Masculine/feminine axis: Various aspects of "masculine" and "feminine" behavior and appearance are innately classified and so can find their way into many symbols that may have little to do with men and women in particular.

Kin/non-kin axis: Kin recognition and detection mechanisms may "push" a symbol along this axis, conceptually classifying a particular symbol as "kinlike" versus "non-kinlike" by either identifying it with other kin symbols or separating it from kin.

Predator/prey axis: Predatory behavior is innately recognized by the perceptual/conceptual system. Any animate symbol that displays predatory versus non-predatory behavior may have a degree of vague "predation" as part of its meaning.

Light/dark axis: The depiction of lightness and darkness in a symbol carries with it all the archetypal meanings of light and darkness previously reviewed. Combination of light and dark, as in a "striped animal," for example, may carry connotations of a combination of these two concepts.

Animate/inanimate: This dimension differentiates all animate things from non-animate things on the basis of behavior; so objects that are normally inanimate can behave "animately" along this dimension and contribute to symbols in this manner. This includes plants, which have similar properties to animals except they do not have intentionality or self-propelled movement, but rather an animate "essence" as well as a "biological" nature that separates them from inanimate objects like rocks or metals.

Vertical dimension: A large array of concepts are associated with vertical dimension, which includes "balance" since our upright posture demands it for proper functioning, and it is hardwired into our equilibrium system. Hence any aspect of verticality in either the environment (cliffs, mountains, caves, towers, etc.) or behavior (flight, falling, rising, etc.) may contain the inherent symbolic aspects of verticality.

Natural/artificial axis: Brain regions devoted to artifact recognition can differentiate symbols along this axis and identify them with humans especially. This is frequently seen in environments that are "natural," such as forests, caves or mountains, versus artifactual environments like shelters, towns, or cities. The degree of involvement and human intent, then, is what defines this axis.

Numerosity axis: The various meanings of the "deep" archetype of number, from one to four, can play a part in *any* symbol, since there is always at least one of them. Two, three, or four similar symbols appearing together may be indicative of separation of opposites, unification of opposing themes (like a synthesis or dynamic triad), or a fundamental division of chaotic data into a coherent system (like the visual system, which is a static quaternity).

Symmetry axis: Related to numerosity is *symmetry*; symmetry is nearly always going to be more positively regarded (in terms of affect) than asymmetry. This vague property can obviously represent a variety of meanings depending on the context, remembering that there are many types of symmetry that will range from perfect (circular) symmetry to complete asymmetry. Note that if two objects are being understood as "symmetric" they must at least be similar enough to warrant such a comparison. Trees are not "symmetrical" with butterflies – they are different "objects"; remember to think using innate concepts and not modern scientific (and hence learned) concepts since these are less likely to be used in symbol construction. In other words, trees and butterflies may be "symmetrical" in that they both comprise typical biological molecules, but at the holistic level, understood unconsciously, they are not symmetrical.

Left/right axis: The various aspects of left and right symbolism, with their origin in the hemispheric specialization, will play a part along this dimension, with "left" usually equating with the emotional, intuitive, less conscious but more informed right brain, and "right" corresponding with the rational, analytic, more conscious but more rigid left brain.

Purity axis: The vague concept of "purity" can also contribute to a symbol's meaning, and in fact this concept is frequently depicted in black/white or clear/opaque terms, and is related to innate folk biology adaptations to avoid infection. "Pure" things will be more positively appraised affectively (like symmetry is).

Fluid/non-fluid axis: Fluids like air and water are conceived differently than solids in terms of object boundaries and whether or not they are thought of in terms of "stuff" or numbered "things." Fluids are more changing and ephemeral but are frequently imbued with "essence" of some sort or another, and water and air have special significance in relation to life and animation.

Size axis: Size is frequently equated with significance, especially in comparison with other symbols, that is, the IMPORTANT IS BIG metaphorical mapping.

Time axis: The different ways in which time is conceptualized, whether linear or cyclical, can play a part in symbol construction. Symbols that change over time versus those that do not imply aspects of permanence versus malleability. Symbols that change but return to their original form imply cyclicity.

Essence axis: Related to change is the concept of "essence" – a symbol that changes must be seen as having the same essence if it is to be considered an "altered" symbol rather than just a completely different symbol altogether. Essence is another innate and hard to define aspect of an object that represents the "irreducible core" of the object.

Causation: Among the other "deep" archetypes, one must consider in the behavior of the symbol its "causal" relationship with other symbols in the narrative. Hindrance, helping, allowing, preventing, and "causing" are all aspects of the behavior of a symbol that will contribute to this dimension of the symbol's meaning, particularly in the way it interacts with other symbols.

Emotional axis: Rather than simply dividing symbols into "positive" or "negative" categories consider all the innate emotional systems that might be contributing to a symbol's meaning, including SEEKING, LUST, PANIC, CARE, RAGE, PLAY, and FEAR. Animate symbols can be understood by their behavior, whether it is aggressive, fearful, caring, or whatever, and inanimate symbols can be understood by the affects they evoke either in other characters or in the subject.

Color axis: All the subtleties of color symbolism will contribute to any particular symbol, be it black, white, red, or whatnot.

Personality axis: Perhaps most important of all is the idea that a symbol has a personality – this makes participation with it rather natural, if sometimes still baffling.

Relational patterns

In addition to a symbol's "dimensions," which are aspects that the symbol has in itself, remember that all metaphors and symbols are relational in nature. Therefore, the relational nature they are depicting will be inherent in the metaphorical structure. Innate relationships will play a large part in their construction, and, as before, will most often be based on evolutionarily relevant relationships. The relationship of a man and his wife, for example, will be more often of concern than the relationship between a man and a mud puddle (a rhinoceros might have a different opinion of this matter, however).

Examples of common relational patterns that a symbol may be depicting (none of these are mutually exclusive) include:

Father–Son
Father–Daughter
Mother–Son
Mother–Daughter
Male–Female
Self–Group
Self–Shadow or Persona (alternatively id–ego–superego interactions)
Conscious self–unconscious system (commonly underlying nearly all symbols)
Conscious self–nature/environment

Example of symbol dimension analysis

Here I will return to the eagle–bat pair I presented in the dream example I gave previously. I will consider each dimension in turn. First of all, the symbol appears as a pair of animals traveling together, and appeared before the dreamer (and therapist) encountered the crossroads. It is two animals, and therefore has a binary nature, but an asymmetrical one, in that there are not two eagles, but a bald eagle and a bat. Both are the "same size," so they seem "equal in significance." Also they are contrasted along the light/dark axis, as the bat was described as "shadowy" and the eagle as a white-headed bald eagle. Bats are normally nocturnal creatures that live in caves, whereas eagles soar in the high sun (these two observations are not likely to be innately known but represent learned aspects of their character that would be commonly incorporated into the symbolism). Both have the dimension of verticality (as do all flying animal symbols), which implies "higher" thinking or "spiritual" (i.e., symbolic or non-physical) thoughts, higher vantage points, freedom, and "divine" inspiration but also possible "precarious" aspects or height in its dangerous aspect. Both symbols could conceivably have a "predatory" aspect; however, they are flying peacefully together in the dream, and so are not behaving in typically predatory ways; therefore, this dimension would likely be considered irrelevant in this particular case.

Birds can fly and roam far and wide, are "independent" and unconnected with the "earth" or "ground," which is often concerned with physical reality. They are also characters of the open outdoors, as opposed to inner enclosed spaces. These features give the eagle a strong SEEKING quality so that it might qualify as a Self symbol. Note that if this is the case it contrasts with the much more ineffectual animus "maintenance workers" in the town later, after the subject separates from the therapist – perhaps a comment on how therapy is affecting this aspect of her personality and subjective world, meaning positively, during therapy, and reflecting the fear of helplessness afterward. The bat, since it is more "grounded" than an eagle, suggests the intimacy, containment, and refuge of the cave and darkness – this poses an interesting contrast to the eagle, in that they are both traveling together as allies. This "union of opposites" suggests further that the two of them together represent a "Self symbol," meaning a metaphorical representation of the subject's "guide toward health" at the time of the dream. Both are obviously animal symbols, and there does not appear to be a hint of kin–non-kin differentiation to this symbol pair.

The natural versus artificial axis is reflected in the setting where the eagle and bat are found – a forest. Note that they disappear when the subject enters the more "artificial" world of the town and its buildings. If it is a Self symbol, it is getting "lost" by disappearing, suggesting a causal implication in the removal of a natural setting which "causes" the eagle and bat to disappear into unconsciousness. The animals themselves are devoid of artificiality because they are animals. The "purity" axis comes into play only in that the bat is not purely dark, but brownish black in color – a very "earthy" tone that further suggests a play of opposites between it and the eagle and shows the color dimension of the symbol pair as well; the eagle is not entirely white, but has a brown body – a completely white eagle would have a dimension of "purity" to it (like the white dove) that the relatively more mundane eagle of the dream does not have. The fact that the birds are flying in the fluid medium of the air, rather than grounded or underwater, suggests aspects of swift change, but only in potential, since they are not "zipping around" but soaring calmly. Note also that the airy medium suggests the "breath of life," that is, wind, that is so important to the respiratory centers of the reptile brain. There is no left/right significance here, since the bat and eagle soar in circles around the dreamer, but with the eagle always closer to the dreamer than the bat – this has a spiral symbolism and also suggests a closeness with the eagle, which by its color appears more conscious; in other words, the bat is further away, which recalls the INTIMACY IS CLOSENESS mapping, wherein the bat is more "distant" and less well-known (i.e. more unconscious).

In time they do not change much, only soaring steadily, then disappearing abruptly. This suggests an aspect of permanence or at least timelessness, rather than rapid or cyclic change within the context of the dream. In terms of essence, the fact that the eagle and bat are traveling together suggests that they somehow share the same essence, which is why it could be a Self symbol – note that the aspect of "superiority" required for it to be a Self symbol is attained in its vertical, that is, "higher," position in space relative to the dreamer (and, I humbly submit, the therapist as well!). It is also superior in that it is an eagle, as opposed to a common wren, for example; the eagle is very important to American symbolism and is the national bird (i.e. the "totem animal" *fylgja* of the entire nation, if I may) – another connotation with the wider social milieu. Finally, in the affective dimension, the pair appear to be SEEKING, exploring serenely without desperation, perhaps a distant place or a new vantage point. They do not, by their behavior, appear to be fearful, angry, lustful, panicking, or concerned with caretaking. The other possibility is that they are flying for sheer joy, and are therefore reflective of PLAY circuitry at work.

As far as the relational pattern is concerned, the eagle and bat seem to be flying of their own accord, without much interaction from either myself or the dreamer. There does not appear to be any parent–child or self–group pattern evident in its behavior. The only pattern that does appear to fit is the conscious–unconscious pattern, wherein if we follow the assumption that the bird and bat are Self symbols, the dreamer appears to be traveling "with" the Self, which is nevertheless moving along of its own accord seemingly unaware of the those of us riding the bicycles.

Notice that this in-depth analysis is time consuming – it is recommended only for symbols that are rather mysterious, such as the eagle and bat in this dream. It is revealing since it uncovers perhaps unseen aspects of the innate brain architecture that contribute to its construction, but notice it does not provide a "final answer" as to its meaning, nor could it because of the ineffable core of meaning behind metaphors – there's no free lunch here. What it does do is highlight aspects of a symbol that may not have been obvious. Further treatment of this symbol might be to imagine a continued journey with it, perhaps engaging it symbolically via some kind of mental ritual or guided imagery – this would amount to participation in the dream symbolism *as if* it were a godlike being. For all the afore-mentioned reasons, I think such practice could lead to positive mind–body effects. McNamara (2009) provides further examples of how interactions with spirit beings can be beneficial in a number of ways, as well as some of the pitfalls of such practices.

Chapter 15

Molecules to mandalas

> Mythology is not allegorical; it is tautegorical. For mythology, the gods are beings that really exist; instead of being one thing and signifying another, they signify only what they are.
>
> Friedrich Wilhelm Scheller (1775–1874)

In this book I have adopted a largely "ahistorical" or cross-sectional approach to symbolism. I have ignored the way symbol systems change over time throughout history – this would be outside the scope of this work however, in future work I will indeed present such an analysis in "longitudinal" terms, because this is very important, too, and a key component of what I'm trying to explore.

As we have seen, the conscious self is only the latest addition to the hominid repertoire of adaptations; it is indeed powerful and highly open to change. It is the source of free will and our capacity for rational analysis as well as soaring complex thoughts. It is not infinitely powerful, however; consciousness has definite limitations. Furthermore, it rests upon a massive unconscious edifice millions of years in the making, but because of the limits of conscious processing – the "filter" – consciousness *feels* as if it contains everything we are and everything we can be. This is an illusion.

The evidence we have suggests that the mind contains an amazing array of instincts and adaptations capable of immense creativity. Furthermore, the unconscious mind is not simply a repository for infantile and irrational impulses. Rather, it contains all the basic plans required for life on earth as *Homo sapiens*, as she evolved in small foraging bands in the ancestral environment. These instincts self-organize and manifest themselves rapidly in development, becoming adaptations and generating common modes of thinking that are universal.

Looking over all the data reviewed thus far, we see that from the very start the genome uses the environment to suit its needs, which are ultimately replication. Over the course of development, every step of the way, it interacts with environmental data, material, and so on, but it does not simply take in "general information"; rather, it takes *specific* environmental data at *specific* times, in *specific* ways, and ignores a whole lot of other things, just as a consequence of the genetic structure. Thus the genome is responsible for *defining* the environment as well as using its information in preset and also emergent ways; hence the question of the innate structure of the mind, and the innate underpinnings of all the images we experience is a tricky one and not easily resolvable into "structure" and "content," since our genome anticipates and formulates human experience in species-specific ways right from the beginning. Recalling that I define things that are "innate" as anything that reliably emerges irrespective of personal historical variations, it appears that Jung's intuition of an innate collective unconscious was well founded, as multiple disciplines have shown the mind to have an impressive array of such innate mechanisms and forces. This is not controversial. Where all the vigorous theorizing and debate come in is when we try to figure out just *how* the innate mind interacts with the world, and what are the *causes* of our symptoms and experiences, which range from archetypal conflicts to idiosyncratic experiences. In psychiatry and psychology, literally hundreds of answers to this question exist.

Medical monotheisms

Theorists over the history of psychology have often tried to reduce everything in the mind to one thing or a small collection of principles. Freud initially attempted to explain everything in terms of the sex drive, later adding the "death instinct" (2010). Alfred Adler emphasized the power drive (Ansbacher and Ansbacher, 1964), where behaviorists emphasized "stimulus," "response," and "rewards" or "reinforcement." Some theorists reduce all symptoms and experiences in therapy to early attachments, making "attachment" the monotheism of these systems. Self psychology (Wolf, 2002) reduces everything we experience to deficits in "mirroring" and "idealization." Such simplification and reduction is a common practice in science, and indeed modern theoretical physics seeks to unify all forces into a single "Theory of Everything." Thus the drive toward unification and simplification seems strong in the human heart.

But whenever I hear such sweeping arguments, reducing everything we experience (even if limited to psychological symptoms) to a small few principles, I get suspicious. I sense the work of the verbal, analytic left hemisphere, for example, which likes to formulate nice, neat, tightly packed stories and ideas and furthermore likes to ignore or deny specifics, contradictions, and complexities. The left hemisphere needs the balance of the non-dominant right hemisphere, which questions, explores, is chaotic, emotional, and symbolic, even vague. And it is a curious fact that so many different theories result in effective therapies (reviewed in Benedetti, 2009);

thus there may be truth to all the above approaches, despite their vastly different theoretical rationale, which suggests that there is likely not a single determinant of psychic development and pathology, but many. Some also have suggested based on multiple comparative studies (Benedetti, 2009: 123–145; also Ahn and Wampold, 2001) that this is due to the commonalities of all therapies, including a thoughtful listener, a ritual-like setting, an introspective attitude, and so forth; this is not contradictory to the idea that multiple forces act upon consciousness, and focusing and differentiating any one of them may help facilitate psychological balance. In any case, evidence strongly supports traditional psychodynamic methods as highly effective modes of therapy (Shedler, 2010).

Jung argued that it was archetypes that organize and moved development and subjective experience, which could include all the above and many more, and he refused to speculate on how many archetypes there were, resisting the temptation to unify everything to simply one force or principle. One might argue that his concept of the Self is the exception to this (Hillman, 1977), but even though Jung felt that the psyche had a central organizing center, he discouraged analysts from reducing all dream images or clinical symptoms to it. If one dreamed of a snake, he argued for "sticking with the image" – that is, not reducing it to some kind of abstract process or developmental issue unless it fits: "The unconscious," said Jung in one of his seminars, always "says what it means" (1984: 30). Thus the snake is best viewed in itself as a complete symbol. It is an animate symbol and so has a personality; thus in the mind one should treat it as such rather than trying to reduce it to some theoretical construct, a past developmental issue, or whatever; in this respect Jung's approach is similar to the popular cognitive behavior therapy since it focuses less on causal speculations and more on present concerns and processes.

Jungian theory is therefore one of the few "polytheistic" theories of the mind, and there are two reasons that this may be a more appropriate and intuitively convincing approach than trying to reduce all psychology to a few basic principles. First, the very genome itself is not unified. It consists of many genes that often conflict with one another, and this conflict carries over into progressively more and more complex levels of "competition." For example, the neuroscientist Patrick McNamara puts forward a very plausible genetic explanation as to why we inherit a mind full of conflicting impulses and desires:

> there exist internal "agents" that differ over ultimate behavioral goals. These agents reflect differing sets of genes, the strategic "interests" of which are opposed to and in conflict with one another. This genetic conflict is reflected in the consciousness of the individual in whom the genes reside. . . . Genetic conflict is ubiquitous throughout the natural world. Organisms are composed of multiple genetic entities that do not

always share the same interests because they have different modes of inheritance.

(2009: 34–35)

Using this framework, and providing many more examples, he produces a model of a conscious self born into conflict:

> These genetic data substantially verify the claim that the default state of most organisms, including human beings, is internal conflict. We are a conglomeration of conflicting sets of genes, all of which are in competition with one another to pass copies of themselves down the generations. They build physiologic systems that assist them in that process, and among these systems are systems of the brain. . . . By far the greatest source of conflict around alternative courses of action arises out of conflicting internal desires that in turn are rooted in evolutionary genetic conflicts.

(38–39)

Later he continues:

> there may be several Minds or subpersonalities within a single person. The multiplicity of minds within a single person can even be seen in normal, healthy individuals when we dream.

(196)

Such comments remind quickly of Jung's theorizing on complexes and archetypal figures that emerge from the unconscious.

Thus these systems, each with separate goals and perspectives, battle with one another over which one will ultimately seize control of consciousness and direct the behavioral result (LeDoux, 1996, 2002). The sheer number of unconscious systems involved, singularly or (more likely) in various combinations, results in countless possibilities for internal conflicts and desires. There may indeed be an overarching Self principle that works toward reining in all this chaos, but to focus solely on that will likely miss many details.

In therapy I often see these conflicting systems waging war within a person's psyche. I was involved in one case of a bulimic who used laxatives and diuretics to induce vomiting by day, only to find himself binging on entire jars of peanut butter at night. Interestingly, this binging took place while the patient was in a semi-conscious altered state. Thus the two conflicting "complexes" that were influenced by the innate push for approval and social stature (among other things) the patient had attributed to relentless thinness, which waged war with the push to obtain nourishment – in this case the latter had been relegated to the unconscious, but that did not erase it; it only allowed it the ability to influence consciousness outside awareness. In many cases of posttraumatic stress disorder, I see a ferocious and warlike complex, obviously infused with a great deal of RAGE activity, conflicting with a terrified FEAR-infused complex, and these two fight one another and the conscious self in dreams and waking life.

The introduction of altered states of consciousness further enriches this interplay, and it may be that the capacity for such altered states evolved in order to help manage all this activity; such states include dreaming or waking activities such as the particular "zone" we get in when intensely involved in creative work, athletic activity, dancing, or especially religious activity such as ritual or enrapt prayer. I include some kinds of psycho-therapy in this list as well. The trance states induced by various techniques or entheogens are another way humankind has attempted to access these states for various reasons (Haule, 2010).

The second reason the "polytheistic" approach may be highly appro-priate is that these gene/environment forces, while certainly interconnected, are most easily visualized and understood *as they appear* in dreaming or otherwise vivid symbolic form, such as spirits, animals, gods, environments, and so forth. A powerful ghost or demon, with its clearly defined physical appearance, mentality, and so forth, when understood as a symbol and not a literal physical being, is the best way to see it because of the Great Mysteries effect of the brain's wiring. It combines all the innate elements (such as the dimensions discussed previously) we understand well and uses them to represent a deeper mysterious thing or process that would other-wise elude our understanding. Thus "sticking with the image" and treating it on its own terms outside too much theoretical reduction remains a very sensible approach.

These various symbols range from very personal images loaded with developmental, idiosyncratic associations, to timeless, primordial, and otherwise *archetypal* symbols that emerge with relative independence from personal factors, the latter of which tend to be rather intense. Most dream characters or otherwise subjectively experienced beings fall under a few overlapping categories: various aspects of ourselves,[1] or images of others that are important in our lives or have been important, such as dead loved ones, are included at this level. Deeper or further "removed" from these characters would be those beings that ancient cultures might classify as spirits, *fylgjur*, elves, fairies, "totem" animals, dwarves, giants, and other creatures of folklore as well as ideals, cultural icons, legendary heroes, and so forth (I include celebrities in this class for modern subjects). These beings are less personal by definition, since they have little content suggestive of any specific person or autobiographical memory but tend to have several generic qualities and are clothed in cultural ideals; moreover, they are never people known personally to the subject. Nevertheless, they still are more "local" due to their cultural group influence, and so like animus or anima

Table 2 Classification scheme for non-physical/symbolic "beings" that can emerge in dream and other altered states of consciousness

"Distance" from consciousness self	Types of beings seen in dream or altered state
Personal	Ego, persona, "spirits" of other people, ancestors, shadows
Semi-personal	Unknown people or spirit beings, anima/animus, faeries, elves
	Dwarves, culture heroes, celebrity "spirits", *fylgjur*
Archetypal	Human-like and animal gods and goddesses, primal environs
	Tripartite universe, Great Tree/Mountain/Ocean
Ultimate	Self, godhead figures, Tao, Wyrd, "demiurge," "Void"

characters they contain some aspects of personal history but not as much as the more personal beings from the first group. Deeper than these are archetypal figures such as gods, who are virtually immune to personal history and simply impose upon consciousness along their own innately driven trajectories; they are often clothed in culturally acquired imagery, but these clothings of names or aspects, however, are conscious afterthoughts, for the gods who emerge into our experience come with a tremendous motivational force, fixing us upon them with world-shattering emotion. We give them vague, abstract names because they exist outside of our typical experiential categories and strain the boundaries of time, space, power, knowledge, comprehension, and so forth; finally, they are profoundly ineffable. To try to comprehend them we clothe them in imagery we can make sense of. Finally, at the deepest level, of course, are the symbols of grand, cosmic integration and transformation such as the Self symbols. All of these beings, forces, and entities likely exist in a nested hierarchy of sorts, but often times are in opposition to one another as well. These hypotheses are presented in Table 2.

No doubt there is overlap in these four categories, as well as numerous interconnections and nested heirarchies. It seems plausible that the further "down" one goes on this list, the stronger weight will be given in the activities of less personal/historical regions of the brain (such as the old mammal and reptile brains) in correlation. Furthermore, it seems that the further down one goes, the less often such images will appear across a person's lifetime.

Gods and emotions

For the vast majority of our history, humankind has understood the world in terms of "gods" or "spirits." This is a natural way to understand our experience that utilizes the best tools our brains have for interacting with our surrounding environment. And notice that what is traditionally thought of as a "god" or "spirit" has much in common with emotions and instincts, which are continually interacting organizers of subjective experience; emotions and/or instincts are universal, as are their modes of expression. They do not die, and they influence us (meaning our autobiographical selves) as if "from outside" ourselves due to their unconscious and more ancient origin. Note also that many gods' names *are actually emotions*; the Greek god Eros means "sexual love" and is the source for our word *erotic*, the goddess Psyche's name means "soul" and is obviously the root for words like *psychology*. The great Germanic god Odin means "fury." Other gods are named after universal elements of the environment; the Vedic mother goddess Mahimata literally means "mother earth," the Indian father god Varuna means "sky," and Thor means simply "the thunderer." A pre-Christian god of the Romans was Dis Pater, which translates as "Wealthy Father," and the Irish Celtic chief god was Dagda, "the Good God." They spoke of "the Good God" (in the case of Dagda) in the same manner as many now refer to "God" – it is easy to let the language barrier confuse the issue here; God is not his "name," as we are named, but rather his title, and the same goes for the gods of the ancients in their own language. Other examples from Norse myth are Freyr ("Lord"), Freya ("Lady"), and Tyr ("God").

In our symbolic way of understanding the world, imperfect as it is, we come to *know* new things about it, however ineffably, that do not require "leaps of faith" to cross the mind–body divide, because there is no divide. If a god happens to be one of them, then so be it, but this means that all efforts to find him or her "out there," then, will naturally fail, since one will never find a god under a rock. But so what? Nothing else meaningful exists out there either without the cooperation of the brain. Furthermore, treating these entities *as if* they were real characters is perhaps not so foolish (depending on how far you take it), because of the involvement of such largely unconscious aspects of brain activities, known to behave with relatively high levels of sophistication, as they interface directly with the physical environment.

Underneath (or above) all of these is an organizing system that probably operates via the mathematics of chaos theory and nonlinear dynamics as a homeorhetic system that adjudicates the activities of these implicit systems[2] – what better way to represent this system than an overarching deity or principle (like Tao or Wyrd) that is utterly mysterious and the "source" of all things we experience, including all the gods, spirits, ancestral ghosts, and so forth?

Jung described that when visiting the Elgyoni tribe of Africa the people worshipped "the moment of the dawn" (Jung, 1961). He initially misunderstood them to be worshipping the sun itself, and when he asked them if this was so, they actually laughed at him. What they were worshipping was actually the particular moment, and no doubt the state of mind that went with it as they contemplated their deity. I don't mean to assert that *all* peoples understand gods in this subtle fashion – certainly, many people take gods to be literal entities wandering about the countryside. But I think that still many more, especially if pressed, will revert to a more symbolic way of describing what they are feeling. And of course, there are many religious thinkers who see religious thought and empirical science as fully compatible. One neopagan religious leader put it to me this way: "We create the gods, and they create us."[3]

So why not simply reduce gods to mental states enrapt in a particular moment? Because *the god* is much more vivid, more descriptive, and perhaps contains deeper significance; this is because it is a symbol, and like all symbols, it describes ineffable things with images, stories, and relationships in preverbal terms that cannot be duplicated with concrete descriptions. Furthermore, the god has a personality, however dimly understood, and can be approached as a being with mentality, intent, and purpose, just like other collections of atoms that we attribute these qualities to as we encounter them every day. Dream characters are such beings, who, though devoid of physicality per se, still have personality and possibly even memory (McNamara, 2009), and so also qualify, and dream characters can be experienced in altered dreamlike states outside of sleep. Interestingly, such characters have a peculiar quality in that they do not seem to be reflectively aware; dream characters have motivation, purpose, and the ability to be interacted with, but they tend not to be terribly introspective, internally conflicted, or dealing with their own subpersonalities – perhaps they do not need to be. Dream characters also share this streamlined quality with the gods and other characters of myth and folklore (Luthi, 1986, 1987). I doubt this is a coincidence. Rather, such beings are fairly straightforward in nature rather than being complex as we are, but have immense motivational muscle, are awesome and have an ineffable and antinomy-like quality to them, but this mysterious nature is due to their symbolic nature and/or our own difficulties comprehending them. Such characters know what they want even if we have difficulty understanding what it is, but they do not seem internally divided on what they want. Unlike us, gods and spirits never need psychotherapy.

The symbolizing brain: Exploring a rational, empirical approach to myth, religion, and ritual

In any case, the central hypothesis of this work is that the continued neurobiological analysis of universal or "archetypal" symbolism will continue to prove useful in further differentiating our understanding of symbol generation, and perhaps open the way to an empirical approach to mythic and religious thinking and being that includes our knowledge of the biological sciences. Anthony Stevens (2002), however, observes that with the exception of a small handful of writers, analytical psychologists appear uninterested in biology. Stevens advises against the continuation of this trend:

> Jungian discourse has become increasingly *disembodied*, as if the physiological correlates of psychic events were of little or no account. . . . This is in marked contrast to Jung's own position: "We keep forgetting that we are primates and that we have to make allowances for these primitive layers in our psyche. . . . Without any body, there is no mind and therefore no individuation."
>
> (55, emphasis in original; Jung quote in McGuire and Hull, 1977)

I couldn't agree more, and I feel this trend is changing. Some analytical psychologists have called for a renewed approach to Jungian psychology that advocates a close alliance with empirical sciences (Haule, 2010; Knox, 2003; Kotch, 2000). I hope analytical psychologists heed this call – I think both fields have quite a bit to offer each other. Jung's theory was originally a biological one, and therefore it should remain so if it is to be useful to physicians and therapists. Furthermore, as I hope I have shown, the evidence backing Jung's concept of archetypes and the "collective unconscious" *as he defined it*, and not as many critics have held up in straw-man effigies, holds up remarkably well to the advances in a multitude of research venues; others have noticed that many of Freud's formulations hold as well (Solms and Turnbull, 2002). Further research, I feel, will continue to refine these ideas.

Everything we know, learn, desire, love, feel, think, fear, and imagine – which includes our symbols – is organized by that most enigmatic and complex creation that has emerged from the mysterious primal chaos of the universe: the brain. This brain is not a blank slate; it is more like a zoo that sees its subjective universe naturally and inevitably in terms of gods, goddesses, animals, lovers, heroes, mothers, fathers, elders, monsters, and demons, as well as heavenly golden realms and fiery kingdoms. This is our inherited birthright; culture and upbringing elaborate on this extensive framework, fleshing out the details, and coloring in the lines. But the framework remains active throughout life, a variously constructive and destructive entity (at least from the point of view of the conscious self) capable of novel creations and unexpected shifts in our experience.

This symbolizing capacity is a fundamental ability of our brains, and encompasses the way we understand everything in our life. In this way it shapes our dream imagery, our twice-told stories, myths, and sacred beliefs, our art and even our science, and when it malfunctions it becomes psychosis, depression, mania or a host of other problems. It can symbolize seemingly anything (though anything the brain *couldn't* symbolize would be outside all speculation by definition!), but preferentially chooses themes that have been important to us over evolutionary time – things that are motivationally most relevant. The most important symbols – the archetypal ones – are those that involve our emotional systems; in neurobiological terms, these include but are not limited to the systems of RAGE, PANIC/ CARE, FEAR, SEEKING/LUST, and PLAY that are extant in all mammals, they subserve all the evolutionary adaptations found buried in even the most complex human behavior, and likely drive a huge part of our subjective world. Indeed, Haule argues that "symbols are the brain's interpretation of the bodily state itself . . . the symbol appears in consciousness as a sort of report from the brain about the state of my body" (2010: 259–260), to which I would add, in a particular inseparable environmental context. Thus they are symbols of the whole of subjective experience, both "internal" and "external." Symbols are thus highly compact statements containing volumes of information.

When viewed like this, the "function" of dreaming becomes nothing more or less than the function of symbolic thought in general, and of other altered states: it is an attempt to grasp things that are not so easily grasped by our limited neurobiological systems. Thus dreaming does not necessarily subserve any particular function such as "threat simulation" (Revonsuo, 2000), "mood regulation" (Kramer, 2007), "sleep protection" (Freud, 1900), or even Jung's more general "compensation" (1974) per se. It may subserve all these things, or none. Ironically, the so-called "neurocognitive" model of dreaming of Foulkes (1999) and Domhoff (2003), which views dreaming as a special type of general cognition involving visuospatial reasoning, most closely matches the model I present here. Domhoff, however, eschewed all psychoanalytic and Jungian interpretations of dreaming and felt they were unsupported by any evidence, and remarked that many Jungian ideas could be understood in terms of "merely" cross-cultural metaphors.

But here's the rub: there is nothing "mere" about metaphors. They permeate everything we do and think about. Moreover, metaphors are rooted in our bodily experience, our visuospatial cognition and our innate capacities such as theory of mind, human recognition systems, or innate folk biology. Pioneers in the cognitive science of religion propose similarly that religious and ritual expressions are a consequence of our normal universal human mental makeup (McCauley and Lawson, 2002), much as I present here (though I emphasize more personal elements such as dreams and psychodynamic processes). When generated unconsciously and tied to our innate emotional systems, they take on a powerful life of their own, and act relatively autonomously in comparison with the conscious self. Therefore, the reason they are cross-culturally appearing (in theme, anyway) is that they are founded upon our shared neurobiological heritage; but any shared neurobiological heritage that forms the basis for metaphors is "archetypal" by definition.

Human brains come into the world prepared for life as a forager in a savannah-like world, but capable of flexible adaptation and creative problem solving. But despite this flexibility, we still formulate experience in terms of a mother and father, an elder, a tribe, an "outside" enemy. We expect animals (particularly snakes and spiders!) and other agents with goals; we expect objects, and a vertically oriented environment, complete with gravity, light and darkness, as well as red, green, yellow and blue things, trees and water. And when the time is right, we expect a mate to exist, and will search for one to the ends of the earth. Thus the most emotionally significant things that we sense consciously or unconsciously will come to be represented by these images to generate meaning, because we understand them best.

And this meaning is our evolutionary birthright. The above expectations have consequences when they are not met, just as not being fed has consequences for hunger. When proper development is disrupted, conflicted, or traumatized, our minds will try to understand the situation, and try to rectify it to serve our emotional needs; these situations will become symbolized with particular furor by our symbolizing brains. Disrupted attachments or emotional traumas will become depicted in this fashion, and the deeper layers of the brain/mind – which is foundational and nearly identical in everyone – will try to find a solution, sometimes in vain, to rectify the archetypal needs of attachment, purpose, self-worth, connection, meaning, power, transcendence, security, love, and many other things yet to discover.

Throughout this book we have explored how our innate emotional systems manifest in a variety of symbolic dimensions; PANIC systems appear correlated with imagery of social isolation and cold/wintery landscapes, darkness, loneliness, and so forth. RAGE correlates with predatory animals, destructive people, rampaging creatures, violent conflict, blood, war and destruction, and so forth; such imagery is particularly evident in posttraumatic stress disorder and manic dreams. SEEKING appears to manifest in "water of life" or deeply meaningful engagement with life, deities, abundance, fertility, and all sorts of powerful religious experiences, and lack thereof often evokes imagery of desolation, lifelessness, emptiness, decay, and death. FEAR often correlates with darkness, being chased, chaos, being trapped, terrifying creatures, or environmental situations. PLAY systems likely correlate with images of activities that involve laughing, undirected rough and tumble behavior, music, or other activities engaged in for pure joy or mischief. And of course LUST involves sexual behavior and imagery. But the possibilities for combinations of these motivating systems, in concert with personal history and cultural learning, expand exponentially in every human lifetime to include all sorts of highly complex symbols, narratives, relationships, and patterns. Thus we all have a great pantheon of beings ranging from prosaic to fantastic, all engaging in timeless patterns of mythic proportion. The particular state of consciousness we are in makes them more or less visible, but the neurobiological activity they are associated with continues on.

Appendix

Affective neuroscience and imagery

As I agree with the idea that a symbol is the "clothing of affect in image" (Colman, 2010), in this appendix I explore some of the finer and more technical details of the innate emotional systems we all share in order to better understand how this may work neurobiologically; I include it here for specialists who want a more detailed account of the emotional systems of the brain that I discuss throughout the book. This section therefore assumes knowledge of brain anatomy and reviews several human and animal studies in greater detail than elsewhere in the book. You have been warned.

Affective neuroscience postulates that emotions derive from ancient, highly conserved regions of the brain, and include the SEEKING, PANIC, FEAR, RAGE, LUST, PLAY, and CARE systems. The SEEKING system (also see LeDoux, 2002: 246–252; and Solms and Turnbull, 2002) is a neurobiological system involved in motivating organisms toward exploration, curiosity, interest, and expectancy that is present in all mammals. This *self-stimulatory* system consists neurobiologically of mostly tonically active (as opposed to cyclically or flexibly active) dopaminergic paths of the lateral hypothalamic corridor, which runs from the ventral tegmental area to the nucleus accumbens – stimulation of these circuits in animals evokes highly energetic exploratory and search behaviors. This system corresponds to "intense interest," "engaged curiosity," and "eager anticipation" in humans, always recognizing that primitive emotional behavior in humans is likely to be overlain by all sorts of social and environmental modulation – but the driving circuitry remains the same. In humans, stimulating this area generates feelings that "something very interesting" is going on (Heath, 1963; Quaade *et al.*, 1974), and is associated with intense "feelings of environmentally engaged aliveness" (Panksepp, 2005: 47), a fact further attested to by the observed effects of psychostimulants such as amphetamines and cocaine, which energize this system. The importance of this system in consideration of archetypal symbolism is its connection with higher brain mechanisms:

there are now many reasons to believe that forethoughts . . . do in fact emerge from the interactions of the SEEKING system with higher brain mechanisms, such as the frontal cortex and hippocampus, that generate plans by mediating higher-order temporal and spatial information processing. Indeed, circuits coursing through the LH can trigger a hippocampal theta rhythm, which . . . is an *elemental signal of information processing in that structure.*

(Panksepp, 1998: 151, emphasis added)

The SEEKING system, then, is an innate, self-generated system involved with exploration and information gathering and processing – key aspects of symbol generation in cognitive terms, especially for a symbolically vigorous species such as *Homo sapiens.* This system has been linked to increased *pattern finding activity* in humans, and when abnormally activated is associated with delusional thinking in schizophrenia (Panksepp, 1998: 161– 162). Working normally, however, it facilitates the recognition of patterns in the environment, which are closely linked with metaphor generation and hence symbol-making activity in humans – it is particularly active, notably, in dreaming. Furthermore, there is evidence that organisms work toward a homeostatis of SEEKING activity as measured through its link to REM sleep, that is, self-stimulation and SEEKING behavior increases in REM-deprived animals (Steiner and Ellman, 1972). It seems that a certain amount of SEEKING is endogenous, innate, and necessary for proper functioning in all vertebrates. The SEEKING system is primed to respond to evolutionarily derived mechanisms and orchestrates the "incentive-directed psychobehavioral 'energy' of the animal" (Panksepp, 1998: 168), which includes higher complex motivations in humans, translating evolutionarily important external and internal information into an appetitive, exploratory, and escalated information-processing response. Just to show how this is linked to human experience, it has been shown that when the SEEKING system is pharmacologically dampened, it is associated with feelings of anergia and dysphoria in humans (Voruganti and Awad, 2004). Being deprived of symbol-making activity, it seems, is strongly associated with depressive mood states. Finally, there are a number of correlates between the SEEKING system and mythic expressions such as the "wellspring of life" and the many descriptions of the various underworlds wherein energy, life, power, and other vague but important things emerge; I explore these in detail elsewhere (Goodwyn, 2010b).

Frustration of the SEEKING system, as well as pain and irritation, can also activate the RAGE system, which "we share from the neurodynamics of subcortical circuits we share homologously with other animals" (Panksepp, 1998: 187). This system, which elicits aggressive, angry attack responses, can be generated by stimulating the same brain regions, notably the periaqueductal gray, the medial, and ventrolateral hypothalamus and the amygdala electrically or pharmacologically in humans and all mammalian species studied (Miczek, 1987). Direct electrical stimulation of the RAGE system in humans results in reports of feelings of intense rage (Hitchcock and Cairns, 1973; Mark *et al.*, 1972). Autonomic response to stimulation of this system results in elevation of heart rate, blood pressure, body temperature, and blood flow. The RAGE system directs, sensitizes, and activates implicit perceptual, judging, and memory systems, and brings anger and plans for revenge to the surface when activated by appropriate environmental conditions (Christianson, 1992; Stein *et al.*, 1990). Like all affective systems, the higher cortical appraisal systems co-opt the older affective motivational systems that direct implicit perceptual, judging, and memory systems, and hence the explicit system that is built upon them. This fact is important to remember in our discussion of how human emotions work to generate affect-laden symbols. The SEEKING system is also closely linked to the LUST system, which has obviously evolved to direct mate-seeking behavior (Panksepp, 1998, 2005).

The FEAR system, which involves the periventricular gray, central, and lateral areas of the amygdala, the anterior and medial hypothalamus and the lower brain stem and spinal cord, can invoke elevated heart rate and blood pressure, the startle and freeze response, and elimination and perspiration in mammals (Panksepp, 1998: 212–213). Electrical stimulation of this area in animals is associated with profound escape and aversion behavior (Panksepp, 2005).

The PANIC system evolved from early reptilian pain circuits and mediates feelings of social isolation, and separation distress in infants. It motivates the organism toward reestablishing broken social bonds. In fact, the mammalian brain contains a highly integrated emotional system involved in maintaining attachments, likely as a result of longer development times and the need to maintain much greater parental care behavior. This system, preceded by brain systems involved in thermoregulation, pain sensation, and avoidance, as well as rudimentary reptilian mother–infant parental bonding, mediates separation distress behavior when animals are socially deprived (associated with reduction in opioid activity in humans, see Zubieta *et al.*, 2003), and social comfort when satisfied (and associated with endogenous opioid release; see Keverne *et al.*, 1989). The PANIC system involves the dorsomedial hypothalamus, ventral septal area, preoptic area, and sites in the bed nucleus of the stria terminalis (which are also heavily involved in the sexual and maternal behavior circuitry). Persistent social isolation and loss appears to activate this system to produce panic, anxiety and later depression *in all mammals* (Panksepp, 1998: 275–276; Panksepp, 2005; cf. Dickinson and Eva, 2006). Social contact appears to be required for survival as abandoned animals exhibit anaclytic depression and usually die (Panksepp *et al.*, 1991), and social environment has been shown to modulate affective responses to pain and increase behavioral indices of pain in humans and animals (reviewed in Panksepp, 2005).

Finally, the PLAY system creates an impulse in all mammals to engage in rough-and-tumble activity that arises spontaneously early in development – this behavior is sensitive to deprivation and animals deprived of play activity will increase play activity once allowed (Panksepp, 1998: 281). The need for play is contingent on satisfaction of basic needs; hunger and fear can inhibit play (Siviy and Panksepp, 1985). With respect to this system,

> The systematic nature of the results . . . affirms that the urge to play is an intrinsic function of the mammalian nervous system . . . the evolutionary roots probably go back to an ancient PLAY circuitry shared by all mammals in essentially homologous fashion.
>   (Panksepp, 1988: 282; Thor and Holloway, 1984)

This source of exuberant joy, useable as an independent reward in humans and animals, then, appears to be hardwired into our neurobiological makeup rather than being solely explainable on the basis of nurture (Panksepp, 2005). This system is distinct from the more serious SEEKING system and in fact appears to operate in opposition to it.

Interestingly, the PLAY system appears to extend into tickling responses, which are observed in all mammals (Panksepp, 1998: 287; see also Panksepp, 2005, 2006), and "play sounds," which resemble laughter in a variety of independently observed ways. Play sounds accompany "tickling" stimulation when applied to conserved areas of the body such as the nape of the neck and upper flank regions, and appear to be a mammalian birthright that promotes social bonding across species (Panksepp, 2005: 55). Note also that laughing is observed in blind and deaf children (Eibl-Eibesfelt, 1989). The play system is also likely to be the neurological substrate for the "theory of mind" ability (Panksepp, 1998: 289), and is mediated by activity in the parafascicular and posterior thalamic nuclei, which are, not surprisingly, associated with human laughter (Sterns, 1972) and unrelated to neocortical regions (Pellis et al., 1992). Overactivity of the PLAY system has been implicated in attention deficit hyperactivity disorder and mania (Panksepp, 1998), and opioids have been shown to increase activity of PLAY circuits in humans and other animals (Panksepp, 2005).

Notes

Chapter 1

1 I provide an in-depth discussion about the "blank slate" idea as it relates to the theory of archetypes and innateness (Goodwyn, 2010a); this essay offers several points of view on the subject for interested specialists.

2 Panksepp knew B. F. Skinner (the founder of behaviorism) personally and actually pled with him in a 1987 letter to abandon the traditional ultrapositivistic behaviorist stance that internal representations and subjective mental states are unsuitable for psychological study – that is, the "black box" mentality. Skinner was unconvinced to his death (Panksepp, 1998: 12).

3 I am indebted to the Jungian analyst Jerry Ruhl (Johnson and Ruhl, 1997, 2000, 2007) for his help in carefully defining the archetype in a way that stays as true as possible to Jung's original intuitions and avoids reductionist and reifying fallacies. Notably, I consider the archetype as more of a process than a "thing."

Chapter 2

1 Panksepp takes issue with evolutionary psychology for a number of reasons that are based more on methodology than content; I explore this and other criticisms of evolutionary psychology more thoroughly elsewhere (Goodwyn, 2010a); what is important here is the agreement that evolution is highly relevant to the mind, particularly in our basic emotional motivations. Note that I am *not* referring to "mental modules," as strictly defined by the philosopher Jerry Fodor (1983), but something less restrictive and much better supported by the literature. As Haule (2010) insightfully observes, instinctive patterns are more like complexities within complexities rather than isolated modules or "building blocks."

2 John Bowlby developed his theory of "attachments," that is, bonds between mother and infant, based on careful studies of rhesus monkeys and other primates, including humans. He noted the startling similarities between human children and young nonhuman primates in their behavior toward their mothers.

3 For those familiar with brain anatomy, the limbic system includes the brain regions known as the hypothalamus, part of the thalamus, the amygdala, hippocampus, fornix, many of the basal forebrain nuclei, septum, part of the cingulate gyrus and the mamillary bodies.

4 There are other models of consciousness (reviewed in Panksepp, 1998: 300–323; cf. also Dennett, 1992), though these do not emphasize neuroscientific data.

5 Lamarck was a predecessor to Darwin who theorized that species could change due to experiences during its lifetime – in other words, for example, giraffes grew

long necks by stretching to reach higher branches, and these experiences were passed on to the next generation. Lamarckianism gave way to Darwinian evolution.

Chapter 3

1 For a critique of behaviorism from the field of affective neuroscience, see Panksepp, 1990.
2 The overlap in sensory processing and mental image generation is large but not perfect (Kosslyn *et al.*, 2001). This should not be surprising, since if it were identical we would presumably not be able to distinguish fantasy from reality (such as may be the case in schizophrenia). The details of these differences are still under investigation, but in general the rule holds.
3 Exceptions such as lucid dreaming (Laberge, 1991) and other variations (Purcell *et al.*, 1993) notwithstanding. These exceptions are beyond the scope of this book but do not contradict my thesis.
4 Strictly speaking, I should refer to these regions as "more conscious" or "less conscious" rather than an either/or "conscious/unconscious" designation, as research shows consciousness to be a "layered" phenomenon rather than a unitary phenomenon (Watt and Pincus, 2004). Jung presaged this idea crudely (1961).
5 Flying is obviously not related to our evolutionary history; however, I suspect this is a common *symbolic* representation for reasons I will explore later.
6 Hobson *et al.*'s original theory that the brain cobbles together a narrative from random deep brain firing assumed that dream content was intrinsically random and meaningless, however, more recently they have retreated from this position to one that is agnostic (2000).
7 The studies cited in Strauch and Meier (1996) showed that fantasy material is more densely populated with characters, and contains more familiar settings, animals and fictional creatures; overall, however, the differences were relatively minor.
8 In the text what I simplify with the word "image" is actually the more technically precise "representations of states of affairs within a given computational system."
9 This measurement as it relates to attractiveness and fecundity is actually somewhat more complex than a simple "lower waist-to-hip ratio is better" rule, but in general it holds cross-culturally. See Sugiyama (2005: 321–326) for complete discussion.
10 Mechanisms for recognition of high genetic quality males exist also, such as muscularity, height, prominent chin and brows, "v-shaped" torso, and so on, and are reviewed in Sugiyama (2005).
11 Here I use the standard practice of all caps for mentalese.
12 Metonymy is the process of making a part of an object represent the whole object and is a common occurrence in language (Pinker, 2007)
13 Provided we recognize it as the subjective aspect of a monistic brain/mind phenomenon (Solms and Turnbull, 2002).

Chapter 4

1 Theriomorphic symbols combine human and animal attributes; examples from mythology include the Minotaur (man-bull), the mermaid (woman-fish) and most of the Egyptian pantheon; there are many others worldwide.

2 More severely brain damaged subjects had a larger number of dream characters than mildly damaged ones (Kramer and Roth, 1975) – further linking consciousness, in this case impaired via brain damage, and complexes to dream imagery/symbols. If consciousness is damaged, and dream characters represent implicit systems, one would expect just such a result because the personality is less coherent and more "divided."

3 For any sticklers out there, I should clarify that when I mention unconscious symbols I mean, unconsciously generated and perceived by consciousness in a state of dream, reverie, trance, intoxication, psychosis, or otherwise altered state of downmodulated processing in conscious brain regions.

4 This filter may be at least in part due to orbitofrontal inhibitory processing, which is, again, downmodulated in dreams and fantasy altered states (Solms and Turnbull, 2002).

5 Identifying information and details have been changed for patient privacy.

6 I am indebted to the author Ben Waggoner, who is fluent in Old Norse and Old English, for his assistance in gathering and interpreting the *fylgja* lore.

7 Waggoner notes (personal communication, 2010) that the only version extant of this saga is a translation from the original Latin, now lost, thus this terminology may not be exact.

8 The Jungian analyst George Hogenson (2009), for example, has observed that artificial intelligence theory shows how simple environment response circuits can generate organized behavior that appears "algorithmic"; these action patterns are therefore unresolvable self-environment systems and illustrate the "blurriness" of the boundary between self/environment that probably applies to most unconscious systems.

Chapter 5

1 It is beyond the scope of the present work to explore complex variations such as might occur in homosexual or transgendered individuals – Jungians have indeed already examined these concepts in detail.

Chapter 6

1 By this I mean that women prefer men who are heterozygous with them at the major histocompatibility alleles. This should be valued in primary partners in order to limit infections within families. The fact that the preference for dissimilar MHC proteins did not vary with ovulation, and the preference for multiply heterozygous mates actually *increased outside* the fertile period suggest that women have an adaptation to prefer these men for long-term partners, because these men would be more likely to produce multiple disease-resistant offspring in a long-term partnership but would confer less of an advantage in short-term matings, since short-term matings are by definition *short term*, so any diseases he may get are less likely to be passed to the female through long-term cohabitation.

Chapter 7

1 Autism, for example, is a neurodevelopmental disorder in which mother attachments are highly impaired no matter what the behavior of the mother is.

Chapter 9

1 And in the absence of severe mental disturbance/brain damage.
2 Other parallels exist in Hebrew, Christian, Greek, and Mithraic symbolism, which see the raven as an oracular symbol capable of communication with the divine spheres (Tressider, 2005).

Chapter 11

1 It should be noted that chimpanzees react strongly to storms and engage in "rain dance" rituals in response to them (Haule, 2010: 186–196).
2 Freudian defense mechanisms, incidentally, also have a strong backing in empirical research. See Luborsky and Barrett (2006) for a review.
3 Note also that when taken to the extreme, this symbolism can create harsh dualisms of what is "good" and "bad," as observed, for example, in the religious reforms of Zarathustra (ancient Persian religion), which were so influential to Christianity (Puhvel, 1987). In this system all the gods and spirits were seen as part of the "truth" (personified as the supreme god Ahuramazda) or "the lie" (personified as the evil god Ahriman)

Chapter 12

1 Knox and I discuss the finer points of what "innate" means in Goodwyn, 2010a; I do not entirely agree with her (2003) definition of the archetype-as-such for reasons that go beyond the scope of this book, but the fundamental assignation of image schemata as deeply archetypal I do not dispute.
2 This is not to say that language shapes our concepts of causation; rather, it is the other way around (Pinker, 2007).
3 What I am calling the "conscious self" is analogous to what Damasio calls the autobiographical self; this construct is correlated with the activity of the dorso-lateral prefrontal cortex, the hippocampus and the association areas of the parietal cortex in the brain.
4 Or also an increased relative activity of the so-called "default network" of medio-cortical and subcortical brain regions (Buckner et al., 2008).

Chapter 14

1 This applies not only to physiological changes but to other sensory information as well: multiple investigators have shown that subliminally presented stimuli come to be symbolically incorporated into spontaneous imagery in dream reports or reports from subjects in quiet wakefulness and sensory deprivation conditions (reviewed in Fiss, 1993). Note, however, that not just any stimuli affect dream imagery; rather, only ones apparently related to evolutionary fitness appear to find their way in.
2 I will be exploring this subject in much greater depth in future work.
3 The opposite of the placebo, or "nocebo" effect has also been demonstrated in a variety of settings; furthermore, there does not appear to be a single placebo effect but many (Benedetti et al., 2005, 2007; Benedetti, 2009).
4 Lakoff and Johnson (1999) argue that ubiquitous metaphors are not "genetic" – which is not the same thing as saying they are innate – but acquired through statistical learning mechanisms; hence it might appear that my appeal to

evolutionary psychology is unwise. But their position on metaphor acquisition has been forcefully challenged by Pinker (2007) on several grounds that go beyond the present work. In any case, the fact that phylogenetically relevant specializations are reliably acquired is not controversial – what is debated is whether or not they are primarily or secondarily acquired, which is of little consequence to my present model.

5 Perhaps until we evolve into something else, that is.

6 I am of course indebted to the famous anthropologist Lucien Levy-Bruhl (1922) for the inspiration for this terminology. This also includes participation in "magic" rituals, the subject of a future volume.

7 Psychologists will recognize that the so-called CONTAINMENT as well as the DIVISION image schemata are included here.

Chapter 15

1 Such as the image Jung referred to as the "persona" – or the "mask" we show the world.

2 Homeorhesis means "similar flow," meaning that a homeorhetic system will tend toward the same flowing dynamic over time. It is contrasted with a homeostatic system in that a homeostatic system is less dynamic, returning to the same "state" rather than being a constant flow. See Prigogine and Stengers (1988) for more detail on these concepts of chaos theory.

3 Diana Paxson, author of numerous books on neopaganism, personal communication, 2010.

Bibliography

Abell, F., Happe, F. and Frith, U. (2000). Do Triangles Play Tricks? Attribution of Mental States to Animated Shapes in Normal and Abnormal Development. *Journal of Cognitive Development*, 15: 1–20.

Aboitiz, F. and Garcia, R. V. (1997). The Evolutionary Origin of the Language Areas in the Human Brain. A Neuroanatomical Perspective. *Brain Research Reviews*, 25: 381–396.

Ackerman, B. (1981). Young Children's Understanding of a False Utterance. *Developmental Psychology*, 31: 472–480.

Ader, R. and Cohen, N. (1982). Behaviorally Conditioned Immunosuppression and Murine Systemic Lupus Erythematosus. *Science*, 215: 1534–1536.

Adler, N. E., Espel, E. S., Castellazzo, G. and Ickovics, J. R. (2000). Relationship between Subjective and Objective Social Status with Psychological Functioning: Preliminary Data in Healthy, White Women. *Health Psychology*, 19: 586–592.

Ahn, H. and Wampold, B. E. (2001). Where Oh Where Are the Specific Ingredients? A Meta-Analysis of Component Studies in Counseling and Psychotherapy. *Journal of Counseling Psychology*, 48: 251–257.

Ahn, W., Kalish, C., Gelman, S., Medin, D., Luhmann, C., Atran, S., Coley, J. and Shaft, P. (2001). Why Essences Are Essential in the Psychology of Concepts. *Cognition*, 82: 59–69.

Akil, M., Pierri, J. N., Whitehead, R. E., Edgar, C. L., Mohila, C. and Lewis, D. A. (1999). Lamina-Specific Alteration in the Dopamine Innervation of the Prefrontal Cortex in Schizophrenic Subjects. *American Journal of Psychiatry*, 156: 1580–1589.

Alvard, M. (1995). Intraspecific Prey Choice by Amazonian Hunters. *Current Anthropology*, 36: 789–818.

Andrews, P. W., Gangestad, S. W. and Matthews, D. (2003). Adaptationism: How to Carry out an Exaptationist Program. *Behavioral and Brain Sciences*, 25: 489–504.

Ansbacher, H. and Ansbacher, R. R. (1964). *Individual Psychology of Alfred Adler*. Harper Perennial.

Antrobus, J. (2000). Theories of Dreaming. In M. Kryger, T. Roth and W. Dement (eds.), *Principles and Practices of Sleep Medicine*, 3rd ed. W. B. Saunders.

Appleton, J. (1990). *The Symbolism of Habitat: An Interpretation of Landscape in the Arts*. University of Washington Press.

Arditi, A., Holtzman, J. D. and Kosslyn, S. M. (1988). Mental Imagery and Sensory Experience in Congenital Blindness. *Neuropsychologica*, 26: 1–12.

Atran, S. C. (2002a). Modular and Cultural Factors in Biological Understanding: An Experimental Approach to the Cognitive Basis of Science. In P. Carruthers, S. Stich and M. Siegal (eds.), *The Cognitive Basis of Science*. Cambridge University Press.

Atran, S. C. (2002b). *In Gods We Trust: The Evolutionary Landscape of Religion*. Oxford University Press.

Atran, S. C. (2005). Strong vs Weak Adaptationism in Cognition and Language. In P. Carruthers, S. Laurence and S. Stich (eds.), *The Innate Mind*. Oxford University Press.

Atran, S. C., Medin, D., Lynch, E., Vapnarsky, V., Ek, E. U. and Sousa, P. (2001). Folkbiology Doesn't Come from Folkpsychology: Evidence from Yukatek Maya in Cross-Cultural Perspective. *Journal of Cognition and Culture*, 1: 3–32.

Austin, W. (1980). Friendship and Fairness: Effects of Type of Relationship and Task Performance on Choice of Distribution Rules. *Personality and Social Psychology Bulletin*, 6: 402–408.

Avis, J. and Harris, P. L. (1991). Belief-Desire Reasoning among Baka Children: Evidence for a Universal Conception of Mind. *Child Development*, 62: 460–467.

Bagley, C. A., Ohara, S., Lawson, H. C. and Lenz, F. A. (2006). Psychophysics of CNS Pain-Related Activity: Binary and Analog Channels and Memory Encoding. *Neuroscientist*, 12(1): 29–42.

Baker, R. R. and Bellis, M. A. (1995). *Human Sperm Competition*. Chapman and Hall.

Bakermans-Kranenburg, M. J., van Ijzendoorn, M. H. and Bokhorst, C. L. (2004). The Importance of Shared Environment in Infant–Father Attachment: A Behavioral Genetic Study of the Attachment Q-Sort. *Journal of Family Psychology*, 18(3): 545–549.

Bales, K. L., Kim, A. J., Lewis-Reese, A. D. and Carter, C. S. (2004). Both Oxytocin and Vasopressin May Influence Alloparental Behavior in Male Prairie Voles. *Hormones and Behavior*, 45(5): 354–361.

Balling, J. D. and Falk, J. H. (1982). Development of Visual Preference for Natural Environments. *Environment and Behaviour*, 14: 5–28.

Bandura, A. (1997). *Self-Efficacy: The Exercise of Control*. Cambridge University Press.

Barber, N. (1995). The Evolutionary Psychology of Physical Attractiveness: Sexual Selection and Human Morphology. *Ethology and Sociobiology*, 16: 395–424.

Barber, N. (2003). Paternal Investment Prospects and Cross-National Differences in Single Parenthood. *Cross-Cultural Research*, 37: 163–177.

Bargh, J. A. and Chartrand, T. L. (1999). The Unbearable Automaticity of Being. *American Psychologist*, 54: 462–479.

Barrett, H. C. (2005). Adaptations to Predators and Prey. In D. Buss (ed.), *The Handbook of Evolutionary Psychology*. John Wiley & Sons.

Barrett, J. L. (2004). *Why Would Anyone Believe in God?* Altamira Press.

Bauer, R.M and Vergaellie, M. (1988). Electrodermal Discrimination of Familiar but Not Unfamiliar Faces. *Brain and Cognition*, 8: 240–252.

Baumeister, R. F. and Twenge, J. M. (2002). Cultural Suppression of Female Sexuality. *Review of General Psychology*, 6: 166–203.

Bayley, H. ([1912] 1951). *The Lost Language of Symbolism*. London.

Beauchemin, K. M. and Hays, P. (1995). Prevailing Mood, Mood Changes and Dreams in Bipolar Disorder. *Journal of Affective Disorders*, 35: 41–49.

Bechtel, W. and Abrahamsen, A. (1991). *Connectionism and the Mind: An Introduction to Parallel Processing in Networks*. Blackwell.

Bedny, M., Pascual-Leone, A. and Saxe, R. (2009). Growing up Blind Does Not Change the Neural Bases of Theory of Mind. *Proceedings of the National Academy of Sciences*, 106(27): 11312–11317.

Belsky, J. (1999). Modern Evolutionary Theory and Patterns of Attachment. In J. Cassidy and P. R. Shaver (eds.), *Handbook of Attachment*. Guilford Press.

Benedetti, F. (2009). *Placebo Effects*. Oxford University Press.

Benedetti, F., Mayberg, H. S., Wager, T. D., Stohler, C. S. and Zubieta, J.-K. (2005). Neurobiological Mechanisms of the Placebo Effect. *Journal of Neuroscience*, 25(45): 10390–10402.

Benedetti, F., Lanotte, M., Lopiano, L. and Colloca, L. (2007). When Words Are Painful: Unraveling the Mechanisms of the Nocebo Effect. *Neuroscience*, 147: 260–271.

Benes, F. M., Davidons, J. and Bird, E. D. (1986). Quantitative Cytoarchitectural Studies of the Cerebral Cortex of Schizophrenics. *Archives of General Psychiatry*, 43: 31–35.

Berlin, B. and Kay, P. (1969). *Basic Color Terms: Their Universality and Evolution*. University of California Press.

Berman, K. F. and Meyer-Lindenberg, A. (2004). Functional Brain Imaging Studies in Schizophrenia. In D. S. Charney and E. J. Nestler (eds.), *The Neurobiology of Mental Illness*. Oxford University Press.

Berns, G. S. (2008). Functional Brain Imaging. *Psychiatry Residents' Symposium*. Palm Beach, FL, Sept. 12–14.

Berns, G. S., Laibson, D. and Loewenstein, G. (2007). Intertemporal Choice – Toward an Integrative Framework. *TRENDS in Cognitive Science*, 11: 482–488.

Bertolo, H., Paiva, T., Pessoa, L., Mestre, T., Marques, R. and Santos, R. (2003). Visual Dream Content, Graphical Representation and EEG Alpha Activity in Congenitally Blind Subjects. *Cognitive Brain Research*, 15: 277–284.

Biederman, I. (1995). Visual Object Recognition. In S. Kosslyn and D. Osherson (eds.), *An Invitation to Cognitive Science*, vol. 2, *Visual Cognition*. MIT Press.

Bienenfeld, D. and Yager, J. (2007). Issues of Spirituality and Religion in Psychotherapy Supervision. *Israel Journal of Psychiatry and Related Sciences*, 3: 178–186.

Bierlein, J. F. (1994). *Parallel Myths*. Ballantine.

Biller, H. B. (1974). *Paternal Deprivation*. Lexington Books.

Bjorklund, D. F. and Pellegrini, A. D. (2002). *The Origins of Human Nature: Evolutionary Developmental Psychology*. American Psychological Association.

Bjorklund, D. F. and Blash, C. H. (2005). Evolutionary Developmental Psychology. In D. Buss (ed.), *The Handbook of Evolutionary Psychology*. John Wiley & Sons.

Blanchette, I. and Dunbar, K. (2000). How Analogies Are Generated: The Roles of Structural and Superficial Similarity. *Memory and Cognition*, 28: 108–124.

Blanchette, I. and Dunbar, K. (2001). Analogy Use in Naturalistic Settings: The Influence of Audience, Emotion, and Goals. *Memory and Cognition*, 29: 730–735.

Bloom, P. (1996). Possible Individuals in Langage and Cognition. *Current Directions in Psychological Science*, 5: 90–94.

Boroditzky, L. (2000). Metaphoric Structuring: Understanding Time Through Spatial Metaphors. *Cognition*, 75: 1–28.

Bosaki, S. and Astingont, J. W. (1999). Theory of Mind in Preadolescence: Relations between Social Understanding and Social Competence. *Social Development*, 8: 237–255.

Bower, G. H. (1972). Mental Imagery and Associative Learning. In L. Gregg (ed.), *Cognition in Learning and Memory*. Wiley.

Bowlby, J. (1969). *Attachment and Loss*, vol. 1, *Attachment*. Hogarth Press.

Boyer, P. (2001). *Religion Explained: the Evolutionary Roots of Religious Thought*. Basic Books.

Boyer, P. and Barrett, H. C. (2005). Domain Specificity and Intuitive Ontology. In D. Buss (ed.), *The Handbook of Evolutionary Psychology*. John Wiley & Sons.

Braitenberg, V. and Schulz, A. (1991). *Anatomy of the Cortex*. Springer-Verlag.

Bremner, J. D., Randall, P., Vermetten, E., Staib, L., Bronen, R. A., Mazure, C., Capelli, S., McCarthy, G., Inis, R. B. and Charney, D. S. (1997). Magnetic Resonance Imaging-based Measurement of Hippocampal Volume in Posttraumatic Stress Disorder Related to Childhood Phsyical and Sexual Abuse: A Preliminary Report. *Biological Psychiatry*, 41: 23–32.

Brody, H. B. and Brody, D. (2000). Placebo and Health – II. Three Perspectives on the Placebo Response: Expectancy, Conditioning, and Meaning. *Advances in Mind-Body Medicine*, 16: 216–232.

Brooke, R. (1991). *Jung and Phenomenology*. Routledge.

Browman, C. and Kapell, L. (1982). Repetitive Sexual Dream Content of Normal Adults. *Sleep Research*, 11: 115.

Brown, D. E. (1991). *Human Universals*. McGraw Hill.

Brown, L. M. (1998). *Raising Their Voices: The Politics of Girls' Anger*. Harvard University Press.

Brüne, M. and Brüne-Cohrs, U. (2006). Theory of Mind – Evolution, Ontogeny, Brain Mechanisms and Psychopathology. *Neuroscience and Biobehavioral Reviews*, 30(4): 437–455.

Buckner, R. L., Andrews-Hanna, J. R. and Schacter, D. L. (2008). The Brain's Default Network. *Annals of the New York Academy of Science*, 1124: 1–38.

Buller, D. J. and Hardcastle, V. G. (2000). Evolutionary Psychology, Meet Developmental Neurobiology: Against Promiscuous Modularity. *Brain and Mind*, 1: 307–325.

Burns, J. K. (2006). Psychosis: A Costly By-Product of Social Brain Evolution in *Homo Sapiens. Progress in Neuro-Psychopharmacology and Biological Psychiatry*, 30: 797–814.

Burnstein, E. (2005). Altruism and Genetic Relatedness. In D. Buss (ed.), *The Handbook of Evolutionary Psychology*. John Wiley & Sons.

Buss, D. M. (1988). The Evolution of Human Intrasexual Competition: Tactics of Mate Attraction. *Journal for Personality and Social Psychology*, 54: 616–628.

Buss, D. M. (1994). *The Evolution of Desire*. Basic Books.

Buss, D. M. (2003). *The Evolution of Desire: Strategies of Human Mating*. Free Press.

Buss, D. M. (2004). *Evolutionary Psychology: The New Science of the Mind*. Allyn and Bacon.

Buss, D. M. (2005). Introduction: The Emergence of Evolutionary Psychology. In D. Buss (ed.), *The Handbook of Evolutionary Psychology*. John Wiley & Sons.

Buss, D. M. (2009). The Great Struggles of Life: Darwin and the Emergence of Evolutionary Psychology. *American Psychologist*, 64(2): 140–148.

Buss, D. M. and Schmitt, D. (1993). Sexual Strategies Theory: An Evolutionary Perspective on Human Mating. *Psychological Review*, 100: 204–232.

Buss, D. M. and Shackelford, T. K. (1997). From Vigilance to Violence: Mate Retention Tactics in Married Couples. *Journal of Personality and Social Psychology*, 72: 605–619.

Buss, D. M. and Duntley, J. D. (1999). Killer Psychology: The Evolution of Intrasexual Homicide. Paper presented to the annual meeting of the Human Behavior and Evolution Society, Salt Lake City, UT.

Buss, D. M. and Duntley, J. D. (2003). Homicide: An Evolutionary Perspective and Implications for Public Policy. In N. Dess (ed.), *Violence and Public Policy*. Greenwood.

Buss, D. M., Shackelford, T. K., Kirkpatrick, L. A., Choe, J. C., Lim, H. K., Hasegawa, M., Hasegawa, T. and Bennet, K. (1999). Jealously and the Nature of Beliefs about Infidelity: Tests of Competing Hypotheses about Sex Differences in the United States, Korea, and Japan. *Personal Relationships*, 6: 125–150.

Butterworth, B. (1999). *The Mathematical Brain*. Macmillan.

Butterworth, B. (2005). The Development of Arithmetical Abilities. *Journal of Child Psychology and Psychiatry*, 46(1): 3–18.

Byrne, R. W. (2003). Tracing the Evolutionary Path of Cognition. In M. Brüne, H. Ribbert and W. Schiefenhövel (eds.), *The Social Brain: Evolution and Pathology*. Wiley.

Campbell, A. (1986). *The Girls in the Gang*. Blackwell.

Campbell, A. (2005). Aggression. In D. Buss (ed.), *The Handbook of Evolutionary Psychology*. John Wiley & Sons.

Campbell, J. (1949). *The Hero with a Thousand Faces*. Pantheon.

Campbell, J. ([1959] 1991). *The Masks of God: Primitive Mythology*. Arkana.

Campbell, J. (1988). *The Power of Myth*. Anchor.

Campbell, L. and Ellis, B. J. (2005). Commitment, Love, and Mate Retention. In D. Buss (ed.), *The Handbook of Evolutionary Psychology*. John Wiley & Sons.

Cann, R. L., Stoneking, M. and Wilson, A. C. (1987). Mitochondrial DNA and Human Evolution. *Nature*, 325: 31–36.

Caramazza, A. and Shelton, J. (1998). Domain-Specific Knowledge Systems in the Brain: The Animate–Inanimate Distinction. *Journal of Cognitive Neuroscience*, 10: 1–34.

Carroll, J. (2005). Literature and Evolutionary Psychology. In D. Buss (ed.), *Handbook of Evolutionary Psychology*. Wiley.

Carruthers, P., Laurence, S. and Stich, S. (eds.) (2005). *The Innate Mind*. Oxford University Press.

Carson, J., Burks, V. and Park, R. D. (1993). Parent–Child Physical Play: Determinants and Consequences. In K. MacDonald (ed.), *Parent-Child Play: Descriptions and Implications*. State University of New York Press.

Carter, C. S. (1992). Oxytocin and Sexual Behavior. *Neuroscience and Biobehavioral Reviews*, 16: 131–144.

Carter, C. S. (1998). Neuroendocrine Perspectives on Social Attachment and Love. *Psychoneuroendocrinology*, 23: 779–818.

Carter, C. S. (2002). Neuroendocrine Perspectives on Social Attachment and Love. In J. T. Caciooppo, G. G. Bertson, R. Adolphs, C. S. Carter, R. J. Davidson, M. K. McClintock, B. S. McEwan, M. J. Meaney, D. L. Schacter, E. M. Sternberg, S. S. Suomi and S. E. Taylor (eds.), *Foundations in Social Neuroscience*. MIT Press.

Cartwright, R. D. and Romanek, I. (1978). Repetitive Dreams of Normal Subjects. *Sleep Research*, 7: 174.

Cartwright, R. D., Dravitz, H., Eastman, C. I. and Wood, E. (1991). REM Latency and the Recovery from Depression: Getting over Divorce. *American Journal of Psychiatry*, 148: 1530–1535.

Castelli, F., Happe, F., Frith. U. and Frith, C. D. (2000). Movement and Mind: A Functional Imaging Study of Perception and Interpretation of Complex Intentional Movement Patterns. *Neuroimage*, 12: 314–325.

Chagnon, N. A. (1988). Life Histories, Blood Revenge, and Warfare in a Tribal Population. *Science*, 239: 985–992.

Chisolm, J. S. (1996). The Evolutionary Ecology of Attachment Organization. *Human Nature*, 7: 1–38.

Chomsky, N. (1980). *Rules and Representation*. Columbia University Press.

Christianson, S. A. (ed.) (1992). *The Handbook of Emotion and Memory: Research and Theory*. Lawrence Erlbaum.

Cicogna, P. and Bosinelli, M. (2001). Consciousness during Dreams. *Consciousness and Cognition*, 10: 26–41.

Ciprian-Ollivier, J. and Cetkovich-Bakmas, M. G. (1997). Altered Consciousness States and Endogenous Psychoses: A Common Molecular Pathway? *Schizophrenia Research*, 28: 257–265.

Cirlot, J. E. ([1971] 2002). *A Dictionary of Symbols*. Dover.

Cleveland, H. H., Jacobson, K. C., Lipinski, J. J. and Rowe, D. C. (2000). Genetic and Shared Environmental Contributions to the Relationship between the Home Environment and Child and Adolescent Achievement. *Intelligence*, 28: 69–86.

Cloitre, M. (1997). Conscious and Unconscious Memory: A Model of Functional Amnesia. In D. J. Stein (ed.), *Cognitive Science and the Unconscious*. American Psychiatric Press.

Colman, W. (2010). Dream Interpretation and the Creation of Symbolic Meaning. In M. Stein (ed.), *Jungian Psychoanalysis: Working in the Spirit of Carl Jung*. Open Court.

Colloca, L. and Benedetti, F. (2005). Placebos and Painkillers: Is Mind as Real as Matter? *Nature Reviews Neuroscience*, 6: 545–552.

Colloca, L., Lopiano, L., Lanotte, M. and Benedetti, F. (2004). Overt Versus Covert Treatment for Pain, Anxiety, and Parkinson's Disease. *Lancet Neurology*, 3: 679–684.

Colloca, L., Siguado, M. and Benedetti, F. (2008). The Role of Learning in Nocebo and Placebo Effects. *Pain*, 136: 211–218.

Corteen, R. S. and Wood, B. (1972). Autonomic Responses to Shock Associated Threat Words. *Journal of Experimental Psychology*, 94: 308–313.

Corter, C. M. and Fleming, A. S. (1990). Maternal Responsiveness in Humans: Emotional Cognitive and Biological Factors. *Advances in the Study of Behavior*, 19: 83–136.

Cosmides, L. and Tooby, J. (1992). Cognitive Adaptations for Social Exchange. In J. H. Barkow, L. Cosmides and L. Tooby (eds.), *The Adapted Mind: Evolutionary Psychology and the Generation of Culture*. Oxford University Press.

Cosmides, L. and Tooby, J. (2005). Neurocognitive Adaptations Designed for Social Exchange. In D. Buss (ed.), *The Handbook of Evolutionary Psychology*. John Wiley & Sons.

Cosmides, L., Tooby, J. and Barkow, J. (1992). Environmental Aesthetics. In J. Barkow, L. Cosmides and J. Tooby (eds.), *The Adapted Mind: Evolutionary Psychology and the Generation of Culture*. Oxford University Press.

Coss, R. G. and Goldthwaite, R. O. (1995). The Persistence of Old Designs for Perception. *Perspectives in Ethology*, 11: 83–148.

Crick, F. and Mitchison, G. (1983). The Function of Dream Sleep. *Nature*, 312: 101.

Crick, F. and Mitchison, G. (1986). REM Sleep and Neural Nets. *Journal of Mind and Behavior*, 7: 229–250.

Cronin, H. (2005). A Critique of Some Current Evolutionary Thought. *Quarterly Review of Biology*, 80(1): 19–26.

Cummins, D. (1996). Evidence for the Innateness of Deontic Reasoning. *Mind and Language*, 11: 160–190.

Cummins, D. (2005). Dominance, Status and Social Hierarchies. In D. Buss (ed.), *The Handbook of Evolutionary Psychology*. John Wiley & Sons.

Cunningham, M. R., Barbee, A. P. and Pilhower, C. L. (2002). Dimensions of Facial Phsycial Attractiveness: The Intersection of Biology and Culture. In G. Rhodes and L. A. Zebrowitz (eds.), *Facial Attractiveness: Evolutionary, Cognitive, and Social Perspectives*. Ablex.

Curlin, F. A., Larence, R. E., Odell, S., Chin, M. H., Lantos, J. D., Doenig, H. G. and Meador, K. G. (2007). Religion, Spirituality, and Medicine: Psychiatrists' and Other Physicians' Differing Observations, Interpretations, and Clinical Approaches. *American Journal of Psychiatry*, 164: 1825–1831.

Daly, M. and Wilson, M. (1985). A Sociobiological Analysis of Human Infanticide. In G. Hausfater and S. Hrdy (eds.), *Infanticide: Comparative and Evolutionary Perspectives*. Aldine.

Damasio, A. R. (1990). Category-Related Recognition Defects as a Clue to the Neural Substrates of Knowledge. *Trends in Neuroscience*, 13: 95–98.

Damasio, A. R. (1994). *Descarte's Error: Emotion, Reason, and the Human Brain*. Penguin.

Damasio, A. R. (1999a). Commentary on Panksepp. *Neuro-Psychoanalysis 1:* 38–39.

Damasio, A. R. (1999b). *The Feeling of What Happens*. Harcourt.

Damasio, A. R., Graff-Radford, N., Eslinger, P., Damasio, H. and Kassell, N. (1985). Amnesia Following Basal Forebrain Lesions. *Archives of Neurology*, 42: 263–271.

Damasio, A., Tranel, D. and Damasio, H. (1990). Face Agnosia and the Neural Substrates of Memory. *Annual Review of Neuroscience*, 13: 90–109.

Davidson, H. E. (1988). *Myths and Symbols in Pagan Europe*. Syracuse University Press.

Davidson, H. E. (1993). *The Lost Beliefs of Northern Europe*. Routledge.

Davidson, R. J. (2003). Affective Neuroscience and Psychophysiology: Toward a Synthesis. *Psychophysiology*, 40(5): 655–665.

Dawkins, R. (1982). *The Extended Phenotype*. Oxford University Press.

Dawkins, R. (1989). *The Selfish Gene*, new ed. Oxford University Press.

Dawkins, R. (2008). *The God Delusion*. Mariner.

Dawson, J. L. M., Cheung, Y. M. and Lau, R. T. S. (1973). Effects of Neonatal Sex Hormones on Sex-Based Cognitive Abilities in the White Rat. *Psychologia*, 16: 17–24.

De Beni, R. and Cornoldi, C. (1988). Imagery limitations in Totally Congenitally Blind Subjects. *Journal of Experimental Psychology: Learning, Memory and Cognition*, 14(4): 650–655.

DeBruine, L. M. (2002). Facial Resemblance Enhances Trust. *Proceedings of the Royal Society of London. Series B, Biological Sciences*, 269: 1307–1312.

Dehaene, S. (1997). *The Number Sense: How the Mind Creates Mathematics*. Oxford University Press.

Deikman, A. (1971). Bimodal Consciousness. *Archives of General Psychiatry*, 125: 481–489.

Delacour, J. (1997). Neurobiology of Consciousness: An Overview. *Behavioral Brain Research*, 85: 127–141.

Dennett, D. (1992). *Consciousness Explained*. Back Bay Books.

Dennett, D. (2007). *Breaking the Spell: Religion as a Natural Phenomenon*. Penguin.

De Pascalis, V., Chiaradia, C. and Carotenuto, E. (2002). The Contribution of Suggestibility and Expectation to Placebo Analgesia Phenomenon in an Experimental Setting. *Pain*, 96: 393–402.

Descartes, R. (1647). The Principles of Philosophy. In *The Philosophical Works of Descartes*, vol. 1, pp. 201–302. Dover.

Devlin, K. (2000). *The Math Gene: How Mathematical Thinking Evolved and Why Numbers Are Like Gossip*. Basic Books.

Dickinson, M. J. and Eva, F. J. (2006). Anxiety and Depression May Have an Evolutionary Role as Negative Reinforcers, Encouraging Socialisation. *Medical Hypotheses*, 66: 796–800.

Dijkstra, P. and Buunk, B. P. (2001). Sex Differences in the Jealousy-Evoking Nature of a Rival's Body Build. *Evolution and Human Behavior*, 22: 335–341.

DiPietro, J. A. (1981). Rough and Tumble Play: A Function of Gender. *Developmental Psychology*, 17: 50–58.

Dodge, K. A. (1986). Social Information-Processing Variables in the Develoment of Aggression and Altruism in Children. In C. Zahn-Waxler, E. M. Cummings and R. Iannotti (eds.), *Altruism and Aggression: Biological and Social Origins*. Cambridge University Press.

Domhoff, G. W. (2003). *The Scientific Study of Dreams: Neural Networks, Cognitive Development, and Content Analysis*. American Psychological Association.

Drevets, W. C., Gadde, K. M. and Krishnan, K. R. R. (2004). Neuroimaging Studies of Mood Disorders. In D. S. Charney and E. J. Nestler (eds.), *The Neurobiology of Mental Illness*. Oxford University Press.

Duchaine, B. and Nakayama, K. (2005). Dissociations of Face and Object Recognition in Developmental Prosopagnosia. *Journal of Cognitive Neuroscience*, 17(1): 249–261.

Duchaine, B. and Nakayama, K. (2006). Developmental Prosopagnosia: A Window to Content-Specific Face Processing. *Current Opinion in Neurobiology*, 16(2): 166–173.

Duchaine, B., Yovel, G., Butterworth, E. J. and Nakayama, K. (2006). Prosopagnosia as an Impairment to Face Specific Mechanism: Elimination of the Alternative Hypotheses in a Developmental case. *Cognitive Neuropsychology*, 23: 714–747.

Duchaine, B., Germine, L. and Nakayama, K. (2007). Family Resemblance: Ten Family Members with Prosopagnosia and within-Class Object Agnosia. *Cognitive Neuropsychology*, 24(4): 419–430.

Duchaine, B., Jenkins, R., Germine, L. and Calder, A. J. (2009). Normal Gaze Discrimination and Adaptation in Seven Prosopagnosics. *Neuropsychologica*, 47(10): 2029–2036.

Duchaine, B., Murray, H., Turner, M., White, S. and Garrido, L. (2010). Normal Social Cognition in Developmental Prosopagnosia. *Cognitive Neuropsychology*, Feb 25: 1–15.

Dunbar, R. I. M. (2003). The Social Brain: Mind, Language, and Society in Evolutionary Perspective. *Annual Reviews in Anthropology*, 32: 163–181.

Dunn, J. (1988). *The Beginnings of Social Understanding*. Basil Blackwell.

Duntley, J. D. (2005). Adaptations to Dangers from Humans. In D. Buss (ed.), *The Handbook of Evolutionary Psychology*. John Wiley & Sons.

Edinger, E. F. (1972 [1992]). *Ego and Archetype*. Shambhala.

Eibl-Eibesfelt, I. (1989). *Human Ethology*. Aldine de Gruyter.

Eiser, A. S. (2005). Physiology and Psychology of Dreams. *Seminars in Neurology*, 25(1): 97–105.

Ekman, P. (1992). An Argument for Basic Emotions. *Cognition and Emotion*, 6: 169–200.

Eliade, M. ([1949] 2005). *The Myth of the Eternal Return*. Princeton University Press.

Eliade, M. ([1952] 1991). *Images and Symbols: Studies in Religious Symbolism*. Princeton University Press.

Eliade, M. ([1958] 1990). *Patterns in Comparative Religion*. Bison Books.

Eliade, M. ([1964] 2004). *Shamanism: Archaic Techniques of Ecstasy*. Princeton University Press.

Ellis, B. J. (1992). The Evolution of Sexual Attraction: Evaluative Mechanisms in Women. In J. H. Barkow, L. Cosmides and L. Tooby (eds.), *The Adapted Mind: Evolutionary Psychology and the Generation of Culture*. Oxford University Press.

Ellis, B. J. and Garber, J. (2000). Psychosocial Antecedents of Variation in Girls' Pubertal Timing: Maternal Depression, Stepfather Presence, and Marital and Family Stress. *Child Development*, 71: 485–501.

Ellis, B. J., McFadyen-Ketchum, S., Dodge, K. A., Pettit, G. S. and Bates, G. E. (1999). Quality of Early Family Relationships and Individual Differences in the Timing of Pubertal Maturation in Girls: Tests of an Evolutionary Model. *Journal of Personality and Social Psychology*, 77: 387–401.

Ellis, B. J., Bates, J. E., Dodge, K. A., Fergusson, D. M., Horwood, J. L., Pettit, G. S. and Woodward, L. (2003). Does Father Absence Place Daughters at Special Risk for Early Sexual Activity and Teenage Pregnancy? *Child Development*, 74: 801–821.

Ellis, L. (1995). Dominance and Reproductive Success among Nonhuman Animals: A Cross-Species Comparison. *Ethology and Sociobiology*, 16: 257–333.

Erdelyi, M. H. (1985). *Psychoanalysis: Freud's Cognitive Psychology*. W. H. Freeman.

Evans, D. L. (2008). Psychiatric Disorders in the Medically Ill. *Psychiatry Residents' Symposium*. Palm Beach, FL, Sept. 12–14.

Evans, E. M. (2001). Cognitive and Contextual Factors in the Emergence of Diverse Belief Systems: Creation versus Evolution. *Cognitive Psychology*, 42(3): 217–266.

Fisher, H. (2004). *Why We Love: The Nature and Chemistry of Romantic Love*. Henry Holt.

Fiss, H. (1993). The "Royal Road" to the Unconscious Revisited: A Signal Detection Model of Dream Function. In A. Moffitt, M. Kramer and R. Hoffmann (eds.), *The Functions of Dreaming*. State University of New York Press.

Fletcher, G. J. O., Simpson, J. A., Thomas, G. and Giles, L. (1999). Ideals in Intimate Relationships. *Journal of Personality and Social Psychology*, 76: 72–89.

Flinn, M. V. (1992). Paternal Care in a Caribbean Village. In B. Hewlett (ed.), *Father–Child Relations: Cultural and Biosocial Contexts*. Aldine.

Flinn, M. V., Ward, C. V. and Noone, R. J. (2005). Hormones and the Human Family. In D. Buss (ed.), *The Handbook of Evolutionary Psychology*. John Wiley & Sons.

Foa, E., Hembree, E. and Rothbaum, B. (2007). *Prolonged Exposure Therapy for PTSD: Emotional Processing of Traumatic Experiences, Therapist Guide*. Oxford University Press.

Fodor, J. (1983). *The Modularity of Mind*. MIT Press.

Fosse, M., Fosse, R., Hobson, J. A. and Sitckgold, R. (2003). Dreaming and Episodic Memory: A Functional Dissociation? *Journal of Cognitive Neuroscience*, 15: 1–9.

Fosse, R., Stickgold, R. and Hobson, J. A. (2001). Brain-Mind States: Reciprocal Variation in Thoughts and Hallucinations. *Psychological Science* 12: 30–36.

Fosse, R., Stickgold, R. and Hobson, J. A. (2004). Thinking and Hallucinating: Reciprocal Changes in Sleep. *Psychophysiology*, 41: 298–305.

Foulkes, D. (1985). *Dreaming: A Cognitive-Psychological Analysis*. Lawrence Erlbaum.

Foulkes, D. (1996). Dream Research: 1953–1993. *Sleep*, 19: 609–624.

Foulkes, D. (1999). *Children's Dreaming and the Development of Consciousness*. Harvard University Press.

Foulkes, D. and Fleisher, S. (1975). Mental Activity in Relaxed Wakefulness. *Journal of Abnormal Psychology*, 84: 66–75.

Foulkes, D. and Rechtschaffen, A. (1964). Presleep Determinants of Dream Content: Effects of Two Films. *Perceptual and Motor Skills*, 19: 983–1005.

Foulkes, D. and Scott, E. (1973). An Above-Zero Waking Baseline for the Incidence of Momentarily Hallucinatory Mentation. *Sleep Research*, 2: 108.

Foulkes, D., Pivik, R., Steadman, H., Spear, P. and Symonds, J. (1967). Dreams of the Male Child: An EEG Study. *Journal of Abnormal Psychology*, 72: 457–467.

Freud, S. (1900). *The Interpretation of Dreams*. Oxford University Press.

Freud, S. ([1923] 1959). Remarks upon the Theory and Practice of Dream Interpretation. In J. Strachey (ed.), *Sigmund Freud: Complete Works*, vol. 14. London: Hogarth.

Freud, S. (1969). *A General Introduction to Psychoanalysis*. Washington Square Press.

Freud, S. (2010). *Beyond the Pleasure Principle*. CreateSpace.

Frith, U. and Frith, C. D. (2003). Development and Neurophysiology of Mentalizing. *Philosophical Transcripts of the Royal Society of London B*, 358: 459–473.

Gallese, V. and Goldman, A. (1998). Mirror Neurons and the Simulation Theory of Mind-Reading. *Trends in Cognitive Science*, 2: 493–501.

Gallistel, C. R. (1995). The Replacement of General-Purpose Theories with Adaptive Specializations. In M. S. Gazzaniga (ed.), *The Cognitive Neurosciences*. MIT Press.

Gangestad, S. W. and Thornhill, R. (1997). The Evolutionary Psychology of Extra-Pair Sex: The Role of Fluctuating Asymmetry. *Evolution and Human Behavior*, 18: 69–88.

Gangestad, S. W. and Thornhill, R. (1998). Menstrual Cycle Variation in Women's Preferences for the Scent of Symmetrical Men. *Proceedings of the Royal Society of London. Series B*, 265: 727–733.

Gangestad, S. W., Thornhill, R. and Garver-Apgar, C. E. (2004). Female Sexual Interests across the Ovulatory Cycle Depend on Primary Partner Developmental Instability. Unpublished manuscript, University of New Mexico.

Gangestad, S. W., Thornhill, R. and Garver-Apgar, C. E. (2005). Adaptations to Ovulation. In D. Buss (ed.), *The Handbook of Evolutionary Psychology*. John Wiley & Sons.

Ganis, G., Thompson, W. L. and Kosslyn, S. M. (2004). Areas Underlying Visual Mental Imagery and Visual Perception: An fMRI Study. *Cognitive Brain Research*, 20: 226–241.

Gardner, R. and Wilson, D. R. (2004). Sociophysiology and Evolutionary Aspects of Psychiatry. In J. Panksepp (ed.), *Textbook of Biological Psychiatry*. Wiley.

Garnham, A. (1991). Did Two Farmers Leave or Three? Comment on Starkey, Spelke and Gelman: Numerical Abstraction by Human Infants. *Cognition*, 39: 167–170.

Gazzaniga, M. S. (1995). Principles of Human Brain Organization Derived from Split-Brain Studies. *Neuron*, 14: 217–228.

Gazzaniga, M. S. (1998). *The Mind's Past*. University of California Press.

Gazzaniga, M. S., Ivry, R. B. and Mangun, G. R. (eds.) (2002). *Cognitive Neuroscience: The Biology of the Mind*, 2nd ed. Norton.

Geary, D. C. (1998). *Male, Female: The Evolution of Human Sex Differences*. American Psychological Association.

Geary, D. C. (2005). Evolution of Paternal Investment. In D. Buss (ed.), *The Handbook of Evolutionary Psychology*. John Wiley & Sons.

Gelman, R. and Gallistel, C. R. (1978). *The Child's Understanding of Number*. Harvard University Press.

Gelman, R., Durgin, F. and Kaufman, L. (1995). Distinguishing between Animates and Inanimates: Not by Motion Alone. In D. Sperber, D. Premack, and A. J. Premack (eds.), *Causal Cognition*. Oxford University Press.

Gelman, S. A., Coley, J. D. and Gottfried, G. M. (1994). Essentialist Beliefs in Children: The Acquisition of Concepts and Theories. In L. A. Hirschfeld and S. A. Gelman (eds.), *Mapping the Mind: Domain Specificity in Cognition and Culture*. Cambridge University Press.

Gentner, D. and Jeziorski, M. (1989). Historical Shifts in the Use of Analogy in Science. In B. Gholson, W. R. Shadish, R. A. Shadish, R. A. Beimeyer and

A. Houts (eds.), *The Psychology of Science: Contributions to Metascience.* Cambridge University Press.

Germine, L., Cashdollar, N., Düzel, E. and Duchaine, B. (2010). A New Selective Developmental Deficit: Impaired Object Recognition with Normal Face Recognition. *Cortex*, 47(5): 598–607.

Ghazanfar, A. A. (2008). Language Evolution: Neural Differences that Make a Difference. *Nature Neuroscience*, 11(4): 382–384.

Ghiglieri, M. P. (1999). *The Dark Side of Man: Tracing the Origins of Violence.* Perseus.

Gianotti, L. R., Mohr, C., Pizzagalli, D., Lehmann, D. and Brugger, P. (2001). Associative Processing and Paranormal Belief. *Psychiatry and Clinical Neurosciences*, 55(6): 595–603.

Goetz, A. T. and Shackelford, T. K. (2006). Modern Application of Evolutionary Theory to Psychology: Key Concepts and Clarifications. *American Journal of Psychology*, 119(4): 567–584.

Goldberg, S. and Lewis, M. (1969). Play Behavior in the Year-Old Infant: Early Sex Differences. *Child Development*, 40: 21–31.

Golinkoff, R. M., Harding, C. G., Carlson-Luden, V. and Sexton, M. (1984). The Infant's Perception of Causal Events: The Distinction between Animate and Inanimate Objects. In L. P. Lipsitt (ed.), *Advances in Infancy Research.* Ablex.

Goodwyn, E. (2010a). Approaching Archetypes: Reconsidering Innateness. *Journal of Analytical Psychology*, 55: 503–522.

Goodwyn, E. (2010b). Mythic Mind–Brain Resonance in Norse Mythology. Unpublished manuscript.

Gopnik, A. and Meltzoff, A. N. (1987). The Development of Categorization in the Second Year and Its Relation to Other Cognitive and Linguistic Developments. *Child Development*, 58: 1523–1531.

Grady, J. (1997). Foundations of Meaning: Primary Metaphors and Primary Scenes. PhD dissertation, University of California, Berkeley.

Grammer, K. (1992). Variations on a Theme: Age Dependent Mate Selection in Humans. *Behavioral and Brain Sciences*, 15: 100–102.

Grammer, K., Renninger, L. and Fischer, B. (2004). Disco Clothing, Female Sexual Motivation, and Relationship Status: Is She Dressed to Impress? *Journal of Sex Research*, 41: 66–74.

Gray, J. A. (1987). *The Psychology of Fear and Stress.* Cambridge University Press.

Haas, O., Schwenk, W., Hermann, C. and Muller, J. M. (2005). Guided Imagery and Relaxation in Conventional Colorectal Resections: A Randomized, Controlled, Partially Blinded Trial. *Diseases of the Colon and Rectum*, 48(10): 1955–1963.

Hagan, E. H. (2005). Controversial Issues in Evolutionary Psychology. In D. Buss (ed.), *The Handbook of Evolutionary Psychology.* John Wiley & Sons.

Hall, C. S. and Van de Castle, R. (1966). *The Content Analysis of Dreams.* Appleton-Century-Crofts.

Hall, C. S. and Nordby, V. J. (1972). *The Individual and His Dreams.* New American Library Classics.

Hall, C. S., Domhoff, G. W., Blick, K. A. and Weesner, K. E. (1982). The Dreams of College Men and Women in 1950 and 1980: A Comparison of Dream Contents and Sex Differences. *Sleep*, 5(2): 188–194.

Hall, J. (1983). *Jungian Dream Interpretation: A Handbook of Theory and Practice*. Inner City Books.

Hamilton, W. D. (1964). The Genetical Evolution of Social Behaviour. *Journal of Theoretical Biology*, 7: 1–52.

Harrington, A. (ed.) (1997). *The Placebo Effect*. Harvard University Press.

Hartmann, E. (1998). *Dreams and Nightmares: The Origin and Meaning of Dreams*. Perseus Publishing.

Hartmann, E., Russ, D., Oldfield, M., Falke, R. and Skoff, B. (1980). Dream Content: Effects of l-DOPA. *Sleep Research*, 9: 153.

Haselton, M. G. and Miller, G. F. (2002). *Evidence for Ovulatory Shifts in Attraction to Artistic and Entrepreneurial Excellence*. Paper presented at the annual meeting of the Human Behavior and Evolution Society Conference, Rutgers, New Jersey.

Haselton, M. G., Nettle, D. and Andrews, P. W. (2005). The Evolution of Cognitive Bias. In D. Buss (ed.), *The Handbook of Evolutionary Psychology*. Wiley & Sons.

Haule, J. R. (2010). *Jung in the 21st Century*, vol. 1, *Evolution and Archetype*. Routledge.

Hauser, M. D. and Spaulding, B. (2006). Monkeys Generate Causal Inferences about Possible and Impossible Physical Transformations. *Proceedings of the National Academy of Sciences*, 103: 7181–7185.

Hayden, B. (2003). *Shamans, Sorcerers, and Saints: A Prehistory of Religion*. Smithsonian Books.

Heath, R. G. (1963). Electrical Self-Stimulation of the Brain in Man. *American Journal of Psychiatry*, 120: 571–577.

Helm, H. M., Hays, J. C., Flint, E. P., Koenig, H. G. and Blazer, D. G. (2000). Does Private Religious Activity Prolong Survival? A Six Year Follow-up Study of 3,851 Older Adults. *Journal of Gerontology, Biological Science and Medical Science*, 55: M400–405.

Henderson, J. L. (1964). Ancient Myths and Modern Man. In C. G. Jung and M.-L. von Franz (eds.), *Man and His Symbols*. Dell.

Hill, K. and Hurtado, A. M. (1996). *Ache Life History: The Ecology and Demography of a Foraging People*. Aldine de Gruyter.

Hillman, J. (1977). *Re-Visioning Psychology*. Harper.

Hinton, G. E. and Nowlan, S. J. (1987). How Learning Can Guide Evolution. *Complex Systems*, 1: 495–502.

Hintzman, D. L. (1988). Human Learning and Memory: Connections and Dissociations. *Annual Review of Psychology*, 41: 109–139.

Hitchcock, E. and Cairns, V. (1973). Amygdalotomy. *Postgraduate Medicine*, 49: 894–904.

Hobson, J. A. (1988). *The Dreaming Brain: How the Brain Creates Both Sense and Nonsense of Dreams*. Basic Books.

Hobson, J. A. (1999). The New Neuropsychology of Sleep: Implications for Psychoanalysis. *Neuropsychoanalysis*, 1(2): 157–83.

Hobson, J. A. (2003). Sleep Is of the Brain, by the Brain and for the Brain. *Nature*, 437: 1254–1256.

Hobson, J. A. and Kahn, D. (2007). Dream Content: Individual and Generic Aspects. *Consciousness and Cognition*, 16(4): 850–858.

Hobson, J. A., Pace-Schott, E. F. and Stickgold, R. (2000). Dreaming and the

Brain: Toward a Cognitive Neuroscience of Conscious States. *Behavioral and Brain Sciences*, 23: 793–1121.

Hogenson, G. B. (2004). Archetypes: Emergence and the Psyche's Deep Structure. In J. Cambray and L. Carter (eds.), *Analytical Psychology: Contemporary Perspectives in Jungian Analysis*. Brunner-Routledge.

Hogenson, G. B. (2009). Archetypes as Action Patterns. *Journal of Analytical Psychology*, 54(3): 325–337.

Hollos, M., Leis, P. E. and Turiel, E. (1986). Social Reasoning in Ijo Children and Adolescents in Nigerian Communities. *Journal of Cross-Cultural Psychology*, 17: 352–374.

Howard, D. V. (1992). Implicit Memory: An Expanding Picture of Cognitive Aging. *Annual Review of Gerontology and Geriatrics*, 11: 1–22.

Hughes, S. M. and Gallup, G. G. (2002). Sex Differences in Morphological Predictors of Sexual Behavior. *Evolution and Human Behavior*, 24(3): 173–178.

Humphrey, N. (2002). Great Expectations: The Evolutionary Psychology of Faith-Healing and the Placebo Response. In N. Humphrey (ed.), *The Mind Made Flesh: Essays from the Frontiers of Evolution and Psychology*. Oxford University Press.

Hurtado, A. M. and Hill, K. R. (1992). Paternal Effect on Offspring Survivorship among Ache and Hiwi Hunter-Gatherers: Implications for Modeling Pair-bond Stability. In B. S. Hewlett (ed.), *Father–Child Relations: Cultural and Biosocial Contexts*. Aldine de Gruyter.

Insel, T. R. (1992). Oxytocin – a Neuropeptide for Affiliation: Evidence from Behavioral, Receptor Autoradiographic, and Comparative Studies. *Psychoneuroendocrinology*, 17: 3–35.

Jackendoff, R. (2002). *Foundations of Language: Brain, Meaning, Grammar, Evolution*. Oxford University Press.

Jacoby, J. (1964). Symbols in an Individual Analysis. In C. G. Jung and M.-L. von Franz (eds.), *Man and his Symbols*. Dell.

Jaffé, A. (1964). Symbolism in the Visual Arts. In C. G. Jung and M.-L. von Franz (eds.), *Man and His Symbols*. Dell.

Jarvinen, D. W. and Nicholls, J. G. (1996). Adolescents' Social Goals, Beliefs about the Causes of Social Success and Dissatisfaction in Peer Relations. *Developmental Psychology*, 32: 435–441.

Jirikowski, G. F., Caldwell, J. D., Stumpf, W. E. and Pedersen, C. A. (1988). Estradiol Influences Oxytocin Immunoreactive Brain Systems. *Neuroscience*, 25: 237–248.

Joe-Laidler, K. and Hunt, G. (2001). Accomplishing Femininity among the Girls in the Gang. *British Journal of Criminology*, 41: 656–678.

Johnson, C. (1997a). Metaphor vs. Conflation in the Acquisition of Polysemy: The Case of SEE. In M. K. Hiraga, C. Sinha and S. Wilcox (eds.), *Cultural, Typological and Psychological Issues in Cognitive Linguistics*. Current Issues in Linguistic Theory 152. John Benjamins.

Johnson, C. (1997b). Learnability in the Acquisition of Multiple Senses: SOURCE Reconsidered. In J. Moxley, J. Juge and M. Juge (eds.), *Proceedings of the Twenty-Second Annual Meeting of the Berkeley Linguistics Society*. Berkley Linguistics Society.

Johnson, M. H. (1990a). Cortical Maturation and the Development of Visual Attention in Early Infancy. *Journal of Cognitive Neuroscience*, 2: 81–95.

Johnson, M. H. (1990b). Cortical Maturation and Perceptual Development. In H. Bloch and B. I. Bertenthal (eds.), *Sensory Motor Organisations and Development in Infancy and Early Childhood*. Kluwer.

Johnson, R. A. and Ruhl, J. M. (1997). *Balancing Heaven and Earth: A Memoir of Visions, Dreams and Realizations*. HarperOne.

Johnson, R. A. and Ruhl, J. M. (2000). *Contentment: A Way to True Happiness*. HarperOne.

Johnson, R. A. and Ruhl, J. M. (2007). *Living Your Unlived Life: Coping with Unrealized Dreams and Fulfilling Your Purpose in the Second Half of Life*. Tarcher.

Jones, I. and Blackshaw, J. K. (2000). An Evolutionary Approach to Psychiatry. *Australian and New Zealand Journal of Psychiatry*, 34: 8–13.

Jung, C. G. (1919). The Structure and Dynamics of the Psyche. In H. Read, M. Fordham, G. Adler, and W. McGuire (eds.), trans. R. F. C. Hull, *The Collected Works of C. G. Jung*, vol. 8. Routledge and Kegan Paul.

Jung, C. G. ([1936] 1966). *Psychology and Religion: Based on the Terry Lectures Delivered at Yale University*. Yale University Press.

Jung, C. G. ([1950] 1976). The Symbolic Life. In H. Read, M. Fordham, G. Adler, and W. McGuire (eds.), trans. R. F. C. Hull, *The Collected Works of C. G. Jung*, vol. 18. Princeton University Press.

Jung, C. G. ([1953a] 1977). Two Essays in Analytical Psychology. In H. Read, M. Fordham, G. Adler, and W. McGuire (eds.), trans. R. F. C. Hull, *The Collected Works of C. G. Jung*, vol. 7. Routledge and Kegan Paul.

Jung, C. G. ([1953b] 1993). Psychology and Alchemy. In H. Read, M. Fordham, G. Adler and W. McGuire (eds.), trans. R. F. C. Hull, *The Collected Works of C. G. Jung*, vol. 12. Routledge and Kegan Paul.

Jung, C. G. (1954). The Practice of Psychotherapy. In H. Read, M. Fordham, G. Adler and W. McGuire (eds.), trans. R. F. C. Hull, *The Collected Works of C. G. Jung*, vol. 16. Routledge and Kegan Paul.

Jung, C. G. (1955). Foreword. In M. E. Harding, "Woman's Mysteries". Shambhala.

Jung, C. G. ([1956] 1990). Symbols of Transformation. In H. Read, M. Fordham, G. Adler and W. McGuire (eds.), trans. R. F. C. Hull, *The Collected Works of C. G. Jung*, vol. 5. Routledge and Kegan Paul.

Jung, C. G. ([1959a] 1979). Aion: Researches into the Phenomenology of the Self. In H. Read, M. Fordham, G. Adler and W. McGuire (eds.), trans. R. F. C. Hull, *The Collected Works of C. G. Jung*, vol. 9ii. Routledge and Kegan Paul.

Jung, C. G. ([1959b] 2006). The Archetypes and the Collective Unconscious. In H. Read, M. Fordham, G. Adler and W. McGuire (eds.), trans. R. F. C. Hull, *The Collected Works of C. G. Jung*, vol. 9i. Routledge and Kegan Paul.

Jung, C. G. (1961). *Memories, Dreams, Reflections*. Random House.

Jung, C. G. (1963). Mysterium Coniunctionis. In H. Read, M. Fordham, G. Adler and W. McGuire (eds.), trans. R. F. C. Hull, *The Collected Works of C. G. Jung*, vol. 14. Routledge and Kegan Paul.

Jung, C. G. (1964). Approaching the Unconscious. In C. G. Jung and M.-L. von (eds.), *Man and His Symbols*. Dell.

Jung, C. G. (1967). Alchemical Studies. In H. Read, M. Fordham, G. Adler and

W. McGuire (eds.), trans. R. F. C. Hull, *The Collected Works of C. G. Jung*, vol. 13. Routledge and Kegan Paul.

Jung, C. G. ([1971] 1976). *The Portable Jung*. J. Campbell (ed.). Penguin Books.

Jung, C. G. ([1971] 2005). Psychological Types. *The Collected Works of C. G. Jung*, vol. 6.

Jung, C. G. (1974). *Dreams*. Princeton University Press.

Jung, C. G. (1984). *Dream Analysis: Notes of the Seminar Given in 1928–1930*. William McGuire (ed). Princeton University Press.

Jung, C. G. (1990). Jung on Film. Interview with Dr. Richard I. Evans. Stephen Segalier (director). University of Houston: Public Media Video.

Jung, C. G. (1997). *Visions: Notes of the Seminar Given 1930–1934*. Claire Douglas (ed.). Princeton University Press.

Jung, C. G. (2008). *Children's Dreams: Notes from the Seminar Given in 1936–1940*. Princeton University Press.

Kabat-Zinn, J., Massion, A. O., Kristeller, J., Peterson, L. G., Fletcher, K. E., Pbert, L., Lenderking, W. R. and Santorelli, S. F. (1992). Effectiveness of Meditation-Based Stress Reduction Program in the Treatment of Anxiety Disorders. *American Journal of Psychiatry*, 149(7): 936–943.

Kahan, T. L., LaBerge, S., Levitan, L. and Zimbardo, P. (1997). Similarities and Differences between Dreaming and Waking Cognition: An Exploratory Study. *Consciousness and Cognition*, 6: 132–147.

Kahn, D., Pace-Schott, E. and Hobson, J. A. (2002). Emotions and Cognition: Feeling and Character Identification in Dreaming. *Consciousness and Cognition*, 11: 34–50.

Kalin, N. H. (2008). How Do Non-Human Primate Models of Psychiatric Disorders Inform the Field? *Psychiatry Resident's Symposium*. Palm Beach, FL. Sept. 12–14.

Kaplan, H. S. and Gangestad, S. W. (2005). Life History Theory and Evolutionary Psychology. Conceptual Foundations of Evolutionary Psychology. In D. Buss (ed.), *The Handbook of Evolutionary Psychology*. John Wiley & Sons.

Kaplan, H. S., Lancaster, J. B. and Anderson, K. G. (1998). Human Parental Investment and Fertility: the Life Histories of Men in Albuquerque. In A. Booth and A. C. Crouter (eds.), *Men in Families: When Do They Get Involved? What Difference Does It Make?* Erlbaum.

Kaplan, H. S., Hill, K., Lancaster, J. B. and Hurtado, A. M. (2000). A Theory of Human Life History Evolution: Diet, Intelligence, and Longevity. *Evolutionary Anthropology*, 9: 156–185.

Kaplan, S. (1992). Environmental Preference in a Knowledge-Seeking, Knowledge-Using Organism. In J. H. Barkow, L. Cosmides, and L. Tooby (eds.), *The Adapted Mind: Evolutionary Psychology and the Generation of Culture*. Oxford University Press.

Karmiloff-Smith, A. (1992). *Beyond Modularity: A Developmental Perspective on Cognitive Science*. MIT press.

Kellog, R. (1969). *Analyzing Children's Art*. National Press Books.

Kemmerer, D. (2005). The Spatial and Temporal Meanings of English Prepositions Can Be Independently Impaired. *Neuropsychologia*, 43: 797–806.

Kennedy, J. M. (1980). Blind People Recognizing and Making Haptic Pictures. In M. A. Hagen (ed.), *The Perception of Pictures*, vol. 2. New York: Academic Press.

Kenrick, D. T., Groth, G. R., Trost, M. R. and Sadalla, E. K. (1993). Integrating Evolutionary and Social Exchange Perspectives on Relationships: Effects of Gender, Self-Appraisal, and Involvement Level on Mate Selection Criteria. *Journal of Personality and Social Psychology*, 64: 951–969.

Kenrick, D. T., Maner, J. K. and Li, N. P. (2005). Evolutionary Social Psychology. In D. Buss (ed.), *The Handbook of Evolutionary Psychology*. John Wiley & Sons.

Keverne, E. B., Martensz, N. and Tuite, B. (1989). Beta-Endorphin Concentrations in CSF of Monkeys Are Influenced by Grooming Relationships. *Psychoneuroendocrinology*, 14: 155–161.

Khan, A., Redding, N. and Brown, W. A. (2007). The Persistence of the Placebo Response in Antidepressant Clinical Trials. *Journal of Psychiatric Research*, 42(10): 791–796.

Kihlstrom, J. F. (1987). The Cognitive Unconscious. *Science*, 237: 1445–1452.

Klatzky, R. L., Pellegrino, J. W., McCloskey, B. P. and Doherty, S. (1989). Can You Squeeze a Tomato? The Role of Motor Representations in Semantic Sensibility Judgments. *Journal of Memory and Language*, 28: 56–77.

Knauff, M., Mulack, T., Kassubek, J., Salih, H. R. and Greenlee, M. W. (2002). Spatial Imagery in Deductive Reasoning: A Functional MRI Study. *Cognitive Brain Research*, 13: 203–212.

Knox, J. M. (2003). *Archetype, Attachment, Analysis*. Routledge.

Koenig, H., Goerge, L., Hays, J., Larson, D., Cohen, H. and Blazer, D. (1998). The Relationship between Religious Activities and Blood Pressure in Older Adults. *International Journal of Psychiatry*, 28: 189–213.

Koshi, E. B. and Short, C. A. (2007). Placebo Theory and Its Implications for Research and Clinical Practice: A Review of the Recent Literature. *Pain Practice*, 7(1): 4–20.

Kosslyn, S. M. (1994). *Image and Brain: the Resolution of the Imagery Debate*. MIT Press.

Kosslyn, S. M. (2005). Reflective Thinking and Mental Imagery: A Perspective on the Development of Posttraumatic Stress Disorder. *Development and Psychopathology*, 17: 851–863.

Kosslyn, S. M., Behrmann, M. and Jeannerod, M. (1995). The Cognitive Neuroscience of Mental Imagery. *Neuropsychologia*, 33(11): 1335–1344.

Kosslyn, S. M., Ganis, G. and Thompson, W. L. (2001). Neural Foundations of Imagery. *Neuroscience*, 2: 635–642.

Kosslyn, S. M., Thompson, W. L., Sukel, K. E. and Alpert, N. M. (2005). Two Types of Image Generation: Evidence from PET. *Cognitive, Affective, and Behavioral Neuroscience*, 5(1): 41–53.

Kotch, W. E. (2000). Jung's Mediatory Science as a Psychology Beyond Objectivism. *Journal of Analytic Psychology*, 45(2): 217–244.

Koukkou, M. and Lehmann, D. (1993). A Model of Dreaming and Its Functional Significance: The State-Shift Hypothesis. In A. Moffitt, M. Kramer, and R. Hoffmann (eds.), *The Functions of Dreaming*. State University of New York Press.

Koulack, D. (1993). Dreams and Adaptation to Contemporary Stress. In A. Moffitt, M. Kramer, and R. Hoffmann (eds.), *The Functions of Dreaming*. State University of New York Press.

Kourtzi, Z. and Kanwisher, N. (2000). Activation in Human MT/MST by Static Images with Implied Motion. *Journal of Cognitive Neuroscience*, 7: 196–208.

Kövecses, Z. (1986). *Metaphors of Anger, Pride, and Love: A Lexical Approach to the Structure of Concepts*. John Benjamins.

Kövecses, Z. (1990). *Emotion Concepts*. Springer-Verlag.

Kradin, R. (2004). The Placebo Response Complex. *Journal of Analytical Psychology*, 49: 617–634.

Kradin, R. (2007). *The Placebo Response and the Power of Unconscious Healing*. Routledge.

Kramer, M. (1993). The Selective Mood Regulatory Function of Dreaming: An Update and Revision. In A. Moffitt, M. Kramer, and R. Hoffmann (eds.), *The Functions of Dreaming*. State University of New York Press.

Kramer, M. (2007). *The Dream Experience: A Systematic Exploration*. Routledge.

Kramer, M. and Roth, T. (1975). Dreams and Dementia: A Laboratory Exploration of Dream Recall and Dream Content in Chronic Brain Syndrome Patients. *International Journal of Aging and Human Development*, 6(2): 179–182.

Kramer, M. and Glucksman, M. L. (2006). Changes in Manifest Dream Affect During Psychoanalytic Treatment. *Journal for the American Academy of Psychoanalysis and Dynamic Psychiatry*, 34(2): 249–260.

Kuritzky, L. (1998). Religious Commitment and Health Status. *Internal Medicine Alert*, 20: 71.

Kurlan, J. A. and Gaulin, S. J. C. (2005). Cooperation and Conflict among Kin. In D. Buss (ed.), *The Handbook of Evolutionary Psychology*. John Wiley & Sons.

Laberge, S. (1991). *Exploring the World of Lucid Dreaming*. Ballantine.

Laidlaw, J. and Whitehouse, H. (2007). Introduction to Religion, Anthropology and Cognitive Science. In H. Whitehouse and J. Laidlaw (eds.), *Religion, Anthropology and Cognitive Science*. Carolina Academic Press.

Lakoff, G. (1997). How Unconscious Metaphorical Thought Shapes Dreams. In D. J. Stein (ed.), *Cognitive Science and the Unconscious*. American Psychiatric Press.

Lakoff, G. and Johnson, M. (1980). *Metaphors We Live By*. University of Chicago Press.

Lakoff, G. and Turner, M. (1989). *More Than Cool Reason*. University of Chicago Press.

Lakoff, G. and Johnson, M. (1999). *Philosophy in the Flesh*. Basic Books.

Lakoff, G. and Johnson, M. (2003). Afterword to *Metaphors We Live By*. University of Chicago Press.

Langlois, J. H. and Roggman, L. A. (1990). Attractive Faces Are Only Average. *Psychological Science*, 1: 115–121.

Langlois, J. H., Ritter, J. M., Casey, R. J. and Sawin, D. B. (1995). Infant Attractiveness Predicts Maternal Behaviors and Attitudes. *Developmental Psychology*, 31: 464–472.

Larson, D. B. and Koenig, H. G. (2000). Is God Good for Your Health? The Role of Spirituality in Medical Care. *Cleveland Clinical Journal of Medicine*, 67(80): 83–84.

Leahy, R. L. (2003). *Cognitive Therapy Techniques: A Practitioner's Guide*. Guilford Press.

LeDoux, J. (1985). Brain, Mind, and Language. In D. A. Oakley (ed.), *Brain and Mind*. Methuen.

LeDoux, J. (1996). *The Emotional Brain: the Mysterious Underpinnings of Emotional Life*. Simon and Schuster.

LeDoux, J. (2002). *The Synaptic Self: How Our Brains Become Who We Are*. New York: Viking Penguin.

Leuchter, A. F., Cook, I. A., Witte, E. A., Morgan, M. and Abrams, M. (2002). Changes in Brain Function of Depressed Subjects During Treatment with Placebo. *American Journal of Psychiatry*, 159: 122–129.

Lever, J. (1978). Sex Differences in the Games Children Play. *Social Problems*, 23: 478–487.

Levin, D. (1985). *The Body's Recollection of Being: Phenomenological Psychology and the Deconstruction of Nihilism*. Routledge and Kegan Paul.

Levy-Bruhl, L. (1922). *Primitive Mentality*. AMS Press.

Lidstone, S. C. and Stoessl, A. J. (2007). Understanding the Placebo Effect: Contributions from Neuroimaging. *Molecular Imaging and Biology*, 9: 176–185.

Lim, M. M., Wang, Z., Olazabal, D. E., Ren, X., Terwilliger, E. F. and Young, L. J. (2004). Enhanced Partner Preference in a Promiscuous Species by Manipulating the Expression of a Single Gene. *Nature*, 429: 754–757.

Llinas, R. and Ribary, U. (1992). Coherent 40–Hz Oscillation Characterizes Dream State in Humans. *Proceedings of the National Academy of Sciences, USA*, 90: 2078–2081.

Llinas, R. and Pare, D. (1996). The Brain as a Closed System Modulated by the Senses. In R. Llinas and P. S. Churchland (eds.), *The Mind–Brain Continuum: Sensory Processes*. MIT Press: 1–18.

Llinas, R., Ribary, U., Contreras, D. and Pedroarena, C. (1998). The Neuronal Basis for Consciousness. *Philosophical Transactions of the Royal Society of London B*, 353: 1841–1849.

Logothetis, N. K. and Sheinberg, D. L. (1998). Recognition and Representation of Visual Objects in Primates: Psychophysics and Physiology. In R. Llinas and P. S. Churchland (eds.), *The Mind–Brain Continuum*. MIT Press.

Luborsky, L. and Barrett, M. S. (2006). The History and Empirical Status of Key Psychoanalytic Concepts. *Annual Review of Clinical Psychology*, 2: 1–19.

Luborsky, L., Crits-Christoph, P., Mintz, J. and Auerbach, A. (1988). *Who Will Benefit from Psychotherapy? Predicting Therapeutic Outcomes*. Basic Books.

Luthi, M. (1986). *The European Folk Tale: Form and Nature*. Indiana University Press.

Luthi, M. (1987). *Fairy Tale as Art Form and Portrait of Man*. Indiana University Press.

McCabe, V. (1988). Facial Proportions, Perceived Age, and Caregiving. In T. R. Alley (ed.), *Social and Applied Aspects of Perceiving Faces*. Earlbaum.

McCarthy, M. M. (1990). Oxytocin Inhibits Infanticide in Wild Female House Mice (*Mus Domesticus*). *Hormones and Behavior*, 24: 365–375.

McCarthy, M. M., Low, L. M. and Pfaff, D. W. (1992). Speculations Concerning the Physiological Significance of Central Oxytocin in Maternal Behavior. *Annals of the New York Academy of Science*, 652: 70–82.

McCauley, R. N. and Lawson, E. T. (2002). *Bringing Ritual to Mind: Psychological Foundations of Cultural Forms*. Cambridge University Press.

McClintock, M. K. (1983). Pheromonal Regulation of the Ovarian Cycle: Enhancement, Suppression and Synchrony. In J. G. Vandenbergh (ed.), *Pheromones and Reproduction in Mammals*. Academic Press.

McDonald, R. J., Devan, B. D. and Hong, N. S. (2004). Multiple Memory Systems: The Power of Interactions. *Neurobiology of Learning and Memory*, 82: 333–346.

McDonald, W. M. and Okun, M. S. (2004). Neuropsychiatry: The Border Between Neurology and Psychiatry. In D. S. Charney and E. J. Nestler (eds.), *The Neurobiology of Mental Illness*. Oxford University Press.

McGuire, W. and Hull, R. F. C. (1977). *C. G. Jung Speaking*. Princeton University Press.

MacLean, P. (1952). Some Psychiatric Implications of Physiological Studies on Frontotemporal Portion of Limbic System (Visceral Brain). *Electroencephalogical Clinical Neurophysiology*, 4: 407–418.

MacLean, P. (1990). *The Triune Brain in Evolution*. Plenum Press.

McNally, R. J., Lasko, N. B., Macklin, M. L. and Pitman, R. K. (1995). Autobiographical Memory Disturbance in Combat-Related Posttraumatic Stress Disorder. *Behaviour Research and Therapy*, 33: 619–630.

McNamara, P. (2009). *The Neuroscience of Religious Experience*. Cambridge University Press.

McNamara, P., Andresen, J., Clark, J., Zborowski, M. and Duffy, C. (2001). Impact of Attachment Styles on Dream Recall and Dream Content: A Test of the Attachment Hypothesis of REM Sleep. *Journal of Sleep Research*, 10: 117–127.

McNeill, D. (1992). *Hand and Mind: What Gestures Reveal about Thought*. University of Chicago Press.

McRae, C., Cherin, E., Yamazaki, T. G., Diem, G., Vo, A. H., Russel, D., Eilgring, J. H., Fahn, S., Greene, P., Dillon, S., Winfield, H., Bjugstad, K. B. and Freed, C. R. (2004). Effects of Perceived Treatment on Quality of Life and Medical Outcomes in a Double-Blind Placebo Surgery Trial. *Archives of General Psychiatry*, 61(4): 412–420.

Mahon, B. Z., Anzellotti, S., Schwarzbach, J., Zampini, M. and Caramazza, A. (2009). Category-Specific Organization in the Human Brain Does Not Require Visual Experience. *Neuron*, 63: 397–405.

Mandler, J. (1992). How to Build a Baby II: Conceptual Primitives. *Psychological Review*, 99(4): 587–604.

Mandler, J. (2004). Thought Before Language. *Trends in Cognitive Science*, 8(11): 508–513.

Mandler, J. and McDonough, L. (1998). Inductive Inference in Infancy. *Cognitive Psychology*, 37: 60–96.

Manning, J. T. (2002). *Digit Ratio: A Pointer to Fertility, Behavior, and Health*. Rutgers University Press.

Mannix, L. K., Chandurkar, R. S., Rybicki, L. A., Tusek, D. L. and Solomon, G. D. (1999). Effect of Guided Imagery on Quality of Life for Patients with Chronic Tension-Type Headache. *Headache*, 39(5): 326–334.

Marcus, G. F. (2005). What Developmental Biology Can Tell Us about Innateness. In P. Carruthers, S. Laurence and S. Stich (eds.), *The Innate Mind*. Oxford University Press.

Mark, V. H., Ervin, F. R. and Sweet, W. H. (1972). Deep Temporal Lobe

Stimulation in Man. In B. E. Eleftheriou (ed.), *The Neurobiology of the Amygdala*. Plenum Press.

Marks, I. (1987). *Fears, Phobias and Rituals*. Oxford University Press.

Marler, P. (1991). Song-Learning Behavior: The Interface with Neuroethology. *Trends in Neuroscience*, 14: 199–206.

Marlowe, F. (2003). A Critical Period for Provisioning by Hadza Men: Implications for Pair Bonding. *Evolution and Human Behavior*, 24: 217–229.

Marmor, G. S. (1978). Age at Onset of Blindness and the Development of the Semantics of Color Names. *Journal of Experimental Child Psychology*, 25: 267–278.

Marmor, G. S. and Zaback, L. A. (1976). Mental Rotation by the Blind: Does Mental Rotation Depend on Visual Imagery? *Journal of Experimental Psychology: Human Perception and Performance*, 2: 515–521.

Matsumoto, D. and Ekman, P. (2004). *Japanese and Caucasian Facial Expressions of Emotion (JACFEE) and Neutral Faces (JACNeuF)*. Paul Ekman & Associates.

Matsumoto, D. and Willingham, B. (2009). Spontaneous Facial Expressions of Emotion of Congenitally and Noncongenitally Blind Individuals. *Journal of Personality and Social Psychology*, 96(1): 1–10.

Mayberg, H. S., Silva, J. A., Brannan, S. K., Tekell, J. L., Mahurin, R. K., McGinnis, S. and Jerabek, P. A. (2002). The Functional Neuroanatomy of the Placebo Effect. *American Journal of Psychiatry*, 159: 728–737.

Meador, K. G. and Koenig, H. G. (2000). Spirituality and Religion in Psychiatric Practice: Parameters and Implications. *Psychiatric Annals*, 30: 549–555.

Mealy, L. and Theis, P. (1995). The Relationship between Mood and Preferences among Natural Landscapes: An Evolutionary Perspective. *Ethology and Sociobiology*, 16: 247–256.

Merchant, J. (2009). A Reappraisal of Classical Archetype Theory and Its Implications for Theory and Practice. *Journal of Analytical Psychology*, 54(3): 339–358.

Mesulam, M. M. (1998). From Sensation to Cognition. *Brain*, 121: 1013–1052.

Miczek, K. A. (1987). The Psychopharmacology of Aggression. In L. L. Iversen, S. D. Iversen and S. H. Snyder (eds.), *Handbook of Psychopharmacology*, vol. 19, *New Directions in Behavioral Pharmacology*. Plenum Press.

Miller, A. H. (2008). Inflammation and the Brain: Role of Innate Immune Responses in the Development and Treatment of Major Depression. *Psychiatry Resident's Symposium*. Palm Beach, FL. Sept. 12–14.

Miller, G. A. ([1956] 1994). The Magical Number Seven, Plus or Minus Two: Some Limits on Our Capacity to Process Information. *Psychological Review*, 101(2): 343–352.

Miller, L., Warner, V., Wickramaratne, P. and Weissman, M. (1997). Religiosity and Depression: Ten-year Follow-up of Depressed Mothers and Offspring. *Journal of the American Academy of Child and Adolescent Psychiatry*, 36(10): 1416–1425.

Miller, L. C. and Fishkin, S. A. (1997). On the Dynamics of Human Bonding and Reproductive Success: Seeking Windows on the Adapted-for-Human-Environmental Interface. In J.A Simpson and D. T. Kenrick (eds.), *Evolutionary Social Psychology*. Erlbaum.

Moeller, M. P. and Schick, B. (2006). Relations between Maternal Input and Theory of Mind Understanding in Deaf Children. *Child Development*, 77: 751–766.

Moerman, D. (2002). *Meaning, Medicine and the "Placebo Effect."* Cambridge University Press.

Moffitt, T. E., Caspi, A., Belsky, J. and Silva, P. A. (1992). Childhood Experience and Onset of Menarche: A Test of a Sociobiological Model. *Child Development*, 63: 47–58.

Mohr, C., Graves, R. E., Gianotti, L. R., Pizzagalli, D. and Brugger, P. (2001). Loose but Normal: A Semantic Association Study. *Journal of Psycholinguistic Research*, 30(5): 475–483.

Moseley, J. B., O'Malley, K., Petersen, N. J., Menke, T. J., Brody, B. A., Kuykendall, D. H., Hollingsworth, J. C., Ashton, C. M. and Wray, N. P. (2002). A Controlled Trial of Arthroscopic Surgery for Osteoarthritis of the Knee. *New England Journal of Medicine*, 347: 81–88.

Moyer, K. E. (1976). *The Psychobiology of Aggression*. Harper and Row.

Musselman, D. L., Miller, A. H., Porter, M. R., Manatunga, A., Gao, F., Penna, S., Pearce, B. D., Landry, J., Glover, S., McDaniel, J. S. and Nemeroff, C. B. (2001). Higher than Normal Plasma Interleukin-6 Concentrations in Cancer Patients with Depression: Preliminary Findings. *American Journal of Psychiatry*, 158(8): 1252–1257.

Myers, D. G. (1999). Close Relationships and Quality of Life. In D. Kahneman, E. Diener and N. Schwarz (eds.), *Well-being: The Foundations of Hedonic Psychology*. Russell Sage Foundation.

Naito, M. and Komatsu, S. (1993). Processes Involved in Childhood Development of Implicit Memory. In G. P. Masson (ed.), *Implicit Memory: New Directions in Cognition, Development and Neurology*. Erlbaum.

Neher, A. (1996). Jung's Theory of Archetypes: A Critique. *Journal of Humanistic Psychology*, 36: 61–91.

Nelkin, N. (1993). The Connection between Intentionality and Consciousness. In G. W. Farthing (ed.), *The Psychology of Consciousness*. Prentice Hall.

Nemeroff, C. B. (2008). HPA Axis and the Pathophysicology of Depression: The Role of Early Adverse Experience. *Psychiatry Resident's Symposium*. Palm Beach, FL. Sept. 12–14.

New, J., Cosmides, L. and Tooby, J. (2003). A Content-Specific Attenuation of Change Blindness: Preferential Attention to Animate Beings in Natural Scenes. Vision Sciences Society, Sarasota, FL.

New, J., Cosmides, L. and Tooby, J. (2007). Category-Specific Attention for Animals Reflects Ancestral Priorities, Not Expertise. *Proceedings of the National Academy of Sciences*, 104: 16598–16603.

Newberg, A. and Waldman, M. R. (2006). *Why We Believe What We Believe*. Free Press.

Newberg, A., Pourdehnad, M., Alavi, A. and d'Aguili, E. G. (2003). Cerebral Blood Flow During Meditative Prayer: Preliminary Findings and Methodological Issues. *Perceptual and Motor Skills*, 97(2): 625–630.

Nielsen, T. A. (2004). Chronobiological Features of Dream Production. *Sleep Medicine Reviews*, 8: 403–424.

Nielsen, T. A. and Levin, R. (2006). Nightmares: A New Neurocognitive Model. *Sleep Medicine Reviews*, 11: 295–310.

Numan, M. (1994). Neural Control of Maternal Behavior. In N.A Krasnegor and R. S. Bridges (eds.), *Mammalian Parenting*. Oxford University Press.

Numan, M. and Insel, T. R. (2003). *The Neurobiology of Parental Behavior*. Springer.

Öhman, A. (1993). Fear and Anxiety as Emotional Phenomena: Clinical Phenomenology, Evolutionary Perspectives, and Information-Processing Mechanisms. In M. Lewis and J. M. Haviland (eds.), *Handbook of Emotions*. Guilford Press.

Öhman, A., Flykt, A. and Esteves, F. (2001a). Emotional Drives in Attention: Detecting the Snake in the Grass. *Journal of Experimental Psychology, General*, 130: 466–478.

Öhman, A., Lundqvist, D. and Esteves, F. (2001b). The Face in the Crowd Revisited: A Threat Advantage with Schematic Stimuli. *Journal of Personality and Social Psychology*, 80: 381–396.

Oken, B. S. (2008). Placebo Effects: Clinical Aspects and Neurobiology. *Brain*, 131: 2812–2823.

Orchard, A. (2002). *Cassell's Dictionary of Norse Myth and Legend*. Cassell.

Orians, G. H. and Heerwagen, J. H. (1992). Evolved Responses to Landscapes. In J. H. Barkow, L. Cosmides and L. Tooby (eds.), *The Adapted Mind: Evolutionary Psychology and the Generation of Culture*. Oxford University Press.

Orr, S. P., Metzger, L. J. and Pitman, R. K. (2002). Psychophysiology of Post-traumatic Stress Disorder. *Psychiatric Clinics of North America*, 25: 271–293.

Pace, T. W., Hu, F. and Miller, A. H. (2007). Cytokine-Effects on Glucocorticoid Receptor Function: Relevance to Glucocorticoid Resistance and the Pathophysiology and Treatment of Major Depression. *Brain, Behavior and Immunity*, 21(1): 9–19.

Pace-Schott, E. F., Gersh, T., Silvestri, R., Stickgold, R., Salzman, C. and Hobson, J. A. (2001). SSRI Treatment Suppresses Dream Recall Frequency but Increases Subjective Dream Intensity in Normal Subjects. *Journal of Sleep Research*, 10: 129–142.

Panksepp, J. (1985). Mood Changes. In P. J. Vinken, G. W. Buyn, and H. L. Klawans (eds.), *Handbook of Clinical Neurology*. Elsevier Science.

Panksepp, J. (1990). Can "Mind" and Behavior be Understood without Understanding the Brain? A Reresponse to Bunge. *New Ideas in Psychology*, 8: 139–149.

Panksepp, J. (1998). *Affective Neuroscience: The Foundations of Human and Animal Emotions*. Oxford University Press.

Panksepp, J. (2005). Affective Consciousness: Core Emotional Feelings in Animals and Humans. *Cognition and Consciousness*, 14: 30–80.

Panksepp, J. (2006). Emotional Endophenotypes in Evolutionary Psychiatry. *Progress in Neuropsychopharmacology and Biological Psychiatry*, 30(5): 774–784.

Panksepp, J. (2007). Emotional Feelings Originate below the Neocortex: Toward a Neurobiology of the Soul. *Behavioral Science*, 42: 101–103.

Panksepp, J. and Miller, A. (1996). Emotions and the Aging Brain. In C. Magai and S. H. McFadden (eds.), *Handbook of Emotion, Adult Development, and Aging*. Academic Press.

Panksepp, J. and Panksepp, J. B. (2000). The Seven Sins of Evolutionary Psychology. *Evolution and Cognition*, 6: 108–131.

Panksepp, J. and Northoff, G. (2008). The Trans-Species Core SELF: The Emergence of Active Cultural and Neuro-Ecological Agents through Self-Related

Processing within Subcortical-Cortical Midline Networks. *Consciousness and Cognition 18(1):* 193–215.

Panksepp, J., Bean, N. J., Bishop, P., Vilberg, T. and Sahley, T. L. (1980). Opioid Blockade and Social Comfort in Chicks. *Pharmacology, Biochemistry and Behavior*, 13: 673–683.

Panksepp, J., Yates, G., Ikemoto, S. and Nelson, E. (1991). Simple Ethological Models of Depression: Social-Isolation Induced "Despair" in Chicks and Mice. In B. Olivier, J. Mos and J. L. Slangen (eds.), *Animal Models in Psychopharmacology*. Birkhauser-Verlag.

Panksepp, J., Nelson, E. and Bekkedal, M. (1997). Brain Systems for the Mediation of Social Separation-Distress and Social-Reward: Evolutionary Antecedents and Neuropeptide Intermediaries. *Annals for the New York Acadamy of Science*, 807: 78–100.

Panksepp, J., Knutson, B. and Pruitt, D. L. (1998). Toward a Neuroscience of Emotion: The Epigenetic Foundations of Emotional Development. In M. F. Mascolo and S. Griffin (eds.), *What Develops in Emotional Development?* Plenum Press.

Park, R. D. (1995). Fathers and Families. In M. H. Bornstein (ed.), *Handbook of Parenting*, vol. 3, *Status and Social Conditions of Parenting*. Erlbaum.

Paus, T. (2001). Primate Anterior Cingulate Cortex: Where Motor Control, Drive and Cognition Interface. *Nature Reviews of Neuroscience*, 2: 417–424.

Pellis, S. M., Pellis, V. C. and Whishaw, I. Q. (1992). The Role of the Cortex in Play Fighting by Rats: Developmental and Evolutionary Implications. *Brain Behavior and Evolution*, 39: 270–284.

Penton-Voak, I. S., Perrett, D. I., Castles, D., Burt, M., Koyabashi, T. and Murray, L. K. (1999). Female Preference for Male Faces Changes Cyclically. *Nature*, 399: 741–742.

Perner, J. and Wimmer, H. (1985). "John Thinks That Mary Thinks . . .": Attribution of Second-Order Beliefs by 5–10 Year Old Children. *Journal of Experimental Child Psychology*, 39: 437–471.

Pesant, N. and Zadra, A. (2006). Dream Content and Psychological Well-Being: A Longitudinal Study of the Continuity Hypothesis. *Journal of Clinical Psychology*, 62(1): 111–121.

Phelps, A. J., Forbes, D. and Creamer, M. (2007). Understanding Posttraumatic Nightmares: An Empirical and Conceptual Review. *Clinical Psychology Review*, 28: 338–355.

Piaget, J. (1929). *The Child's Conception of the World*. Routledge and Kegan Paul.

Pinker, S. (1997). *How the Mind Works*. Norton.

Pinker, S. (2002). *The Blank Slate: The Modern Denial of Human Nature*. Viking.

Pinker, S. (2007). *The Stuff of Thought: Language as a Window into Human Nature*. Viking.

Platek, S. M. (2003). *Paternal Uncertainty, the Brain, and Children's Faces: Neural Correlates of Child Facial Resemblance*. Paper presented at the 15th annual meeting of the Human Behavior and Evolution Society, Lincoln, NE.

Platek, S. M., Burch, R. L., Panyavin, I. S., Wasserman, B. H. and Gallup, G. G. (2002). Reactions to Children's Faces: Resemblance Affects Males More than Females. *Evolution and Human Behavior*, 23: 159–166.

Ploog, D. W. (2003). The Place of the Triune Brain in Psychiatry. *Physiology and Behavior*, 79: 487–493.

Pollington, S. (2008). *Leechcraft: Early English Charms, Plantlore and Healing.* Anglo-Saxon Books.

Popik, P., Vetulani, J. and Van Ree, J. M. (1992). Low Doses of Oxytocin Facilitate Social Recognition in Rats. *Psychopharmacology*, 106: 71–74.

Premack, D. and Premack, A. (2003). *Original Intelligence.* McGraw-Hill.

Prentice, N. M., Manosevitz, M. and Hubbs, L. (1978). Imaginary Figures of Early Childhood: Santa Claus, Easter Bunny, and the Tooth Fairy. *American Journal of Orthopsychiatry*, 48(4): 618–628.

Price, D. D., Milling, L. S., Kirsch, I., Duff, A., Montgomery, G. H. and Nicholls, S. S. (1999). An Analysis of Factors that Contribute to the Magnitude of Placebo Analgesia in an Experimental Paradigm. *Pain*, 83: 147–156.

Prigogine, I. and Stengers, I. (1988). *Order out of Chaos: Man's New Dialogue with Nature.* Bantam Books.

Puhvel, J. (1987). *Comparative Mythology.* Johns Hopkins University.

Purcell, S., Moffitt, A. and Hoffmann, R. (1993). Waking, Dreaming and Self-Regulation. In A. Moffitt, M. Kramer and R. Hoffmann (eds.), *The Functions of Dreaming.* State University of New York Press.

Putz, D. A., Gaulin, S. J. C., Sporter, R. J. and McBurney, D. H. (2004). Sex Hormones and Finger Length: What Does 2D:4D Indicate? *Evolution and Human Behavior 25:* 182–199.

Pyysiäinen, I. (2009). *Supernatural Agents: Why We Believe in Souls, Gods, and Buddhas.* Oxford University Press.

Quaade, F., Vaernet, K. and Larsson, S. (1974). Stereotaxic Stimulation and Electrocoagulation of the Lateral Hypothalamus in Obese Humans. *Acta Neurochir*, 30: 111–117.

Quinlan, R. J. (2003). Father-Absence, Parental Care, and Female Reproductive Development. *Evolution and Human Behavior*, 24: 376–390.

Quinn, P. C. and Eimas, P. D. (1996). Perceptual Cues That Permit Categorical Differentiation of Animal Species by Infants. *Journal of Experimental Child Psychology*, 63: 189–211.

Raison, C. L., Capuron, L. and Miller, A. H. (2006). Cytokines Sing the Blues: Inflammation and the Pathogenesis of Depression. *Trends in Immunology*, 27: 24–31.

Ramachandran, V. S., Levi, L., Stone, L., Rogers-Ramachandran, D., McKinney, R., Stalcup, M., Arcilla, G., Zweifler, R., Schatz, A. and Flippin, A. (1998). Illusions of Body Image: What They Reveal about Human Nature. In R. Llinas and P. S. Churchland (eds.), *The Mind–Body Continuum.* MIT Press.

Rauch, S. L., Van der Kolk, B. A., Fisler, R. E. and Alpert, N. M. (1996). A Symptom Provocation Study of Posttraumatic Stress Disorder Using Positron Emission Tomography and Script-Driven Imagery. *Archives of General Psychiatry*, 53: 380–387.

Reber, A. S. (1993). *Implicit Learning and Tacit Knowledge: An Essay on the Cognitive Unconscious.* Oxford University Press.

Rees, A. and Rees, B. (1961 [1998]). *Celtic Heritage: Ancient Tradition in Ireland and Wales.* Thames and Hudson.

Reinsel, R., Wollman, M. and Antrobus, J. (1986). Effects of Environmental

Context and Cortical Activation on Thought. *Journal of Mind and Behavior*, 7: 259–275.

Reinsel, R., Antrobus, J. and Wollman, M. (1992). Bizarreness in Dreams and Waking Fantasy. In J. Antrobus and M. Bertini (eds.), *The Neuropsychology of Sleep and Dreaming*. Erlbaum.

Revonsuo, A. (2000). The Reinterpretation of Dreams: An Evolutionary Hypothesis of the Function of Dreaming. *Behavioral and Brain Sciences*, 23: 793–1121.

Richardson-Klavehn, A. and Bjork, R. A. (1988). Measures of Memory. *Annual Review of Psychology*, 39: 475–543.

Robertson, L. (1998). Visuospatial Attention and Parietal Function: Their Role in Object Perception. In R. Parasuraman (ed.), *The Attentive Brain*. MIT Press.

Roffe, L., Schmidt, K. and Ernst, E. (2005). A Systematic Review of Guided Imagery as an Adjuvant Cancer Therapy. *Psychooncology*, 14(8): 607–617.

Rose, R. M. (1980). Endocrine Responses to Stressful Psychological Events. In E. J. Sachar (ed.), *Advances in Psychoneuroendocrinology*. Saunders.

Rossi, E. (1992). *Mind Body Therapy: Methods of Ideodynamic Healing in Hypnotherapy*. Norton.

Rotenberg, V. S. (1993). REM Sleep and Dreams as Mechanisms of the Recovery of Search Activity. In A. Moffitt, M. Kramer and R. Hoffmann (eds.), *The Functions of Dreaming*. State University of New York Press.

Rubenstein, A. J., Langlois, J. H. and Roggman, L. A. (2002). What Makes a Face Attractive and Why: The Role of Averageness in Defining Facial Beauty. In G. Rhodes and L.A Zebrowitz (eds.), *Facial Attractiveness: Evolutionary, Cognitive, and Social Perspectives*. Greenwood Publishers Group.

Ruby, P. and Decety, J. (2001). Effect of Subjective Perspective Taking During Simulation of Action: A PET Investigation of Agency. *Nature Neuroscience*m, 4: 546–550.

Rumelhart, D. E., McClelland, J. L. and the PDP Research Group (1986). *Parallel Distributed Processing: Explorations in the Microstructure of Cognition*, vol. 1, *Foundations*. MIT Press.

Sabbagh, M. A. and Taylor, M. (2000). Neural Correlates of Theory-of-Mind Reasoning: An Event-Related Portential Study. *Psychological Science*, 11: 46–50.

Sadalla, E. K., Kenrick. D. T. and Venshure, B. (1987). Dominance and Heterosexual Attraction. *Journal of Personality and Social Psychology*, 52: 730–738.

Safran, J. D. and Greenberg, L. S. (1987). Affect and the Unconscious: A Cognitive Perspective. In S. R. Hillsdale (ed.), *Theories of the Unconscious and Theories of the Self*. Erlbaum.

Sapirstein, G. and Kirsch, I. (1998). Listening to Prozac but Hearing Placebo? A Meta-Analysis of the Placebo Effect of Antidepressant Medication. *Prevention and Treatment*, 1: 3–11.

Saunders, P. and Skar, P. (2001). Archetypes, Complexes and Self-Organization. *Journal of Analytical Psychology*, 46: 305–323.

Saxe, R., Carey, S. and Kanwisher, N. (2004). Understanding Other Minds: Linking Developmental Psychology and Functional Neuroimaging. *Annual Reviews in Psychology*, 55: 87–124.

Schacter, D. (1983). Amnesia Observed: Remembering and Forgetting in a Natural Environment. *Journal of Abnormal Psychology*, 92: 236–242.

Schacter, D. (1987). Implicit Memory: History and Current Status. *Journal of Experimental Psychology, Learning, Memory and Cognition*, 13: 50–518.

Schacter, D. (1996). *Searching for Memory: The Brain, the Mind and the Past*. Basic Books.

Schacter, D. and Graf, P. (1986). Effects of Elaborative Processing on Implicit and Explicit Memory for New Associations. *Journal of Experimental Psychology: Learning, Memory, and Cognition*, 12(3): 432–444.

Schacter, D. and Scarry, E. (2000). *Memory, Brain and Belief*. Harvard University Press.

Schmitt, D. P. (2005). Fundamentals of Human Mating Strategies. In D. Buss (ed.), *The Handbook of Evolutionary Psychology*. John Wiley & Sons.

Schmitt, D. P., Shackelford, T. K. and Buss D. M. (2001). Are Men Really More "Oriented" Toward Short-Term Mating than Women? A Critical Review of Theory and Research. *Psychology, Evolution and Gender*, 3: 211–239.

Segerstrom, S. C., Taylor, S. E., Kemeny, M. E. and Fahey, J. L. (1998). Optimism Is Associated with Mood, Coping, and Immune Change in Response to Stress. *Journal of Personality and Social Psychology*, 74(6): 1646–1655.

Seligman, M. E. P. (1971). Phobias and Preparedness. *Behavior Therapy*, 2: 307–320.

Shapiro, A. K. and Shapiro, E. (1997). *The Powerful Placebo: From Ancient Priest to Modern Physician*. Johns Hopkins University Press.

Shedler, J. (2010). The Efficacy of Psychodynamic Therapy. *American Psychologist*, 65(2): 98–109.

Simek, R. ([1993] 2007). *Dictionary of Northern Mythology*. D. S. Brewer.

Simpson, J. A. and Campbell, L. (2005). Methods of Evolutionary Sciences. In D. Buss (ed.), *The Handbook of Evolutionary Psychology*. John Wiley & Sons.

Simpson, J. A., Fletcher, G. J. O. and Campbell, L. (2001). The Structure and Function of Ideal Standards in Close Relationships. In G. J. O. Fletcher and M. Clark (eds.), *Blackwell Handbook of Social Psychology: Interpersonal Processes*. Blackwell.

Simpson, T. (2005). Toward a Reasonable Nativism. In P. Carruthers, S. Laurence and S. Stich (eds.), *The Innate Mind*. Oxford University Press.

Simpson, T., Carruthers, P., Laurence, S. and Stich, S. (2005). Nativism Past and Present. In P. Carruthers, S. Laurence, and S. Stich (eds.), *The Innate Mind*. Oxford University Press.

Sinclair, A., Siegrist, F. and Sinclair, H. (1983). Young Children's Ideas about the Written Number Systems. In D. Rogers and J. Sloboda (eds.), *The Acquisition of Symbolic Skills*. Plenum.

Singh, D. and Bronstad, P. M. (2001). Female Body Odour Is a Potential Cue to Ovulation. *Proceedings of the Royal Society of London, Series B, Biological Sciences*, 268: 797–801.

Siviy, S. M. and Panksepp, J. (1985). Energy Balance and Play in Juvenile Rats. *Physiology and Behavior*, 35: 435–441.

Skinner, B. F. (1953). *Science and Human Behavior*. Macmillan.

Smiley, J. (ed.) (2001). *The Sagas of the Icelanders*. Penguin.

Smith, J. Z. (2004). *Relating Religion*. University of Chicago Press.

Smuts, B. (1995). The Evolutionary Origins of Patriarchy. *Human Nature*, 6: 1–32.

Sober, E. and Wilson, D. S. (1998). *Unto Others: The Evolution and Psychology of Unselfish Behavior*. Harvard University Press.

Solms, M. (1997). *The Neuropsychology of Dreams: A Clinico-Anatomical Study*. Erlbaum.

Solms, M. (2000). Dreaming and REM Sleep Are Controlled by Different Brain Mechanisms. *Behavioral and Brain Sciences*, 23: 793–1121.

Solms, M. (2002). Neurosciences and Psychoanalysis. *International Journal of Psychoanalysis*, 83: 233–237.

Solms, M. and Turnbull, O. (2002). *The Brain and the Inner World: An Introduction to the Neuroscience of Subjective Experience*. Other Press.

Sotirova-Kohli, M., Rosen, D. H., Smith, S. M., Henderson, P. and Taki-Reece, S. (2011). Empirical study of Kanji as archetypal images: Understanding the collective unconscious as part of the Japanese language. *Journal of Analytical Psychology*, 56: 109–132.

Spelke, E. S. (1988). Where Perceiving Ends and Thinking Begins: The Apprehension of Objects in Infancy. In A. Yonas (ed.), *Perceptual Development in Infancy*. Erlbaum.

Spelke, E. S. (1990). Principles of Object Perception. *Cognitive Science*, 14: 29–56.

Spelke, E. S., Breinlinger, K., Macomber, J. and Jacobson, K. (1992). *Psychological Review*, 99: 605–632.

Sperber, D. (1994). The Modularity of Thought and the Epidemiology of Representations. In L. A. Hirschfeld and S. A. Gelman (eds.), *Mapping the Mind: Domain Specificity in Cognition and Culture*. Cambridge University Press.

Spiegel, D. (1990). Hypnosis, Dissociation, and Trauma: Hidden and Overt Observers. In J. L. Singer (ed.), *Repression and Dissociation: Implications for Personality Theory, Psychopathology, and Health*. University of Chicago Press.

Spiegel, D. and Li, D. (1997). Dissociated Cognition and Disintegrated Experience. In D. J. Stein (ed.), *Cognitive Science and the Unconscious*. American Psychiatric Press.

Sproul, B. C. (1979). *Primal Myths: Creation Myths Around the World*. HarperOne.

Squire, L. R. and Cohen, N. J. (1984). Human Memory and Amnesia. In G. Lynch, J. L. McGaugh and N. M. Weinberger (eds.), *Neurobiology of Learning and Memory*. Guilford.

Stein, D. J. (2006). Evolutionary Theory, Psychiatry and Psychopharmacology. *Progress in Neuropsychopharmacology and Biological Psychiatry*, 30(5): 766–773.

Stein, D. J. and Young, M. B. (1997). Rethinking Repression. In D. J. Stein (ed.), *Cognitive Science and the Unconscious*. American Psychiatric Press.

Stein, M. (1988). *Jung's Map of the Soul*. Open Court Publishing.

Stein, N. L., Leventhal, B. and Trabasso, T. (eds.) (1990). *Psychological and Biological Approaches to Emotion*. Lawrence Erlbaum.

Steiner, S. S. and Ellman, S. J. (1972). Relation between REM Sleep and Intracranial Self-Stimulation. *Science*, 177: 1122–1124.

Sterns, F. R. (1972). *Laughing: Physiology, Pathophysiology, Psychology, Pasthopsychology and Development*. Charles C. Thomas.

Stevens, A. (1993). *The Two Million Year Old Self*. Texas A&M University Press.

Stevens, A. (1995). *Private Myths: Dreams and Dreaming*. Harvard University Press.

Stevens, A. (1998). *Ariadne's Clue: A Guide to the Symbols of Humankind*. Princeton University Press.

Stevens, A. (2002). *Archetype Revisited: An Updated Natural History of the Self.* Routledge.

Stevens, A. and Price, J. (2000). *Evolutionary Psychiatry: A New Beginning.* Routledge.

Stiner, M. (1991). An Interspecific Perspective on the Emergence of the Modern Human Predatory Niche. In M. Stiner (ed.), *Human Predators and Prey Mortality.* Westview.

Storms, G. (1948). *Anglo Saxon Magic.* Martinus Nijhoff.

Strauch, I. and Meier, B. (1996). *In Search of Dreams: Results of Experimental Dream Research.* State University of New York Press.

Sugiyama, L. S. (2005). Physical Attractiveness in Adaptationist Perspective. In D. Buss (ed.), *The Handbook of Evolutionary Psychology.* John Wiley & Sons.

Sugiyama, L. S., Tooby, J. and Cosmides, L. (2002). Cross-Cultural Evidence of Cognitive Adaptations for Social Exchange among the Shiwiar of Ecuadorian Amazonia. *Proceedings of the National Academy of Sciences of the United States of America*, 99: 11537–11557.

Surbey, M. K. (1990). Family Composition, Stress, and the Timing of Human Menarche. In T. E. Ziegler and F. B. Bercovitch (eds.), *Socioendocrinology of Primate Reproduction.* Wiley-Liss.

Sweetser, E. (1990). *From Etymology to Pragmatics: Metaphorical and Cultural Aspects of Semantic Structure.* Cambridge University Press.

Tajfel, H., Flament, M. C., Billig, M. and Bundy, R. P. (1971). Social Categorization and Intergroup Behavior. *European Journal of Social Psychology*, 1: 149–178.

Taub, S. (2001). *Language from the Body: Iconicity and Metaphor in American Sign Language.* Cambridge University Press.

Thomas, K. B. (1987). Medical Consultations: Is There Any Point in Being Positive? *British Medical Journal*, 133: 455–463.

Thompson, J. J., Ritenbaugh, C. and Nichter, M. (2009). Reconsidering the Placebo Response from a Broad Anthropological Perspective. *Cultural Medical Psychiatry*, 33: 112–152.

Thompson, M. B. and Coppens, N. M. (1994). The Effects of Guided Imagery on Anxiety Levels and Movement of Clients Undergoing Magnetic Resonance Imageing. *Holistic Nursing Practice*, 8(2): 59–69.

Thor, D. H. and Holloway, W. R. (1984). Social Play in Juvenile Rats: A Decade of Methodological and Experimental Research. *Neuroscientific and Biobehavioral Reviews*, 8: 455–464.

Thornhill, R., Gangestad, S. W., Miller, R., Scheyd, G., Knight, J. and Franklin, M. (2001). MHC, Symmetry, and Body Scent Attractiveness in Men and Women. Unpublished manuscript, University of New Mexico.

Thorpe, S. J., Gegenfurtner, K. R., le Fabre-Thorpe, M. and Bulthoff, H. H. (2001). Detection of Animals in Natural Images Using Far Peripheral Vision. *European Journal of Neuroscience*m, 14: 869–876.

Todd, P. M., Hertwig, R. and Hoffrage, U. (2005). Evolutionary Cognitive Psychology. In D. Buss (ed.), *The Handbook of Evolutionary Psychology.* John Wiley & Sons.

Tooby, J. (1976a). The Evolutionary Regulation of Inbreeding. *Institute for Evolutionary Studies Technical Report*, 76(1): 1–87.

Tooby, J. (1976b). The Evolutionary Psychology of Incest Avoidance. *Institute for Evolutionary Studies Technical Report*, 76(2): 1–92.

Tooby, J. and Cosmides, L. (1992). The Psychological Foundations of Culture. In J. Barkow, L. Cosmides and J. Tooby (eds.), *The Adapted Mind*. Oxford University Press.

Tooby, J. and Cosmides, L. (2005). Conceptual Foundations of Evolutionary Psychology. In D. Buss (ed.), *The Handbook of Evolutionary Psychology*. John Wiley & Sons.

Tooby, J., Cosmides. L. and Barret, H. C. (2005). Resolving the Debate on Innate Ideas: Learnability Constraints and the Evolved Interpenetration of Motivational and Conceptual Functions. In P. Carruthers, S. Laurence and S. Stich (eds.), *The Innate Mind*. Oxford University Press.

Tracy, J. L. and Matsumoto, D. (2008). The Spontaneous Expression of Pride and Shame: Evidence for Biologically Innate Nonverbal Displays. *Proceedings of the National Academy of Sciences*, 105(33): 11655–11660.

Tresidder, J. (ed.) (2005). *The Complete Dictionary of Symbols*. Chronicle Books.

Turkheimer, E. (2000). Three Laws of Behavior Genetics and What They Mean. *Current Directions in Psychological Science*, 9(5): 160–164.

Turkheimer, E. and D'Onofrio, B. M. (2005). Analysis and Interpretation of Twin Studies Including Measures of the Shared Environment. *Child Development*, 76(6): 1217–1233.

Turville-Petre, G. (1972). *Nine Norse Studies*. Viking Society for Northern Research, University College London.

Turville-Petre, G. (1975). *The Myth and Religion of the North*. Greenwood Press Reprint.

Vallance, A. K. (2007). A Systematic Review Comparing the Functional Neuroanatomy of Patients with Depression Who Respond to Placebo to Those Who Recover Spontaneously: Is There a Biological Basis for the Placebo Effect in Depression? *Journal of Affective Disorders*, 98: 177–185.

Van de Castle, R. L. (1994). *Our Dreaming Mind*. Ballantine Books.

Van den Berg, O., Vrana, S. and Eelen, P. (1990). Letters from the Heart: Affective Categorization of Letter Combinations in Typists and Nontypists. *Journal of Experimental Psychology, Learning, Memory and Cognition*, 16: 1153–1161.

van Eenwyk, J. R. (1997). *Archetypes and Strange Attractors: The Chaotic World of Symbols*. Inner City Books.

Vase, L., Robinson, M. E., Verne, G. N. and Price, D. D. (2004). Increased Placebo Analgesia over Time in Irritable Bowel Syndrome (IBS) Patients Is Associated with Desire and Expectation but Not Endogenous Opioid Mechanisms. *Pain*, 115: 338–347.

Viamontes, G. I. and Beitman, B. (2007). Mapping the Unconscious in the Brain. *Psychiatric Annals*, 37(4): 243–256.

von Franz, M.-L. (1964a). The Process of Individuation. In C. G. Jung and M.-L. von Franz (eds.), *Man and His Symbols*. Dell.

von Franz, M.-L. (1964b). Science and the Unconscious. In C. G. Jung and M.-L. von Franz (eds.), *Man and His Symbols*. Dell.

von Franz, M.-L. (1980). *Alchemy: An Introduction to the Symbolism and the Psychology*. Inner City Books.

von Franz, M.-L. (1988). *Psyche and Matter*. Shambhala.

von Franz, M.-L. (1996). *The Interpretation of Fairy Tales*. Shambhala.

von Franz, M.-L. (1999). *Archetypal Dimensions of the Psyche*. Shambhala.

von Raffay, A. (2000). Why It Is Difficult to See the Anima as a Helpful Object: Critique and Clinical Relevance of the Theory of Archetypes. *Journal of Analytic Psychology*, 45: 541–560.

Voruganti, L. and Awad, A. G. (2004). Neuroleptic Dysphoria: Toward a New Synthesis. *Psychopharmacology*, 171: 121–132.

Waggoner, B. (2009). *The Sagas of Ragnar Lodbrok*. Troth Publications.

Wakefield, J. C. (2005). Biological Function and Dysfunction. In D. Buss (ed.), *The Handbook of Evolutionary Psychology*. John Wiley & Sons.

Walters, S. (1994). Algorithms and Archetypes: Evolutionary Psychology and Carl Jung's Theory of the Collective Unconscious. *Journal of Social and Evolutionary Systems*, 17(3): 287–306.

Watt, D. F. and Pincus, D. I. (2004). Neural Substrates of Consciousness: Implications for Clinical Psychiatry. In J. Panksepp (ed.), *Textbook of Biological Psychiatry*. Wiley-Liss.

Wedekind, C. and Füri, S. (1997). Body Odor Preference in Men and Women: Do They Aim for Specific MHC Combinations or Simply Heterozygosity? *Proceedings of the Royal Society of London. Series B, Biological Sciences*, 264: 1471–1479.

Weinberger, J. and Weiss, J. (1997). Psychoanalytic and Cognitive Conceptions of the Unconscious. In D. J. Stein (ed.), *Cognitive Science and the Unconscious*. American Psychiatric Press.

Weise, H. (2003). *Numbers, Language, and the Human Mind*. Cambridge University Press.

Weisfeld, G. E. (1999). *Evolutionary Principles of Human Adolescence*. Basic Books.

Weiskrantz, L. (1986). *Blindsight*. Oxford University Press.

West, M. L. (2007). *Indo-European Poetry and Myth*. Oxford University Press.

Whitehouse, H. and Laidlaw, J. (eds.) (2007). *Religion, Anthropology, and Cognitive Science*. Carolina Academic Press.

Whiting, B. B. and Edwards, C. P. (1988). *Children of Different Worlds: The Formation of Social Behavior*. Harvard University Press.

Wichlinski, L. J. (2000). The Pharmacology of Threatening Dreams. *Behavioral and Brain Sciences*, 23: 1016–1017.

Wilmer, J. B., Germine, L., Chabris, C. F., Chattergee, G., Williams, M., Loken, E., Nakayama, K. and Duchaine, B. (2010). Human Face Recognition Ability Is Specific and Highly Heritable. *Proceedings of the National Academy of Sciences USA*, 107(11): 5238–5241.

Wilson, D. S. (2003). *Darwin's Cathedral: Evolution, Religion, and the Nature of Society*. University of Chicago Press.

Winson, J. (1985). *Brain and Psyche*. First Vintage Books.

Witelson, S. F. (1991). Neural Sexual Mosaicism: Sexual Differentiation of the Human Temporo-Parietal Region for Functional Asymmetry. *Psychoneuroendocrinology*, 16: 131–153.

Wolf, E. (2002). *Treating the Self: Elements of Clinical Self Psychology*. Guilford Press.

Wood, J. N. and Spelke, E. S. (2005). Infants' Enumeration of Actions: Numerical Discrimination and Its Signature Limits. *Developmental Science*, 8(2): 173–181.

Wyatt, R., Goodwyn, E. and Ignatowski, M. (2011). A Jungian Approach to Dreams Reported by Soldiers in a Modern Combat Zone. *Journal of Analytical Psychology*, 56(2): 217–231.

Young, L. J. and Insel, T. R. (2002). Hormones and Parental Behavior. In J. B. Becker, S. M. Breedlove, D. Crew, and M. M. McCarthy (eds.), *Behavioral Endocrinology*. MIT Press.

Yu, N. (1999). *The Contemporary Theory of Metaphor: The Chinese Perspective.* John Brightmans.

Zárate, M. A. and Smith, E. R. (1990). Person Categorization and Stereotyping. *Social Cognition*, 8: 161–185.

Zebrowitz, L. A. (1997). *Reading Faces: Window to the Soul?* Westview Press.

Zimecki, M. (2006). The Lunar Cycle: Effects on Human and Animal Behavior and Physiology. *Postepy Higieny i Medycyny Doswiadczalnej* (Online), 60: 1–7.

Zimler, J. and Keenan, J. M. (1983). Imagery in the Congenitally Blind: How Visual Are Visual Images? *Journal of Experimental Psychology: Learning, Memory and Cognition*, 9(2): 269–282.

Zimmer, H. ([1942] 1972). *Myths and Symbols in Indian Art and Civilization.* J. Campbell (ed.). Princeton University Press.

Zubieta, J. K., Ketter, T. A., Bueller, J. A., Xu, Y., Kilbourn, M. R., Young, E. A. and Koeppe, R. A. (2003). Regulation of Human Affective Responses by Anterior Cingulate and Limbic Mu-Opioid Neurotransmission. *Archives of General Psychiatry*, 60: 1145–1153.

Index

Page references to the endnotes show in brackets the chapter referred to when the same note number appears under different chapters on the same page. For example 208n1[7] indicates page 208, note 1, found under the heading Chapter 7.